Praise for Note For

'A truly inspirational odyssey. The author's musical journey will motivate and encourage everyone – his determination and disciplined long term endeavours in music makes for a compelling, unique read.' *Murray McLachlan, Concert Pianist & Educator, Head of Keyboard, Chetham's School of Music*

'A unique insight into how journeying into music can enhance and transform our lives in ways we had perhaps never imagined. The distinctive blend of biography with music theory takes the reader on unexpected twists and turns as Howard's story unfolds, and his musical adventure intertwines with daily life. *Note For Note* is hugely captivating, touching and inspiring – a must-read for anyone who has dabbled with taking up music.' *Victoria Williams, MyMusicTheory, LmusTCL, BA (Hons)*

'Highly recommended. Will resonate with all those who understand the compulsion to play or improvise music, the psychological need this fills and the exhilaration felt when practice is rewarded by an audience's response to an amateur's performance. A brutally honest personal testimony of a human experience that enriches life via the intimate physical act of working with a musical instrument.' *Marie McKavanagh, Amateur Pianist, LTCL & Performing Arts Clinician BAPAM*

'Could this be the next *Play It Again*? Written by an amateur pianist for amateur pianists, Howard Smith lays out the landscape, signposts and challenge of coming to music as a mature adult. His "late returner" story will provide a sense of relief that no one need be on their own and that it is never too late.' *Ophelia Gordon, Pianist & Music Teacher, B.Mus (Hons), ATCL, LTCL*

'Uplifting. I suspect this engaging tale will be appreciated by pianists and songwriters alike. His joy, frustration and love for music and musicians comes across strongly. The author brings a refreshingly scientific inquisition to the challenge of switching tracks in later life and learning a complex art. His theory experiments had me jumping to the piano on numerous occasions!' *Rob Foster, Piano Teacher, DipLCM, London Piano Meetup Group*

'A powerful message. Not only is the record of the author's adventures on the musical escalator entertaining and affecting but I absorbed a good deal of sage wisdom along the way.' *Martin Ouvry, Writer & Musician*

'In this candid and informative account, Howard Smith captures the excitement and frustrations, pleasures and practicalities of taking up the piano as an adult. Howard's fable is sure to resonate with other adult amateur musicians – and teachers too. His book provides important support to those considering embarking on a similar journey as well as to those who are already fully committed to it.' *Frances Wilson, pianist, writer and blogger on classical music and pianism as 'The Cross-Eyed Pianist'*

'Facing me from the opposite side of the piano, we rehearsed the song one more time. Maintaining eye contact throughout, the emotion of the piece – a plea to my wife and a reflection of my insecurity – overcame us. As my tutor sang the final verse, she blushed, and I looked away embarrassed. It was the power of my music. We broke off and fell about laughing. How on earth was I going to perform "Unbound" for my wife? It was not the lyrics, though I do struggle with speeches at family gatherings, despite having spent much of my working life presenting keynotes at industry events. No, my apprehension about performing the love song was more prosaic than simple butterflies or stage fright. I could not sing.'

For forty years, HOWARD SMITH worked hard as a technologist and consultant, a career he loved. Approaching retirement, and facing an intractable problem at the office, he discovers the one thing that had been missing all along: a piano. Regretful of not having had the discipline to persevere with lessons as a child, the author embarks upon an urgent quest: to lead a new creative life and to achieve this in just three years. Encountering many obstacles and rescued by a blue snowman, he finally comes to understand what it means to be a musician. Blending theory and practice, this unique memoir describes how the author navigated his transition from the digital to the analogue: from the bits and bytes of the computer industry to the world of melody, harmony and musical performance. Join our hero as he jumps onto a distinctly bumpy escalator in what becomes a relentless pursuit of his dream.

Howard lives in Surrey with his wife. Their cat, Adagio, occupies the same premises.

NOTE FOR NOTE

BEWITCHED, BOTHERED & BEWILDERED

HOWARD SMITH

Fairdene Press ♦ LONDON

First published in Great Britain in 2020
by Fairdene Press

Enquiries to Fairdene Press
fairdenepress@gmail.com

www.note4notethebook.com
#Note4NoteTheBook

A catalogue record for this book is available from the British Library.

ISBN 978 1 9998467 1 8

1 2 3 4 5 6 7 8 9 10

Typeset in Adobe Caslon, Waverly CF & Isabel
Copyediting by Martin Ouvry
Typography & book design by the author

This book is manufactured-on-demand, printing units only as ordered, reducing excess production. The ink used is chlorine free, and the acid-free paper stock is supplied by a Forest Stewardship Council-certified provider. The paper is made from 30% minimum post-consumer waste recycled material.

Dedicated to all those who bring the joy of music to their pupils and audiences, whose lives, livelihoods and passion have been disrupted by Covid-19

#SaveTheArts

The events narrated in this book took place between
Friday, February 14, 2014 and New Year's Day, 2018

CONTENTS

A Warning xv

PRELUDE

1 Katy steps onto an escalator 3

VERSE

2 Week one 25

3 The next lesson 30

4 The lead sheet 39

5 Nemesis 45

6 Unblocking 53

7 The fourth 59

8 The circle 68

9 The musical mind 74

10 Two-five-one 79

11 On technique 85

12 Modes 91

13 The theory exam 98

MIDDLE EIGHT

14 Pookin' dookin' 107

15 Rock school 113

16 Piece in a day 118

17 My imaginary piano 125

18 On education 132

19 Moving in diatonic circles 140

20 A pleasant day 146

21 Grade six theory hiatus 153

PRE CHORUS

22 *The Blue Snowman* 159

23 Losing track 172

24 Life intervenes 184

25 Six strings 190

26 Lawns 198

27 A parting of ways 202

CHORUS

28 Reharmonize me 209

29 Under my nose 214

30 A growing excitement 221

31 Songwriting 223

32 As trees we stand 232

33 Ear training 242

34 Unbound 250

FINALE

35 Dreams and coincidences 261

36 The living-room concert 268

37 Shattered 277

38 Gig 293

Acknowledgements 297

POSTLUDE

Right to be wrong? 301

What Katy did next 302

The returning adult 319

Conquering anxiety 323

Further reading 329

About the type

'Music is ... a mother's lullaby. It gives sound to our feelings when we have no voice, words when we are silent. In it we praise, love, hope and remember. The breath of the soul, the contours of the path of a hummingbird in flight, and the wind that carries it, music shapes and shivers into endless colours, nuanced and diverse, and eternally creative. It is Spirit taking form.'

Jason Martineau, *The Elements of Music*

A WARNING

I admit it. I wrote this book for myself. A journey such as this – the bumpy escalator I rode – sure needs bolstering. If you are contemplating a similar voyage or have already embarked on one, may I offer a word of advice? There will be times when the good folks around you may not understand what you are doing, or why. Not everyone can accept the freedoms you will need for the ride. And you, embroiled in the immense effort, its details and complexities, may not recognise how others perceive what is happening. Expect a little craziness at times. Realise that your ups and downs, so important to you, may not matter so much to them. Where you may hope for praise, it might not come. When you choose to 'put yourself out there' the responsibility for whatever happens next lies with you and you alone. Such is the creative life. Get over it. You will need several large cushions to protect yourself from harm. Only you can find those cushions and, if your journey turns out to be anything like mine, support will come from the most unexpected places.

Little of this is easy. Nor is it always 'fun'. Look to your teachers to show you the way but recognise that even they, with decades of experience, will not have all the answers you need. I found it necessary to wallow in a good deal of self-reflection during my time on the escalator. Writing this book was part of that introspection, a roughly hewn 'working out' of where my journey might lead and what might be lurking around the corner, waiting to pop up and poke fun at me.

Lastly, a suggestion. Thank your friends and family for their patience and tolerance. Do so often and in large doses. If my experience is anything to go by, you may be unable to hide your needs and frustrations from those you love. And they, no doubt, will not only have to endure your obsessive woodshedding but also your compositions and performances, all of which could be dreadful.

Let none of the above prevent you from pushing ahead through the choppy waters. Navigating this particular ocean is, I found, the only way to make progress. Yet only embark on such a costly expedition if you are clear that it is what you need, and must do. The road ahead will be more than a little rocky. I hope my book can help you to find your own shock absorbers and escape pods, whatever they turn out to be.

Oh yes, I almost forgot: there is some music theory among these pages. Fast forward if required. Rest assured, it tails off as things get somewhat, shall we say, creative?

Howard Smith

PRELUDE

'I've got a right to be wrong,
My mistakes will make me strong,
I'm stepping out into the great unknown,
I'm feeling wings though I've never flown'

Joss Stone, 'Right To Be Wrong'

1

KATY STEPS ONTO AN ESCALATOR

In which I decide my life must change, ask for a piano lesson and reflect on my abundant good fortune. I find two delightful teachers and the value of a penfriend willing to join me for the ride.

This is the story of how, in later life, I learnt to play the piano and became a musician, of sorts. Three years were spent in the glorious effort. While I did not achieve all I had hoped, I was, nevertheless, pleased with my modest progress. How did I do it? There are many ways to learn. This is my journey, nothing more nor less. You might regard it as unusual: others might react, 'Yeah. So what. Of course!' You be the judge.

I am sixty. How did I get here? Like so many, I took piano lessons as a child. I started when I was ten. Also, like many, I threw in the towel when I should have stayed the course. I was twelve, going on thirteen.

Here's the problem many of us faced. My childhood music teacher was a kind but a somewhat crusty and rather unimaginative lady. She taught 'pianoforte' the traditional way – learn a scale, practise a piece, sit an exam, pass a grade – move to the next square or go back to jail. It was soulless. I enjoyed tinkering with many of the pieces she set, but something was missing. My teacher never identified the problem, and I, a child, could not figure it out. Daily practice was … uninspiring. And not for lack of time at the keyboard. Despite its age and poor condition, I loved our family piano and could spend hours pressing random combinations of keys to hear what sounds I could conjure. Fascinated by how the instrument's strings vibrated with one another, I would turn my head to one side and listen carefully, ear pressed tight against the soundboard. Resonance: it was addictive. A favourite pastime was to hold down keys at the bottom of the keyboard (so their strings could vibrate freely) while striking notes at the top in what I later came to learn was 'staccato'. I would then reverse this formula: open strings in a high register and play staccato in a low register. By such means I could summon up the most mysterious harmonies and sustain these 'voices of the night' (as I called them) for what seemed minutes at a time, only removing my hands when I could no longer hear the faint reverberations.

If there was a problem with the way I was being taught, it was not for lack of interest. Quite the opposite. Classical, jazz, old, new, tonal, atonal ... I have always loved music of all kinds. Yet – and perhaps this is telling – repertoire was never discussed with my teacher; our relationship was barren in that regard. Was it this missing personal connection that prevented me from taking my teacher's weekly prescription seriously? Perhaps if I had spent as much time doing what she asked as I squandered in undisciplined random experimentation, things could have turned out differently. But it was not to be. Inexorably, the scant practice I did manage evaporated. After several weeks of this delinquency, I had nothing new to show my teacher; at least nothing that would impress her. The dreaded 'next lesson' – always the same format – became more and more, well ... embarrassing. Our time together had become a facade. And behind the facade, unbeknown to her, my interest in music had morphed from the practical to the theoretical.

What parent can know what is truly going on in the mind of a teen-ager? My loving parents assumed they were giving me music lessons. To me, however, our piano was more an object of curiosity, an engineering marvel, than it was a musical instrument. I remember the occasions when I removed the front panel and watched, fascinated, as the hammers and levers, pecking and bobbing like birds at the taut strings, moved in synchronisation with my fingers. I was not playing the piano, I was performing a physics experiment. It was a laboratory demonstration accompanied by a cacophony of dissonance, shifting and dancing in time with the intricate mechanism. Had our piano been a musical box or fairground automaton, I suspect I would have been equally satisfied just studying its movements for hours on end in an attempt to discern its inner workings. The 'engineer' in me was rearing its head.

Observing my unusual response to the piano, my parents must have been frustrated. It was not that they wished to show off a virtuosic son to all and sundry, to have him perform musical parlour tricks (though they would have loved this, no doubt). No. Any disappointment they felt at my lack of discipline arose, I am sure, from their understanding of the joy that playing a musical instrument adds to life.

My mother adored the piano. She could rattle off a handful of set pieces and would do so on almost every conceivable occasion. There was one – if only I could recall its name – that she must have played a thousand times. She was, however, far from an accomplished musician. This did not matter to her, nor did it detract from my enjoyment of listening to her play. Watching her hands fly up and down the keyboard, I saw my mother come to life. Prone to mild depression, no doubt related to what she described as the 'tedium of domesticity', music (and poetry) were her escape. She was a product of 1950s postwar Britain.

My father, a hard-working and diligent civil servant, had never played a musical instrument, at least not to my knowledge. He never touched our piano, not even out of curiosity. Odd, for it had belonged to his mother and, judging by its age, perhaps a grandparent, too! A modest upright (though intricately decorated), the elegant machine was strictly off-limits to him. The lid could have been nailed shut. Were such activities, in his eyes, the preserve of those with a more aesthetic and 'artistic' temperament? Yes, that must be it. I think he saw the world as divided between those who work and those who do not; between commerce and the arts; an artificial segregation I have never accepted. And sitting at the apex of what my father no doubt perceived as a remote, other-worldly pyramid of non-working artists, were the celebrities and maestros of the day.

Whenever a great pianist or orchestral conductor appeared on television (André Previn being omnipresent at the time), my parents sat in awe, silent, immobile, wrapped in reverence. No one was allowed to speak for fear of breaking the magic. Did they imagine how I might one day perform? This was never stated or even implied, but I felt a gulf between that which I witnessed on TV and the awkward indignity of my weekly lesson. There I was, perched on a two-seater stool, next to a person who must have seemed, to a child, ancient indeed; prehistoric, no less. Cramped in the small back room of her fusty semi-detached, she, her piano and the furnishings of the room hailed from a different age. They held nothing for me. I could not reconcile my mother's love of music with the 'tuition' I was enduring. It must have been a vexation for her (less so for my father) when my piano teacher informed them I was making negligible or no progress. Unless I could be 'more disciplined', she wrote in a letter – a letter I was required to bring home in a sealed envelope – there would be 'little point in me continuing to see Howard'.

And so, for a few more painful weeks, I was again urged to practise, practise, practise ... but found I could not. My parents had no choice; we were not a wealthy family. There was scant spare cash to throw around. I remember once overhearing their anxious discussion of a hire purchase contract: we needed a new sewing machine. And so my father withdrew his support for my dysfunctional music lessons, with my total agreement and relief. I had moved on to other interests.

It was 1970. 'Technology' was teasing society with a plethora of new gadgets. On the racks of newsagents and in many bookshops, and alongside more conventional hobbies (model trains, knitting, and so on) was a new kid on the block: *Popular Electronics* magazine. Brightly coloured illustrations of eager boys and girls adorned the covers of this exciting new title. Wide-eyed, beaming, studious, staring at a bundle of wires and components strewn on a table around which they sat attentively, the impression created was so space-age, so thrilling. Whatever were they building, I wondered? I had to find out. And so my father began to fund my next teenage diversion.

The third Saturday of the month was precious. I would travel to London, specifically to the Edgware Road, north of Marble Arch. Here was a cluster of specialist shops able to provide any component required for any electronics project, no matter how bizarre or impractical. For like-minded young people in the early 70s, this was an unlikely meeting place. Many browsed, often without aim, digging through dusty shelves and boxes, hunting for something we didn't know we needed but which might just spark an idea for a project. Having soaked up the atmosphere and listened to other enthusiasts, I would return home excited, my bag packed with an assortment of switches, resistors, transistors and integrated circuits, my pocket money much depleted.

To those of a certain age, the Edgware Road cluster is now a distant memory. Google it. Ah, nostalgia. Today, our Aladdin's caves have all but disappeared, replaced by smarter outlets selling – what? A potpourri of pre-packaged domestic security systems, home audio, garden lighting and other consumer gadgetry. Dull. Nothing to build here. How the world has changed. Little did we baby-boomers know that our Saturdays spent on the Edgware Road were the spark that would lead some, myself included, to become the geeks and the nerds of the digital age (viewed with a healthy dose of ambivalence by those to whom 'engineering' was strictly a no-go area). Nor could I have imagined, decades later, that I would revisit the same London street, this time to hire a practice space in the basement of a smart piano showroom: the venue for my first songwriting class! As a teen, I could never have imagined such a leap forward and fundamental change, and only remembered the strange connection while writing this book. Uncanny. A randomly chosen venue where I would work with a songwriting tutor, yards from the spot where I had spent so much of my youth. The coincidence connects my past and my present, the decisions I made as a child and the change I sought in later life.

My childhood obsession with electronics is a story in its own right. It will never be written and will not appear here, other than to explain that I was good at science and maths (at least that was what my form teacher was always telling my parents). Was I being channelled? Maybe. Yet I did find the practical side of science a delight. I have always loved making things. If something needs fixing, sticking or assembling, and especially if it involves many parts and a plethora of nuts and bolts, I am interested in it. Instruction booklets have never appealed; I prefer to make mistakes as I go along. Not necessarily the best recipe for learning a musical instrument. As a teenager, the time I spent with a soldering iron, the blank canvas of a copper-clad circuit board and a zoo of wonderfully diverse and colourful electronic components does not bear thinking about. Misspent youth? Perhaps. From the vantage point of post-middle life, I cannot escape the conclusion that, as with the family piano, I may also have been tinkering when it comes to electronics. Again, was something missing? By 1975 I had discovered its name: software.

It is difficult to imagine how strange this ethereal substance must have seemed to the general public (if indeed they had even heard of it) when I first recognised its potential to change the world. The programmable microprocessor, and later the Personal Computer, gave me two things no other hobby had before: control *and* creativity. No longer was I merely assembling a kit, I was now creating! And that which could be created was limited only by my imagination. Joy. Fewer rules to follow. Like the musical notation I came to study decades later, this software was infinitely malleable. I began writing all manner of code in earnest. In hindsight, the connection between programming and music theory now seems obvious. Was I composing in bits and bytes when writing code?

To older engineers of the era, the newfangled software, and the computer languages in which it was written, were often dismissed as a minor extension of the control-logic circuitry with which they had grown up. We upstarts, however (I was now sixteen), knew better. No doubt about it: software was the future! Obviously. The fact that, to people outside our circle, 'code' was so mysterious only added to its appeal. We were racing headlong to the computer age. Our quiet hobby set the stage for what would become today's computer science and software engineering: the subject of prestigious academic degrees.

By 1977 I had joined the first cadre of enthusiasts who built, customised and programmed the earliest personal computers. Little more than bare-board systems, often without a case, these remarkable devices became the innovations that led to the likes of Apple, Microsoft and, eventually, to cloud computing … to Amazon, Google, Facebook and the rest. Many of my compatriots were writing the first computer games. That particular pastime held no interest for me. I was fascinated by theory, and specifically abstraction: the way low-level assembly code – instructions close to the hardware function – could coax my gadgets to speak in high-level, more human-readable programming languages. I still have one of those machines and it still (just about) works. A career was born; my life as a programmer and IT engineer was settled. Did I select this path? I suspect I was guided by influences and market forces far more powerful than any contrary idea I may have unconsciously harboured to pursue a life dedicated to music.

My parents were mystified. The wires and half-built circuits strewn across the corner desk of my tiny bedroom (I was still living at home) meant nothing to them. My father may once have looked inside a valve radio, drawn by the enigmatic orange glow of its vacuum tubes, but that was the extent of his engineering curiosity. To my mother, my projects were nothing more than annoying dust traps that prevented her from cleaning my room. Under strict instruction never to touch, let alone move, my contraptions, she had no choice but to accept that my bedroom was now to be omitted from her obsessive housework. And if I tried to explain what I was up to, I am sure that I failed. 'What on earth is that boy talking about?' they must have asked themselves. 'What *is* a computer scientist, anyway? Is that a profession?' My parents knew what a physicist was because my teacher had explained to them that 'physics was the future' and that one day I would be admitted to a great university to learn the theories of Einstein, Feynman and Heisenberg. And they knew what an engineer was … didn't they build bridges? As for software – if it were soft, did it even exist? It was an utter enigma to them. And yet my parents tolerated my new obsession. More than tolerate it, in fact, they funded it, encouraged it, even if they did not understand it. I can imagine them thinking 'Perhaps it's a sign we have raised a clever boy?'

By the time I was thirty and had completed my first professional software projects, I was on a different planet, and my parents had been left behind. To the end of their days they never touched a personal computer or a web browser. The gulf between their life experience and the potential of what we now call 'digital' was simply too great. I was never able to explain its consequences to them. Who, from the perspective of the late

70s, could have imagined the growth of that nascent industry? Had I announced the intention to become a concert pianist, my parents would no doubt have regarded this as a more reliable and secure career choice than the 'computing' of which they knew nothing. But any anxiety they had once harboured about my direction proved more than unfounded. To build a high-flying career in the rapidly expanding computer industry was like falling off a log to those of a 'making things' kind of mentality. And yet, despite my accelerating success at work, largely the result of teenage experimentation and unrelated to any academic achievement (schools did not own computers in those days, and nothing close to programming was taught), music still tugged at my heart. And so it was, a few years later, that I discovered the electronic synthesiser. Oh my!

It is no exaggeration to admit that I was as obsessed with synthesisers as I had been with electronics. I still am. Programmable machines that conjure never-before-heard sounds, synthesisers were a marvel. Far beyond vibrating piano strings, yet built on precisely the same physics, these astonishing instruments were full of the electronics I loved but also sported a keyboard that looked for all the world like a piano! That connection between electronics and music I found thrilling. And the sounds these machines made ... delicious. The future was clear. Computers would take over the world, and the soundtrack of our lives would be an electronic form of music our parents would hate. Perfect. Entranced by these miracles, I spent much of my free time concocting new timbres and experimenting with oscillators and filters. Just as with the vibration and resonance of the piano (a remarkable technology in its own right, as any quality piano maker will attest) I found the new method of synthesis addictive. Not only did I have keys to press, but I had knobs to turn, sliders to push and a plethora of parameters to tweak. Yet for all this 'creativity', there was no ... music. Adrift in a sea of sound, without direction or progression, I was treading water once again: free-wheeling experimentation without a goal or purpose.

The sterile relationship with my childhood teacher may have stifled any chance I had of deliberately choosing to become a musician. Still, I can thank her for one gift, a gift whose significance I could never have understood at the time. She had taught me the correct way to sit at the piano, how I should position my hands and, crucially, the fingerings I should adopt to avoid tripping over myself. I had been given a modicum of keyboard technique, albeit limited. It was a shame, therefore, that she never spotted or engaged with my latent interest in the theory behind musical composition. Where she expected me to observe the maxim that 'practice makes perfect' in readiness for the next exam, I was more interested in dissecting the notation of the piece she had assigned or, better still, writing my own! But in such endeavours I was left entirely to my own devices, seeking out whatever books I could find at the local (and rather dismal) library – no Internet in those days. But books were there for the taking if one cared to look. And I did. How I eventually lost my precious copy of *Traité de l'harmonie* (*Treatise on Harmony*) I have no idea. It was a gem, and I have since learnt that many academics and musicologists regard the work as one of the most important in the history of music. Written in 1722, the book was the first to codify the principles of tonality that dominated Western composition for over two centuries. In over five hundred pages, Rameau's tome sets out an entire harmonic system. It explains musical intervals, chords and modes, and the practical rules of modulation and progression. I found the author's explanations fascinating but, without guidance from a teacher interested in theory, the bulk of the text proved impenetrable. Put simply: I knew I loved music. I responded emotionally. But I did not understand why, or how.

My school friends were, I believe, perplexed by my enthusiasm for the music of Benjamin Britten and Sir Michael Tippett. As for Maxwell Davies and Harrison Birtwistle, well, whenever I eulogised those guys, I fear my chums concluded that I was a pretentious show-off. Not so. I loved the feeling such music evokes if one chooses to listen. And listen, I did. Close and deep. Even as a teenager, I could cry for Ellen and Peter in Britten's *Grimes* and wonder at the mysteries of heaven and earth during the finale to Tippett's *Child of Our Time*. Of how I came to know of such works I have no clear recollection. Certainly not via my piano teacher. Perhaps a flirtation with the school's music department? Possibly. Yet I did not take music O level, let alone A level … far too many physics and mathematics tests for that. I had been pigeon-holed as the scientist/engineer. And not sitting 'music' prevented me from being entrusted with the key to the lid of the music department's gorgeous grand piano. Annoying.

Notwithstanding the direction my schoolwork was taking, music continued to tease. And while listening to my modest collection of vinyl records, sitting there on our bookshelf was Rameau's intriguing book, pregnant with potential. Was it able to explain how the great works of the twentieth century … worked? I needed to find out. After studying the first few chapters, much to my surprise I discovered I could now compose short musical sequences. There was a logic here. Intriguing. And in my naïve enthusiasm I began to imagine how it might be possible to turn these fragments into completed works, compositions that would (one day) be performed by a great orchestra. Yet these sporadic and clandestine attempts to make music (of which not even my parents were aware) amounted to just a few bars, sometimes a few staves, only two sheets of which survive to this day. One is a two-part fugue in G minor. On it, my teenage handwriting proudly asserts that I intended it to be performed by 'two treble recorders'. The other sheet, now faded, contains a single and unduly atonal melodic line, to be sung, it states confidently, by 'the baritone voice' and 'similar in style' to that adopted by Britten in the final recitative of his masterwork, Opus 66, the *War Requiem*. The tenor Peter Pears, his partner in life and music, sings words from Wilfred Owen's famous poem:

> 'It seemed that out of battle I escaped
> Down some profound tunnel, long since scooped
> Through granites which titanic wars had groined.'

My own melody, in no particular key, sometimes descending in semitones, at other times leaping atonally, is set to words from Mark 16.9:

> 'Now, when Jesus was risen, he appeared first to Mary Magdalene, out of whom he had cast devils.
>
> 'And she went and told them that had been with him, as they mourned and wept.'

Sitting at my piano today, picking out the notes of this music written four and a half decades earlier, I find they echo the style of a recitative from William Walton's *Belshazzar's Feast*, another work I loved as a teen. Had I been imitating? Probably. Certainly. But I'd like to think, not always. I vaguely recall something else I had 'composed' … if only I could find the sheet upon which it was scrawled … a short but terribly complex piece for the piano, involving patterns of notes I could hardly play, and, to the untrained ear, no doubt indistinguishable from the more dissonant works of Stockhausen! Did I compose this, or was it a charade: fragmentary random noise? I remember being proud of the piece, yet I never showed it to my piano teacher, nor indeed to anyone else. Had I done so, she would no doubt have been dismissive, or worse.

And so, as months turned to years and years to decades, real life took over from childhood fantasies. I was never to be a musician, let alone a composer. The dream of making music faded as dreams often do, preoccupied as many of us are by the work needed to support a growing family. Yet I continued to fiddle with keyboards of all kinds, whenever and wherever I could. My musical output over those four decades was, however, laughable. It consisted of little more than a series of strange sounds emanating from my many synthesisers (grown in number around the house), fragments of works I imagined (and pretentiously named) but never completed. Doomed to play these naïve ideas over and over, ad nauseam, the repetitive motifs and rudimentary chord sequences became, I fear, a family joke.

Fast forward. Forty years.

On that wintry day, Friday, February 14, 2014, I was struck by a sudden and startling realisation. It hit me hard: I had wanted to play the piano all along! No electronics, no synthesis, sequencing or distracting software between me and my instrument, just my mind and my hands: raw, unprocessed, analogue. It may sound self-centred, churlish even, but there is no other way to say it: I harboured a profound regret. Despite a glorious life with my wife and soul mate. Despite a rewarding career in the booming computer industry of the 80s and 90s. Despite watching as our children took their first steps, teaching them everything we knew, our hopes and our pride as they embarked on their own adventures at university to emerge at last as adults. I had every reason to be more than content and no reason to regret anything. But I did. I regretted giving up on music. Terribly.

Forty years! Fear welled up in the pit of my stomach. Was I too late? Was it even possible to learn at my age? Would the effort pay off if I tried? What standard could I hope to achieve? I knew from childhood experience how hard it would be to make progress. I was never a 'natural' at the piano. Was this why I gave up so early? The thought horrified me. But, I argued, if I did not restart now, right away, this minute, I would never find out. And so, with that spectre hanging in the air, everything clicked into focus: I was in the Last Chance Saloon. Lacking the plastic mind of a child, I figured maybe five or six years, no more, to make an attempt at the marathon before an ageing brain gave up the ghost, unable to take on a challenging new skill. 'Too late' became my inner mantra.

Why does one choose to do anything? What prompt or encouragement leads, inexorably, to the decision to act? I was out shopping, something mundane no doubt ... and yet ... almost without thinking ... I stepped into our local music shop, approached the front desk, drew a breath and asked the young man behind the counter whether I could buy a lesson. And as if my question were the most natural in the world, he replied, 'Sure you can.'

And I did.

And this book is the story of what happened next.

The shop assistant, polite, softly spoken, sporting a T-shirt adorned with the dark image of an electric guitar, asked about the kind of music I listened to and wished to play. I muttered something inarticulate about jazz, and before I could say more he had suggested the name of a suitable teacher, one of several on their books. Quick as a flash an appointment was made for a trial lesson. The young man had not even asked which instrument I wished to learn. I thought this odd at the time, but let it go. I still had my shopping to collect.

My assigned teacher's name does not concern us here, but if he ever reads this book he will know who he is. He was, still is, and always will be a talented jazz musician. He plays, he writes, he arranges. He directs a gospel choir. And, as it turned out, he does not teach piano technique, even though he plays all keyboards wonderfully. His passion is the bass, electric and acoustic. He is what I longed to be all along, and still wish to become, that rarest of things … the multi-talented creative musician-composer. When you have the good fortune to meet a teacher like this, there are only two things that can prevent you from learning: a congenital lack of talent or an inability (or unwillingness) to take on the work required. I cannot speak about the former, but I have never been shy of the latter. I therefore had one thing going for me at least! I also suspect (I know) that I am presumptuous enough to believe that all blocks or deficiencies of aptitude can eventually be surmounted given sufficient time and effort. Time and this story will tell.

A far cry from the grandiose piano showrooms found in the fashionable centre of many large cities, this music shop, my music shop, was unassuming in every sense, and very much on the wrong side of town. It sat amid a series of cheap restaurants and low-life outlets. Yet, smartly presented and efficiently run, the shop did quite a trade in music lessons, serving a broad community. The staff were polite, helpful and knowledgeable. The place positively buzzed. The large shop window, displaying mostly guitars, both acoustic and electric, was littered with what looked to my eyes a random selection of accessories and other paraphernalia. Presumably, each had a clear purpose in the life of a musician. Which would I need? I wondered.

Inside the shop, set out along one wall and intruding into the central aisle, was a selection of digital pianos. They varied in price, but none was expensive. The wall opposite held a series of tiered racks displaying a bewildering variety of sheet music, theory books and course materials for those pupils wishing to sit 'graded examinations'. The effect was workman-like, no-nonsense, straightforward. This was a place for the practical musician, I judged. And it was here that I was to meet my teacher in just a few days' time. I could have been alright nervous, or at least a touch apprehensive, but I was not. More than excited, I was champing at the bit. But where were the practice rooms?

To my surprise, the lesson was to take place in the basement. I asked to see. The shop assistant directed me down a flight of steep, narrow stairs, at the bottom of which were several small claustrophobic performance rooms. The keyboard room seemed particularly cramped, hardly enough space for an upright. My heart sank. Was this how my journey was to begin? Yet as I looked more closely, as with the retail floor above, each room was eminently practical, orientated to whichever instrument was taught there. It was adequate. I could cope. After all, I was only committing to a trial lesson. Wasn't I?

Looking back, it seemed so simple an act to step into that shop and ask for tuition. Why had I not done so a decade before? Two decades before? Procrastination? Distraction? All the clues had been there: my love of music, of keyboards, of sound. Couldn't I have found the time to weave an hour's practice into family life? Was I really so tired after a day at the office? What would have prevented me from finding the time for a few scales and arpeggios before setting off on my commute? Nothing. What about after dinner, or later in the evening? Indeed: what had stopped me?

I loved my work.

I was a computer fanatic and, as my family often reminded me, talked of little else. My job, designing complex computing systems, had led to real improvements in the world. I was an engineer, a researcher. It was marvellous, creative, all of that. Surely there was no time for anything else but work and family, family and work; the daily grind. Yet, approaching retirement, our children young adults in the throes of leaving the nest, I often found myself reflecting on how I should spend the second half (OK, the remaining third) of my life. And so I made a vow. Whatever my post-working life was to become, it needed to be different in kind from all that had come before. If my past had been dominated by engineering and science, my future should be dedicated to the arts. And not as a post-retirement hobby. Absolutely NOT a 'pastime'. A new vocation! Yes. The simple idea buried itself deep in my subconscious. And from this seed I convinced myself that I needed a new purpose, one that would take me out of my engineering/computing comfort zone: something to scare the willies out of me. Music! Could I, even now in middle-age, become a musician? This (frankly ridiculous) goal seemed to fit the bill perfectly. Music in all its guises: ill-defined, fuzzy, difficult to pin down, this darn-right mysterious wonder would surely demand a different kind of creativity than the 'innovation' expected of me in the lab. Wouldn't it?

There was a moment. I cannot say precisely when, but there was a moment during the last few difficult years of my working life when everything and everyone around me at the office felt artificial, removed from … life. And my mind flipped one-eighty degrees. I'm reaching for a metaphor. Yes, that's it … I needed to switch from the digital to the analogue, from bits and bytes, arcane systems, software code and the rigour of consulting, to a world of sound, harmony and beauty. I'd always known this world existed. I'd craved it without ever realising its significance. Goodness, I get goosebumps merely writing about it. And now, with a music lesson firmly in my diary, the first since childhood, the seed of that lure was growing. Still listening to a great deal of new music – indie pop, modern folk, jazz, contemporary, classical and everything in between – a spectre appeared at the back of my mind. I got to wondering … could I play that? Could I compose that? Am I creative? Could I have conceived that music? And I became determined to find out. As Jodi Picoult once observed, 'The music we listen to may not define who we are, but it's a damn good start.' And even before my first lesson, in the basement of that modest shop in which I'd placed so much trust, I knew my journey would be more than learning set pieces by rote. It was to be about musicianship in the fullest sense of the word. Don't think nooks and crannies. Think freewheeling highways, wide-open vistas, beautiful valleys and mountains; a lifetime of exploration. Excited, I did what I always do when I make an important decision, I wrote an email to a dear and lifelong friend. Let's call him the penfriend; for this is the role he plays in my story. We have known each other forever, having met at primary school – coincidentally around the time I was taking my ill-fated steps as a child pianist.

As you can imagine, my penfriend knows me well. Too well. Still working, but adrift of the certainty of long term employment, I found myself needing to share the ups and downs of the unremitting struggle to become a musician. Yet he never seemed to mind my frequent, and often jarring, intrusions into his inbox. Week by week, month by month, he heard all of my frustrations; in real time. He never once failed to reply, always offered encouragement, and always continued our conversation by asking a thoughtful question or by prompting me to think about my goal in a new light. While he would never regard himself as 'musical' and has no ambition to learn an instrument (other than a flirtation with the drums), he has one of the most inquiring minds I know. He read biology at university and has retained a particular interest in neuroscience. Music offered a bridge between us. How is harmony heard? Why is certain music so emotional? These were themes to which we would often return.

I remember the time my penfriend and I visited the Natural History Museum in London. He wanted to show me 'the most complex object known to man': the human brain. There it was, preserved in some evil brew, its spinal cord hanging beneath. Ugly. So unlike the beautiful music *it* must have heard, I thought to myself. The experience set the tone for much of our later discussion. I doubt our conversations helped him with neuroscience, but I want him to know that he helped me, enormously. Our frequent interactions crystallised my thoughts. His questions forced me to explain what I thought I knew, and revealed what I did not. He became my sounding board and agony aunt. The back and forth of our correspondence proved a much needed pulse of reinforcement along the way. By setting ambitious (some would say over-ambitious) goals that were then chiselled in stone within our exchange of email, I was more able to keep the promises I was making to myself and to him. How easy to forget a commitment made without fear of the indignity of losing face to a close friend. It was a boon for which I shall be eternally grateful; he kept me going during the most difficult – and occasionally dark – periods of my journey. How many emails? Too many. They number in the thousands. My penfriend, you see, is a real friend. True to form, his careful archive of our discussion became a valuable aide-mémoire for the details set out in this book. This volume is not, however, a music theory text, and absolutely not a scientific treatment of the subject. Sorry, there are plenty of those available elsewhere. All I offer is an honest description of how I felt and reacted to the musical challenges I was tripping over along the path of the escalator on which I found myself.

I seem to have been so lucky. I was fortunate to find a teacher who, as you will learn, gelled so perfectly with the only way I found I could learn as a returning adult. And I was blessed to have a close friend willing to listen as the story unfolded in all its glory and horror. Moreover, two years into my quest, I met another musician, a talented singer-songwriter, who became both an unexpected friend and later my mentor. She showed me another side to music, far from arcane theory; the mysterious process that she calls songwriting and I call voodoo magic. I shall never be a successful songwriter, nor do I have any pretences in that direction. Still, the act of hatching a beautiful song (music and lyrics as one) takes us about as close as we dare go to the frightful precipice I call 'creativity'. I felt I needed to feel that cliff edge if the change I sought in retirement was to be authentic. My beguiling dip into songwriting, about which there will be much to say later, became a revealing complement to the rigours of piano technique and music theory and an essential element in my transition from the digital to the analogue. Songwriting, perhaps more than anything else, fitted my 'everything must change' prescription perfectly.

So why this book?

To be clear: I did not set out to write. I had no intention of doing so. It takes time to hatch a book, and I had far too many scales to practise and chords to learn to be distracted by what some will no doubt regard as a self-indulgent vanity-publishing project. To catch up on lost years, anything that ate into the spare time I had, needed to be eradicated. After all, I was still working a demanding day job. Yet the book is here, in your hands. How? Forgive me, but that (most painful) part of the story will have to wait until later.

So here it is: *Note For Note*. Buckle up, sit up straight and, if you have the patience, follow me on the escalator as best you can. Who knows, something I found along the way might help you. Writing it down certainly helped me. And if my tale of the twists, turns, immovable walls and blind alleys of this highly unusual mode of transport nudge you to make a similar decision – to walk in, bold as brass, and ask for a lesson – then hang on tight. It will be the mental thrill-ride of your life.

Did I reach my goal? Maybe 30 per cent, perhaps a little more. Was that enough? No way. But that's just me: Mr Never Satisfied. Is my story unusual? I think so, but you must be the judge of that. Let's get started.

VERSE

'I never liked jazz music because jazz music doesn't resolve. But I was outside the Bagdad Theater in Portland one night when I saw a man playing the saxophone. I stood there for fifteen minutes, and he never opened his eyes. After that I liked jazz music. Sometimes you have to watch somebody love something before you can love it yourself. It is as if they are showing you the way.'

Donald Miller, *Blue Like Jazz*

2
WEEK ONE

In which, as if by magic, I am given a glimpse of what it means to be a musician. At least, that's what I thought.

My teacher turned out to be the nicest guy. We got on like a house on fire from the get-go. Ten years younger than me, approaching fifty, I learnt that his family grew up in the Caribbean. While steeped in gospel and jazz, his musical knowledge and instincts far exceeded any specific genre. After a few words of introduction, we were right down to business.

As he quizzed and probed me to figure out where I was on the musical spectrum, I told him I remembered something about 'grade three' as a child, but could not be sure and had absolutely no idea what that would mean four decades later. He then asked me to do something or other on the keyboard … which I fumbled.

'I suspect you know more than you realise,' he observed.

Was he merely being kind? Then came the surprise:

'You understand I am not a piano teacher, right? I do not teach technique. If you need a qualified piano tutor, you should look elsewhere. I'm a semi-professional bass player who also plays keyboards.'

I should have noticed the electric bass in the corner of the room: a marvellous instrument, six strings (unusual), at least four different hardwoods, beautiful grain, and handmade by the look of it.

The next few minutes were confusing. I did need a piano teacher, didn't I? Wasn't that why I had asked for a lesson? He suspected not. His view was that I needed to learn about how music works. The playing, he said, would be 'something I could teach myself'. I was doubtful about this but, for the time being, suspended disbelief. His personality was irresistible, and I wanted to trust him.

At ease with the piano, he could improvise over a set of chords and magically, effortlessly, make music, modulating fluidly between keys and all while weaving (to my ear) exquisite harmonies and bewitching tunes. Most remarkable of all, however, was his encyclopaedic knowledge of the history of music, the depth of which became apparent in the weeks and months ahead.

I would mention a band or a tune, and whether he knew the song or not he was able to determine (with considerable precision) the origin of its style and the basis of its harmony. More often than not, he could also pinpoint the specific musical influences of prior composers and songwriters that had led to the music being written and recorded. To perform such miracles, he had only to listen to a piece once. A delightful example of his insight occurred in our first thirty minutes together. And it gave me my first lesson in harmony.

Having failed to adequately answer a question about my own musical interests, I threw in the name of an obscure progressive folk-rock band from the 70s, hoping this might allow him to draw the right conclusion.

'Never heard of them', he said, flatly.

Asking if I could use his laptop, I pulled up a track from the group's second (wonderful) album.

'Ah yes, I see. Interesting. When did you say this LP was released?' he inquired, now engaged.

Confident, I replied that it was 1972. More questions followed.

'How old would these guys have been when they made the record?'

'I guess about twenty-two.'

'Ah,' he exclaimed, 'so, as teens, depending upon what their parents were listening to, these young men might have heard this ...' and quick as a flash he dialled up a 50s jazz tune. There it was, precisely the same harmonic sequence. Even I could tell! Different song. Different era. Utterly different genre. Same harmony. Wow. My new teacher had performed this extraordinary mental feat in less than five seconds. It was a kind of magic, or so it appeared to me.

This first gestalt experience cemented the teacher–pupil relationship. While having limited knowledge of classical music, and appearing uninterested in my (relatively recent) infatuation with modern folk-pop, we collided in the rich brew that is jazz/fusion/gospel/R&B: the creamy soup from which so many influential musical forms and compositional ideas had hatched. How lucky I was. A teacher, chosen at random by the simple act of stepping into the first music shop I tripped over while out shopping, shared many of my musical tastes.

Over the next two years, we would often use our time together to explore a specific tune and try, as he put it, to 'understand where it came from'. His ability to find connections between vastly different styles was repeated time and again. It was how he taught and a delightful way to introduce what to me were entirely new concepts: how basslines 'move'; how chords 'progress'; how a melody is woven into and extends the 'signature notes' of a 'prevailing key'. Week one, and I was being exposed to ideas my childhood teacher would never have invoked.

If my adult teacher was, as he claimed, not a piano tutor, he was clearly some kind of serious musicologist. How he acquired such extensive knowledge is unclear. I never did ask him, but, as the weeks rolled by, as my journey edged forward, I began to get a feel for his methods.

He claimed that the music we listen to during our formative years has an indelible impact on the kinds of music we can improvise or compose in later life. Much had happened, he explained, to develop musical language since the 70s and 80s. 'You must stretch your ears,' he insisted, 'if you are to contribute to the development of new music yourself.' Frankly, this sounded like an impossibly distant and ridiculously lofty goal, but what a statement! Again, my childhood teacher would never have suggested such a thing. To improvise, to compose, I needed to listen far more carefully to the music I was already listening to, he insisted. Memorising a tune is one thing; understanding why it sounds the way it does is something else entirely. I needed new ears, not just new hands and fingers. My first 'piano lesson' was moving in a direction I could never have predicted.

Every one of our lessons was a joy. No more so than when he occasionally played me one of his own compositions. Impressive. He admitted that even he was, however, 'stuck in the 70s', the result of the pervasive influence of the film music and TV tunes of the era. And as if to prove his point, he kept on performing the magic trick: 'Ah yes, Howard, this reminds me of the theme from …' and proceeded to play a few bars, note perfect. He had what I now call an 'instant musical recall', far beyond typical 'ear training'.

How did my first lesson end? With an assignment, of course. My homework for the week was to:

- Write out, on stave paper, each of the triads (three-note chords) that fall on the seven notes of the C major scale.
- Repeat in all twelve keys, C to B (including all the black notes.) Add the correct key signature to each.
- Do the same for the (so-called) '7th' chords (four-note chords).
- Spell (i.e. name) each of the chords above, stating their quality: major, minor, dominant or diminished.

Yes, that's one hundred and sixty-eight chords (7 x 12 x 2). And having written them down – 'neatly mind you' – I was tasked with playing them on the piano, one at a time, 'as slowly as necessary', up and down the keyboard, through all the scales, taking note (pun intended) of the patterns formed. Specifically, I was asked to 'look carefully at how the shapes of the chords of different qualities fall on the notes of the scale'. It sounded impossibly complex, but my teacher described the exercise clearly enough and gave a worked example. I agreed to try but warned him I did not expect to get far in a week. Dismissing this caveat, he promised advice via email, if needed.

As I left the shop that day, I purchased two thick pads of music paper.

Sitting at home in front of my piano – pencil in hand, a blank stave daring me to write – the exercises were awakening something that had lain dormant for a lifetime. I felt a palpable sense of excitement.

Adagio – curled up peacefully on the opposite side of the room – shifted lazily in his basket, not a care in the world. Tilting his head, with a sideways glance at me, our pet's expression revealed little. An implied question? And just as quickly he buried his face between his paws. I returned to the task at hand. Chords! Hundreds of them.

A few days into this laborious activity and my rudimentary harmonic knowledge was expanding. For the first time in decades, my repetitive four-chord pop progressions were being challenged. It was the start of a journey which, under my new teacher's guidance and the gaze of Adagio, would expose me to a bewildering zoo of new-to-me concepts. I was finally learning something about music.

The 'playing' did indeed appear to be entirely incidental.

3

THE NEXT LESSON

In which I learn that music has an inner logic, that improvisation can break the code when pushed too far, and that root movement, chord inversion and voice-leading are vital anchoring skills for any musician.

Hoping to curry favour with my new teacher, I completed all but one of the exercises he had assigned at the end of my first lesson. How different from the recalcitrant child, never willing to take my teacher's instruction, always poking around inside the mechanics of our piano – avoiding practice in favour of experimentation. Intent on progress, my homework was perfect, a thing of beauty. No more putting off practice in the mistaken belief that my next lesson could *be* my practice. No more panic as the days counted down to that frightful day when, once again, you are expected in the musical psychiatrist's chair. As I learnt over the coming weeks and months, my adult teacher would never allow it. And to illustrate the point, he told a story about an ex-voice-pupil of his (yes, he taught singing as well as bass and piano).

'She seemed unable to grasp that progress means work,' he explained. 'Like a lot of kids these days, she was looking for instant gratification. There is no such thing in music,' he asserted.

After a few weeks trying to turn the lazy girl around, he asked her to leave and not waste his time further. It cleared the decks for him to work with more a motivated student. Memories of childhood embarrassment came rushing back. No more. As a returning adult, I needed this clarity of purpose. He would never put it this way, but the implication was clear:

'Step up or don't waste my time.' I think he sensed how desperate I was to play the piano and was signalling an irrefutable truth. What he actually said was this:

'If you are not practising,' he told me, 'you are not a musician.'

For my teacher, musicianship *was* practice; period. Well, he never did have to remind me to practise, but as if to hammer home the message, he would occasionally open up about his own practice regime.

'You know, Howard, I felt like a child again this week,' he admitted.

He went on to explain some esoteric improvisation technique he had been struggling with. And as my own work piled up over the coming weeks, I reciprocated in kind and told him of my struggles. He always found a way to help, either by explanation or demonstration. More than patient, he was a saint. He needed to be. As you will see, I have a tendency to push on beyond any natural limits. It's the only way I find I can make progress. Don't get me wrong: practising to reinforce technique is necessary but by itself does not guarantee success. Some things are just hard, no matter how one tries. I call them blocks. And I encountered many in my time on the escalator. One early example concerned that staple of jazz and popular music, the 'lead sheet'. We'll get to that soon, but ... What was teacher saying? Chords. Something about 'inversion'? Sensing I had no idea what he was talking about, he took a step back and began with the basics.

The C major chord, for example, consists of the notes C, E and G, of which there are many across the eighty-eight notes of the piano keyboard, albeit in different registers. Thus, no matter which C, E or G you play together, and in whatever order, you always end up playing a C major chord. Go try it. Hear how every combination, no matter how chosen, sounds curiously similar. And while doing so, feel free to duplicate any note: you'll still perceive the C major harmony. Why? My teacher explained that the way we hear music is not in terms of absolute frequencies but of intervals and the ratios between tones. Hearing this from the horse's mouth, it brought to mind my teenage experiments with piano-string resonance. Had I been on the right lines all along? Over--eager to impress him, I bragged that I had once worked out the mathematical relationships within the notes of a rather unusual chord. I expected him to be interested. He was not. He held a disdain for overly academic approaches to music-making. He placed a significant emphasis on ear training and, more specifically, upon the exploration of the combinations of 'horizontal' and 'vertical' intervals that 'make sense' aurally and therefore musically.

'Listen to everything you can,' he urged, 'music of different genres, eras and styles.

'Not to have absorbed the music of the past would be like learning a foreign language having never visited the country in which it is spoken.

'How could you possibly understand the culture if you had never engaged in meaningful conversation?'

Music was, for him, practical first and foremost, a tool no different from speech. I suspect he was frustrated by my tendency to veer towards the theoretical, not that he would ever say so. There we'd be, he demonstrating how chords 'progressed' and me attempting to emulate his magic, hands hovering tentatively over the keys. Then, abruptly, I'd stop short and throw a curveball.

'Surely,' I asked, 'notes have mathematical relationships whether we like it or not. Can't I use numbers to help me make music?'

'Yes,' he said, 'but that's not interesting. Music just *is*. Hear it. What you just did ... it sounds good, doesn't it?'

And of course he was right. It did.

Notes do form aural relationships, whether played together (vertical alignment or 'harmony') or in sequence (horizontal alignment or 'melody'); and as I was to learn, any progression can be mashed around and still sound just like the song that originated it. It's hard to break the logic of a good tune. Ask any jazz musician. They exploit this aural physics spontaneously as they improvise. But even they can push logic too far: the song can … get lost. The trick of improvisation, I was told, is to sit on the boundary between a literal rendering of the original harmony, and chaos.

'That's where jazz resides,' he said, and suggested an experiment.

Try this: tune your radio to a 'modern jazz' channel. Wait until they play a jazz standard, a well-known tune. Can you hear the original under the expansive improvisation? Does what you hear resemble anything more than a jumble of random sounds? Are your ears sufficiently attuned and sympathetic to the aural language the musicians are using? Contemporary jazz can (and often does) take harmony to extremes, pushing the boundary of the acceptable for the casual listener. An analogy: when a non-native speaker enters a room full of people holding a dense, complicated, fast-moving conversation, with all its subtleties and nuances, they will miss much of what is being discussed. Music is just like that.

Learning to play the piano, I was beginning to realise, is not only about ensuring that our fingers find their way to the right places at the right time but also about orienting our mind to the form and structure of the music. To perform by rote, without such understanding, is little more than a party trick. And I was not interested in party tricks. I'd had quite enough of those in the previous forty years – the same chords, over and over. Had I known then what I know now, I could have been far more creative, even within the constraints of popular music. Pop uses only a small number of chords, yet every tune is different. How? My teacher explained that there are a zillion ways to play even a handful of notes.

Add the variations that arise from different rhythms and instrumentation, and the possibilities become endless. Step by step, lesson by lesson, my teacher was introducing me to ideas that shape the 'vibe' of a song and how tiny changes can radically alter how music is heard. And that's just pop. What about Bach, Brahms and Britten? What about Birtwistle!?

Eager to unlock more of the musical code, I encouraged my teacher to spill more of the beans on the riddles of composition. How could the same twelve notes have led to such a vast and diverse repertoire?

'Hey, slow down, Howard,' he advised, 'first things first. What do you know about chord inversion?'

A chord is inverted when a note other than the root moves to the bass. Take F-A-C, the F major triad. That's root position because the bass of the chord is also the name of the chord: F. Play the same notes in the order A-C-F, and we have the same F major harmony but with A in the bass. This is 'first inversion'. In musical notation, it is written as F_b or F/A (F *over* A in the bass). Play the chord as C-F-A and we have 'second inversion', written as F_c or F/C.

Don't be confused by the subscripts $_b$ and $_c$. These do not refer to the notes B and C. They are just labels, F_a being root position, F_b being the first inversion and F_c being the second inversion. If a chord has four notes, it has a 'third inversion', notated F_d.

I found these details fascinating and had begun to write about them to my penfriend, eager to share my developing knowledge with him. We'd spoken about music theory before, but now I had something to say.

'Hey, I've just learned this. Take a look.'

My penfriend, who has never (to my knowledge) sat at a piano, found my email explanations less than illuminating. I lost him completely when I first introduced the much feared (by many students) 'figured bass' and the joy of notation such as 6-3, 6-4, 5-♯6, ♭9-8-5 and (many) others.

When I explained that these terms could also be abbreviated (6 meaning 6-3 for example) and that specific notes were assumed to be played with no need to spell them out on the stave, he made his view perfectly clear:

'That kind of arbitrary, illogical, archaic shorthand would frustrate the hell out of me,' he wrote. With obvious irritation, he continued:

'What you have just described, that's not theory. It may be a language, but if so it's an exceedingly odd one. Whatever it is, it alone would prevent me from ever embarking on any kind of a musical journey.'

Of course, I disagreed.

Many of the elements of music which at first sight appear to hail from some arcane corner of history make perfect sense, each serving a specific purpose. At times idiosyncratic, musical notation allows the most intricate works to be written succinctly. Entire symphonies can be transcribed in relatively few pages.

'Lighten up,' I urged my friend. 'If we are to have a meaningful conversation about music, the eccentricities of notation are going to be our necessary evil. After all, it's not mathematics! Trust me. This stuff is the easy part, even if physics does determine the ratio of tones in a mysterious chord and the intervals of a beautiful melody.'

The explanation did not convince him.

'Does any of this have anything to do with being a musician?' he asked, citing jazz. 'Don't they just "jam"? Surely jazz musicians past and present don't learn this stuff, Howard?'

Hmm.

Yes, musicians who improvise can take advantage of the aural logic without necessarily assigning numbers or symbols. We marvel when they create a soundscape for their listeners without the distraction of a complicated score. But does this imply that they are untrained in theory? No. Any significant musician, in any genre, has been to music college.

Haven't they? Many hold advanced degrees – those who do not, often work with a co-writer who has. Surely, theory is not just important but vital. But I digress. Back to chords.

The presence of a selected bass note in each inversion casts a subtly different sound to the harmony, but the chord retains its root from a theoretical (and aural) perspective. This feature turns out to be incredibly useful when writing music. The ability to move the bass note allows chords to flow into and between each other, allowing basslines (the sequence of lowest tones) to evolve organically and harmonic progressions to ... well ... progress! Get the idea of chord inversion, in theory and in practice, and you are well on the way to understanding another vital concept for any keyboard player: the oddly named 'voice-leading'.

I cannot remember when my teacher first told me about voice-leading. Certainly no later than lesson four. He continually emphasised its importance. I am still, even now, far from happy with my ability to use voice-leading at the keyboard, in real time. It takes more than practice – something I cannot quite put my finger on needs to be internalised. The best jazz musicians do it without thinking.

In music theory, the word 'voice' refers not only to the singing voice (tenor, bass, alto, soprano) but also to the specific melodic lines within a score. It could, for example, be a flute part, a cello part, or the separate lines of music created by two hands and five fingers when playing the piano. In a Bach fugue or 'invention' (two-part, three-part), there will be several such 'voices' at play. These combine to form chords when notes sound together. Voice 'leading' refers to the art of allowing the individual voices within the harmony to move smoothly, avoiding unnecessary leaps (large intervals) between consecutive notes. A simple example:

Suppose I wish to play a C major chord followed by an F major chord. I could play the notes C-E-G followed by the notes F-A-C. In which case the lower voice would be C to F, the middle voice A to E and the upper voice G to C. All three would be ugly jumps, but that would be precisely the way I *would* have played those two Plain Jane chords before I had been taught inversion. It amazes me that I was never told about this as a child. But perhaps it's not so surprising. My childhood lessons consisted entirely of the repetitive learning of set pieces in which all the twists and turns intended by the composer were set out, in precise detail, on the sheet music. There was no reason to explain anything more than to point to the verbatim notes. Here, with my adult teacher, no stone was left unturned, and every possible nuance of the music was unravelled, clarified and demonstrated. And I was lapping it up.

Look what happens if I use the second inversion of C before playing the F chord. The sequence is G-C-E (the C chord) to F-A-C (the F chord). Try it out at the keyboard. See how the lower voice is now G followed by F, an interval of a tone, a single step in a musical scale. That's good voice-leading! Yet in this example, the C still jumps to A and the E to C: not ideal. Now see what happens if I play it this way: root position C followed by second inversion F. Now the sequence is C-E-G followed by C-F-A. Notice how the bass note of each chord is the same, C: no movement required! Only the upper two voices change, and only by one step. That's *really* good voice-leading. A choir could sing that sequence and it would sound great. Indeed, the art of voice-leading emerged from the practice of choral composition over centuries, and it is central to how the vast majority of music is written today.

When my teacher played the piano, he exhibited perfect voice-leading. Stunning. His fingers hardly seemed to move, yet the changes of harmony emanating from his improvisation were startlingly beautiful. Magical. It was as if he were conjuring music from the keyboard as a magician releases doves from beneath a cloak. Had he not revealed the trick,

I could never have understood. I was not ready.

More homework was required.

Over the next seven days, I was asked to:

- Write out, on stave paper, the root position and first and second inversions of each of the seven possible triads, in each of the twelve major keys. That's two hundred and fifty-two chord shapes (3 x 7 x 12).
- Find all these chords on the keyboard. Play with them. Pick out their inversions. Listen to each carefully.
- Mark the pairs of chords that share one, or two, notes. Notice how, with a simple inversion, these chords can be brought closer together on the keyboard.

I was being told, in effect, to 'sit in the corner' and write 'I shall never pull Mary's hair again' … a thousand times. Similar instructions followed lesson by lesson, step by step. In contrast to repetitive technique exercises designed to work the fingers, my teacher was giving me tasks intended to work the musical brain. Seeing how the notes fell on the written stave helped me to find chords by name, and this in turn helped cement their shapes under my hands and in my muscle memory. In his efforts to turn me into a musician, my teacher was playing a game. Subconsciously, I was taking the critical first steps towards the essential art of voice-leading.

4

THE LEAD SHEET

In which I learn the value of ambiguity, as contrasted with rote learning, performing monkeys and pianistic automatons. And that's jazz!

I believe it was week four when I was first asked to 'play' a lead sheet. One page of music, melody only, chord symbols above each bar or measure. The title revealed that it was a well-known tune, a 'jazz standard', one of thousands my teacher could have chosen. I knew the song, but had never played it. It looked innocuous enough.

I was able to read the notes. And I knew what a key signature was. The chord symbols, however, were new to me. C^7 was a dominant seventh chord. $E\text{-}^7$ was an E minor chord with an added minor seventh note. Those I understood, but C^{13sus}? And what to make of $F^{7(alt)}$ or indeed $G^{13(\sharp 11)}$, let alone $B\flat^{7(\sharp 9 \sharp 5)}$? I had absolutely no idea. A few minutes of explanation followed, and the mud began to clear.

This was not so hard. Anyone can understand such weird-looking chord conventions, even my penfriend – *if* he can keep his head and chooses to try. Still, recognition is merely the tip of an enormous iceberg, or should I say an unfathomably deep rabbit hole? Understanding a notation and being able to use it in a musical context, during a performance, are very different things. The lead sheet did not help. It was like nothing I had ever encountered before.

My childhood piano lessons had consisted of learning set-pieces and supporting these with exercises, scales and arpeggios. The music, typically by well-known classical composers, was transcribed in minute detail.

Every note. Every rest. Their length, emphasis, connection to other tones and expression. If a note was to played staccato, it was so marked. If two notes were to be slurred, a curved line would be drawn between them. The lead sheet was the polar opposite of such mathematical precision. Only the barest bones of the melody was illustrated. This hardly told my right hand what to do. As for the left, was the performer supposed to make it up, or guess?

The mysteries of the lead sheet, sometimes called a 'fake sheet' by jazz musicians, deepened. My teacher explained that the chord symbols were themselves only a guide. Precisely how they were to be played or 'voiced' was left to the creative artist. The sheet might state C^7 signifying a C dominant seventh chord (C E G B♭). Still, the musician might decide to drop the 3rd, the E, or choose to add the 9th of the scale, the D one octave above the root C. The lead sheet was deliberately incomplete to allow for a degree of improvisation. The notation also appeared to be ambiguous, revealing few, if any, clues to help the musician divide the notes between the two hands. Nor did it state which notes to duplicate to add depth to the sound. It provided no advice on voice-leading (how to get from one chord to another smoothly) and few details of rhythm. It did, however, specify the structure of the song in terms of its different sections: verses, chorus, introduction and repeats. The lead sheet was in effect a skeleton of the music, and a poor one at that. A fake. Guidelines, not rules. And I was supposed to *play* this? Yikes.

My wife once told a friend of ours, a professional cellist, about the 'fun' Howard was having with lead sheets and how they differed from traditional sheet music. Never having been involved in the world of jazz, our friend found it fascinating that, based on so little information, such vibrant performances could be conjured. Classically trained to accurately reproduce and interpret the composer's intentions, she admitted she would not have known where to start. Jazz musicians are not, however, randomly 'experimenting'. They hear the way the music is developing and respond to it. They call this 'the changes'. Anticipating shifts in harmony, they judge which musical scale to use at any moment: the pool of notes from which to craft a melody line. Since the harmony, and therefore the available notes, is continually changing, one can imagine how complex it is to pull off this 'trick' of improvisation. It's a mind-boggling mental game and presumably why it is so fascinating to watch a live jazz performance as the artist or band take off into a flight of fancy never imagined by the originator of the tune.

For the child enduring a traditional piano lesson, 'playing' a piece requires them to accurately reproduce the notes of the music as written on the stave. The child is essentially learning by rote, hence the agonising advice, to practise, practise, practise. Then, in the exam room, they are rigorously tested: can they move their fingers in sync, and strictly in time, to the patterns of notes and measures of music in front of them? Putting 'expression' and 'interpretation' (let alone 'art') to one side for the time being, the child becomes in effect a music box, or perhaps one of those auto-magical street barrel organs with a monkey sitting atop. The child learning by rote is little more than an automaton, a wind-up doll. They perform in lockstep with the notation as it rolls by. Is this categorization of their hard work a cruel misrepresentation? Yes. But it is precisely how piano lessons felt to me as a child. Compared to a jazz musician improvising from a lead sheet, the child that was me might as well have been linked mechanically to the piano hammers via a series of pulleys, joints and push–pull levers. A performing monkey!

Let this sink in. The gap between a child performing a graded exam piece and the jazz musician improvising from a lead sheet is a chasm. As an adult, I was being asked to take what felt like a giant leap into the unknown. Was there a middle ground? Were my feelings about the strictures of childhood pianism wrong, misleading and unfair to the legions of hard-working teachers schooled in classical pedagogy as promulgated by the leading music boards? Years later, I would come to understand that my bleak view of classical technique was wrong. Dead wrong. But back to the here and now.

Placing the lead sheet on the stand above the keyboard, my teacher asked me to begin to play.

'Go on, try this,' he urged.

I stared at it. I thought about it. I read the first chord symbol. At least it was one that I recognised. I positioned my left hand in root position on the bass note of the chord. I placed my right hand so that my little finger (pinkie) rested on the first note of the melody. I was hoping something would ... well ... happen, but I simply did not know what to do next. I could not 'play' one bar of the music in front of me. It was terrifying. A wellspring of emptiness opened in the pit of my stomach.

Silence.

My teacher, realising that nothing was going to happen, stepped in to demonstrate. And the piano came to life in his hands.

Over the next few minutes, he showed how it was possible to beat out a basic rhythm by playing each chord in sequence while also picking out the melody. Unable to hold back, his talent was irresistible. Magical. There appeared to be no relationship between what his hands were doing and the sparse notation of the lead sheet. Yet the resultant music sounded ... well ... wonderful. There it was, set out before me, the thing I had always longed to do: 'make music'. And at that precise moment, in this my fourth lesson, I realised that my desire to play the piano was far more than a casual whim. Not a pastime to while away the twilight years of a gentle retirement. No. I was not in thrall to the *idea* of playing the piano.

I *had to* play the piano. This was never going to be a hobby I could drop when the going got tough. This was a hunger; an urgent need.

I knew now that I would spend the next few years with this teacher and that my adult lessons would continue week by week. No way was I going to choose to step off the escalator I had joined. I had no idea, however, how hard the ride would be or where it might take me, but I was committed to the path and wrote several over-excited emails to my penfriend to demonstrate my delight. The words 'vocation' and 'new life' most likely amused him and tempted him to sarcasm. Yet he was, as usual, calmly pleased for me and sent encouraging replies. And over the months ahead, his curiosity about what I was attempting, and specifically *how* I was learning, deepened.

My friend once asked whether I thought that the musical 'intervals' I had told him about were, in some inscrutable fashion, coded in the human brain; that perhaps *Homo sapiens* was pre-wired to appreciate consonant music from birth. I had no clear answer and concocted some baloney about 'learning processes'. My half-baked, incomplete and unscientific theories only served to expose my lack of understanding. And his questions continued to pile up. He has an acute mind and was applying it fully in the spirit of my new venture. Emails flew to and fro in a frantic attempt to unlock the mysteries that reared up at every juncture. All too often, however, our interaction would end with 'I'll have to ask Teacher about that'. One difficulty was that my weekly lesson was frustratingly short, typically thirty minutes, or, if my teacher had a free slot, maybe forty-five minutes to an hour. We could easily spend half the lesson talking about a single song! No sooner had we looked at this week's lead sheet, discussed its details, listened to the piece and decoded its chord symbols, than our time would be up: the clock on the wall always ticking. If, as I often did, I threw in a tricky 'theoretical' question, it often occupied the remaining time. My teacher would then assign a task for the coming week. All too soon I was packing my bag, squirrelling away any notes I had made and hastily leaving the room, only to glance at the next person sitting patiently in the cramped waiting area. What kind of musical enlightenment were they seeking, I wondered?

My task this week centred on the lead sheet I had failed to play and which my teacher had brought to life so effortlessly. I was to 'study the sheet carefully', 'decode the chord symbols' and see whether I could 'hear the changes'. Then, 'and only then', he allowed, I should 'play it'. One page of music – surely that could not be so onerous? Compared to a fully notated classical piece, my first lead sheet was an inconsequential trifle. And I had a whole week ahead of me to crack it. So I made a promise to myself: to work hard, hours a day if necessary. I committed to 'play' the music and show my teacher what I could do during our next lesson.

Little did I know how tortuous this task would prove to be.

5

NEMESIS

In which my failure to play a simple lead sheet reveals a truth about the importance of being able to play in every key. I draw a new conclusion about how a child is taught.

Week five. Problems. I knew there would be more lying in wait during my time on the escalator, but this week's nemesis will be forever etched in my memory.

The single page of music I had been asked to study exposed how little I could play. My teacher's flush of enthusiasm for my latent ability (from childhood) was premature. Here, I am not speaking of scales, arpeggios and the like, but rather the movement of my hands across the keyboard to make … music. I honestly thought six days would be enough to crack what was, let's face it, trivial music. Not so. Sitting at the piano, the lead sheet propped in front of me, I must have spent hours making sense of it, mostly to no avail. Why was this so hard? It was plain as day that I was starting from rock bottom. Whatever grade I had achieved as a child, if indeed I ever did, meant little. Zilch. Returning to the piano is nothing like getting back on that old bike.

My frustration with the lead sheet grew with every passing hour. Adagio sensed my unease and rarely stayed longer than a few minutes in the room where we kept our piano. Nothing I did could tease the music from its notation. I could (just about) pick out the melody line, but could not retain it well enough for it not to be a distraction while I tried, in vain, to play the left hand. I could play the chords by themselves, but they did not flow smoothly into one another. My voice-leading was terrible!

Worse, my rhythm proceeded in fits and starts, uneven, unsure and irregular. This was far from a musical performance. I decided there and then that my ability, or rather inability, needed more than a makeover or repair shop. It needed wholesale replacement before I could ever find it in me to sit in front of another lead sheet.

As the next lesson drew near, I had to admit defeat.

The first ten minutes in front of teacher were a fumbling attempt to play the opening few bars. He was kind but had to acknowledge that I needed 'a few more foundations in place' before making that particular journey again. To my great surprise, I was not at all fazed by the admission of failure. How different from the embarrassment I felt (and remember all too keenly to this day) as a child. With this teacher, I felt no reluctance to explain my struggle and no resistance to taking his advice on board and putting it into practice. I was self-motivated and just needed to be pointed in the right direction. No one was telling me what to do, what to play, which exercise to focus on next. I relished this freedom and became obsessed with the challenges he set. The escalator was, so far, moving only slowly, but I knew that would not always be the case. I needed to orientate and steady myself for what was ahead. Music was becoming a game in my mind, one I was determined to win.

And so it was that pupil and teacher took a step back and I learnt how to move between chords elegantly and fluidly. My teacher insisted that I needed to become familiar with a minimal set of standard 'voicings' for any harmony to work well in a contemporary or jazz context. He explained that by having a variety of chord shapes 'under my fingers', I would be able to focus on the music and hesitate less at each bar and beat.

A voicing is a deliberate choice of notes from which to build a chord. The simplest voicing of a major (or minor) chord, as taught to a child, would be 135. That is: the root note, the 3rd of the chord and the 5th.

Since such vanilla triads, perfectly acceptable in folk music, are manifestly simplistic in a jazz context, my teacher suggested we should 'start with 7th chords consisting of four notes. Later we will try 9th chords, that's five notes,' he declared. Goodness.

A typical 7th voicing, I was told, was the four notes of the chord in the order 1357 or 5713 (second inversion). My teacher added that jazz musicians will often 'add colour' to their harmony (chords) by replacing the 5th with the 6th thus: 1367 or 6713. This sounded illogical to me, but I simply accepted what he told me. And he was right. Try it yourself and hear the difference. Cute. So I now had four voicings for each chord. Soon, he assured me, I would be able to spot such voicings while listening to a tune. I was doubtful, but he emphasised that I needed to 'hear' and not just 'listen'. Good grief. Forget my ears, I was finding it hard enough to get my hands accustomed to chord shapes; they altered radically depending upon which key I was playing in.

Play 5713 in C and the white notes are relatively (I stress *relatively*) straightforward to locate. Play in E♭, or B, and the shape of the chord outlines the contours of the black and white keys. It's as if they are mirror images of each other: black for white, white for black. These physical differences proved useful, distinguishing otherwise harmonically indistinguishable chords and therefore building an intuitive familiarity with the keyboard. I'll be saying a lot more about this later but let me highlight one suggestion right away. If I were to pick out one piece of advice from this book, it would be this: whatever scale, exercise or chord sequence you choose to practise, play it in every key. Always. Every time. Why?

It is oh, so easy to be lazy and play on the white notes alone. Great music can be had in C (witness *In C* by Terry Riley), but not being fluent in the other twenty-two key signatures (major and minor) will substantially limit your freedom to perform with other musicians. There are a few reasons for this. At a practical level, it is highly unlikely that C will be appropriate for all music. A musician may well need to choose a key and a register that suits their instrument. Yes, not everyone plays the piano! Choices of key signature become especially problematic when a mix of instruments play together, each with their unique physical constraints. To a piano player, it can come as a surprise that it is almost impossibly difficult to play (and improvise) in certain keys on instruments such as the sax and brass. However, the primary reason for being comfortable with *every* key is that few pieces, if any, remain strictly in the same key throughout.

Music modulates, and the competent musician must be familiar with the corresponding scales. Besides, music often 'steals' harmony, or melody, from related keys, creating variety and interest in the music. It is common for music to shift between major and minor, if only for one chord. For example, the minor chord on the 3rd note of the major scale (E minor in C) might be replaced by the major chord. Another popular idiom is to replace the minor chord on the 3rd with a major chord on the flattened 3rd (E♭ major in C). If your eyes are glazing over, don't worry. Mine did, at first. In any case, for all these reasons, and probably a few more besides, it is vital that everything we do at the keyboard – scales, arpeggios, finger exercises, chords, progressions – we do in every key. I cannot stress this enough. Make it a habit. Yes, it means playing each exercise twelve times over. Yes, that means extra practice. Trust me. It will pay off. You will grow as a well rounded musician.

Back to the lesson. There I was, powerless to play an undemanding lead sheet. My teacher was right. I needed to get back to basics. He set the following exercise for the week ahead:

- Write out, always on stave paper, the two standard voicings (1357 and 5713) for four-note 7th chords.
- Do this for all seven notes of the major scale, in all twelve keys,

'spelling' (naming) each chord.

- If you have time, do this again replacing fifths with sixths, creating two more voicing options (1367 and 6713).
- Play all four voicings in all twelve keys, in the order that works for you. Listen to the subtle differences each makes. Explore their shapes. Feel the way they sit on the keyboard.

Goodness, how many chords is that? Four voicings, seven notes each scale, twelve major keys: three hundred and thirty-six. Using stave paper, however, made writing these down absurdly simple, if somewhat tedious. Why? Wherever a particular voicing is placed on the stave, its *visual* shape stays constant. The key signature, a symbol to the left of each stave, stamps the harmony on the music. So it turns out that chords are easier on recognise on paper, less so on the keyboard. Their shape on the piano – and therefore the hand positions to play them – varies considerably from key to key. Yet in due course even these grow weirdly familiar. How?

When a child looks at a piano keyboard for the first time, all they see is a jumble of black and white notes: a right royal mess. Thus, teachers tend to introduce new key signatures gradually, adding one more 'black' sharp (♯) or 'black' flat (♭) each time the previous scale is mastered. Having learnt C on the white notes, the child is taught that G contains an F♯. They practise the new G scale over and over and are then given a simple piece to play in that key. Having mastered G, they are then taught D, adding C♯ to the F♯. And so on through all twelve keys. Exam boards take a roughly similar approach. My teacher, by contrast, placed no emphasis on any one key; none. Each was as important as any other. He rejected the stepwise key-by-key approach because he believed it slowed, rather than aided, progression. I could not judge, but one experience at home was evidence of his claim.

A young member of our family, who was also learning to play the piano, had been practising her new piece. The music was in F major. The scale contains a single black note, B♭. She had performed the piece for us – beautifully, I might add – but I was curious about whether she knew what a key signature actually was. She did not understand the question. When I explained that the pattern of notes was precisely the same for a piece in C, in G (with its F♯), in F (with its B♭) or even in G♭ (with its six flats), she was amazed. Working together, we counted the steps and half steps – the tones and semitones – between each of the notes of the major scale. Her teacher had never shown her this pattern! Once I had demonstrated that all major scales employ precisely the same scheme, the child could pick out the simple melody she had learnt in F and play it in any key I requested. Suddenly she was a more able musician.

Another example. A professional accompanist who plays the piano for my wife's choir, when confronted by an unfamiliar score, can more or less play it 'at sight'. The rumour, moreover, is that he can also transpose the music to any desired key, in real time. The sheet music might be written in F, but he can play it in E♭, G, A, etc. How is this possible? Clearly, he is not translating notes one by one. No, he must have internalised key signatures across the keyboard to such an extent that he is reading in relative intervals, not absolute note values. Thus he plays what he sees in whatever key he wishes. This experienced accompanist's feat of transposition is not merely a case of him positioning his hands at different starting points on the keyboard and hoping for the best when the conductor picks up the baton. That would certainly not work, since the mix of black and white notes changes during modulation. For example, the key of E♭ starts on black, continues as white, then returns to black. A key such as A, however, begins on white, continues on white, then move up to black, before returning to white. The shape of these scales on the keyboard is diverse, yet the logic of their intervals remains constant. Thus, musicians who practise in every key develop a deeper awareness of each key-centre, and each possible scale. Their familiarity with their instrument is profound and far exceeds that of the 'I play on the white notes' musician. My conclusion: getting 'stuck on the white keys' – being able to only play in C – is a sure-fire way to kill your chance of becoming a musician.

'Playing in every key' became a religion and a mantra for me, an obsession. Even something as simple as 'Three Blind Mice' I would play twelve times over. Any child would surely love this game; and it would hasten their progress. It did mine. Though I was never sure that Adagio appreciated the work I had to do; I suspect my short repetitive sequences, at piano volume, upset his cat demeanour. A few minutes into one of my more obsessive sessions and he would quietly leave the room.

Well, I began this week's lesson with a nemesis and ended it with the recognition that to play from a lead sheet requires considerable facility with chord patterns and the associated voicings. Of course, had my nemesis sheet been written out in detail, note for note, left hand and right hand, I would have been able to read the score, practise the movements by rote, and (perhaps) learnt to play the piece well. Without strong 'sight reading' skills, how long would this have taken? Several weeks. And what would I have achieved at the end? A modest party piece, no more. I did not wish to return to childhood and my lessons never did move to 'sheet music'. Quite the opposite.

I am notorious, among family and friends, for a tendency to purchase a surfeit of support materials – in bulk, quantity and variety – to bolster any new hobby, interest or pastime I set my mind to. It's an expensive but necessary habit. My new-found enthusiasm for music was no exception. Led by my teacher, I had already bought three fat books describing the breadth of jazz harmony and two sets of jazz exercises (to complement the classical exercise books – Czerny and the like – which had been sitting unused in a cupboard for decades). In addition, I treated myself to a massive book of lead sheets, over five hundred tunes, a so-called *Real Book*: one of several widely used compilations of jazz and popular music, accurately transcribed from recordings (by ear) and collated by students at the Berklee College of Music during the 1970s. The odd name was chosen, I learnt later, to distinguish 'official' collections from the equally oddly named *Fake Books* (hence 'fake sheet'). These pirated copies were circulating underground among jazz musicians but were often nothing more than poor quality photocopies of published music. As is so often the case, published jazz music is simplified or inaccurate when compared with the original performance. *Real Books*, by contrast, are new transcriptions and typically of much higher quality.

With my harmony library expanding and my *Real Book* to hand, I now had everything I needed to be a musician, I imagined. Even if I could not play the lead sheets, I figured I could learn a lot through study alone. Yes, theory was essential I argued: that must be what I was missing. How could my teacher have expected me to 'play' a sparse lead sheet, let alone improvise from it, without a deeper understanding of 'how music works'? Wasn't that the phrase he had used when we first met? Surely, I argued in an email to my penfriend, I need to know where the music is heading at any point, and intuit where it could legitimately go next? Theory.

'If you say so,' he pinged back.

6
UNBLOCKING

In which I get a measure of the blocks lying ahead in the road, feel their edges, concentrate fully and wrestle them to the ground.

My shiny new jazz-oriented theory books had opened a veritable Pandora's box. The chords my teacher had introduced during our lessons – the harmonies that I had thought fell into the 'advanced' category – were the tip of an iceberg; the voicings he demonstrated, merely a start. I was overwhelmed. With so many chord shapes to master – hundreds – in so many keys – twenty-four if you include the minors – I feel I should explain something about my approach to practice. Repetition. I enjoy it. I really do. Sometimes I think I enjoy scales, arpeggios and chord progressions more than what most people regard as their primary purpose … to make music! I can sit at the piano for hours and never play a single piece, let alone from start to finish. Let's call it aimless improvisation. It's certainly not music, but it is entirely absorbing. I can do this early in the morning, late at night or anywhere in between. Night-time is the best. The dark. The quiet lends a particular focus to the proceedings. I feel I am falling into the piano, descending into the body of the instrument and experiencing its resonance first hand – a glorious place. Turn down the lights, light a candle, string up some fairy lights. Create your own den. Bliss.

Concentration is required. It is too easy to drift, to allow our thoughts to roam while our fingers do all the work. I fought this tendency with all my strength. Nothing I practised sank in until I was entirely focused on the task, hands and mind engaged. During this period, as I played a scale I watched the pattern of tones and semitones meticulously, internalising their contour. This had the knock-on effect that it became more comfortable to play the same scale or chord in other keys. And speaking the corresponding note names and chord spellings out loud reinforced my muscle memory. Progress! But sometimes even concentrated practice is not enough.

Blocks.

I've already mentioned these capricious creatures more than once in recounting my time on the escalator. They came up and slapped me in the face, from so many directions, more often than I care to admit – vexatious and mischievous blocks in all shapes and sizes. Imagine a ten-ton weight placed in front of an empty lot when the local council wants to prevent the space being used as a car park! That's a block.

Blocks cannot be tackled to the ground through the normal process of daily practice. No. Well-intentioned advice to 'slow down', 'build speed gradually', 'break the music into sections' – none of this is likely to help when faced with a block. Blocks are immovable objects. Impenetrable. Stuck. No matter how slowly you play, nothing gives. We fail, even at the first bar, perhaps on the first beat. And it is not only in the area of technique (practical work) where blocks exist. Look for them also in ear training and sight-reading – blocks and more blocks … for me at least.

Here is my take. Blocks are a conjunction of physical limitation (insufficient technique), intellectual misunderstanding (lack of theory) and, typically, psychological inhibition. The latter should not be underestimated. How did I know when I was facing a block? When I had been working for days and my hands still wouldn't do what I needed them to. Then I knew. And that's the time when we all need some full-on, no-compromise, deadly serious unblocking.

Here is what not to do. Do not, under any circumstances, avoid a block by ignoring it. Walk around too many and you will end up in a pianistic cul-de-sac, limiting your progress on every front. I learnt this truth early. Hand independence was a block for me, something all too familiar to adults who come to the piano late in life. Another was playing in 3^{rds}. I told myself I could skip that. I was wrong: music is stacked full of them. The same goes for 6^{ths} by the way, another of my blocks, especially in those tricksy flat-minor keys. These are blocks any intermediate pianist will face. And worse is yet to come. Expect some nasty surprises.

Without my penfriend's patient kindness, I am not sure I could have survived the first few miles on the escalator, lined as it was with blocks. Whenever I was facing a block, and not merely a situation demanding more practice, I would send him an email explaining how I saw it, and then await his reply.

'Dear friend,' I wrote. 'This week has been particularly tough. I simply don't know what to do next. Teacher is calling out the names of chords during our lesson. I am learning much about theory. But he expects me to keep my hands on the keyboard and quickly move to those chords. Here's the problem, I know which notes they comprise, but to move my hands from where they are to where they need to be ... it's like watching paint dry. This is really slowing down the lesson. Worse, I am expected to do this with good voice-leading!'

To such correspondence, my penfriend – not able to understand the depth of what I was struggling with – often replied with a string of carefully worded sentences that added up to 'You can do it, boy!' Helpful, eh? Well, yes, actually. His encouragement and gentle nudges kept me going through my darkest days.

Unblocking. How? Here is what I would do. I'd name the block and allocate a specific day to face it head-on. Still in full-time employment, my unblocking work, never less than a full day, was always on the weekend; often the whole weekend. This, I accept, was unfair to my family, but needs must. I would disappear into the music room after an early breakfast, lock the door (metaphorically speaking) and get to work. I would not allow myself to leave, barring a family emergency, until I had made significant progress. The discipline required was painful. I endured sessions like this maybe once every six weeks. I had no choice. Time was running out for me. Nearing sixty, I needed to get the bulk of my base-camp training completed in a few short years, before my mind lost any more agility. I called this horizon my Zone of Possible Learning. To leave a block in the road, to ignore it, to avoid its gaze, would be a cop-out. It would also be dangerous given the knock-on effect of leaving the illness untreated. Antidotes and vaccines were required.

So there I was, in the woodshed, tackling some block or other, finding my way through the maze. Food and drink were provided through a hatch in the cell window. My penfriend, seeing how I was driving myself and worried that I was ignoring my family, called it obsessional. 'This is not good for you,' he advised, 'Not good at all. You need to relax a little.'

That, my dear penfriend, is not an option.

If you have ever sat alone, desperately trying to perform a difficult task, for twelve hours on the trot, uninterrupted, and only managed to move a small way towards your goal, you have some idea of what it means to tackle a block. It's a mind thing. Repetition, while important, will never cut it. Mind you, I am good at repetition. Very. But what to do when you sense that further repetition is futile?

Mental images helped. I objectified my blocks as substantial weights, or mountains to climb, or walls in which I needed to create a chink so I could push out the first brick. And not just physical metaphors; I also regarded my blocks as intellectual puzzles. As if meditating, I would sit quietly, contemplative, considering my conceptual blocks from all angles, devising new plans of attack.

Here's an example – an attempt to play a particularly complex chord sequence. You know the type of thing: dense chords, no single tonal centre, unexpected shifts of harmony, altered notes, divided between the hands – a puzzle. I could play it at a snail's pace, but nothing I tried had me anywhere near the tempo directed by the sheet. Instinctively, I turned off the light, lay down in the semi-dark and imagined playing the phrase at speed. Visualising the piano, I watched as my virtual hands and fingers moved over the keys as though a spectre flying over a dead body. I 'played' the challenging sequence in my head. This mental feat was tough at first, requiring the utmost focus, but I eventually became adept at what I call 'mental performance'.

It's common knowledge that young pianists should look straight ahead at the music in front of them and not down at their hands. I took this principle to extremes during my first year on the escalator. Undistracted by visual confirmation, often performing exercises 'eyes closed' or 'blindfold', I was attentive to the feel and shape of the music.

As the blocks started to fall, I became increasingly convinced that my head-on approach was on the right lines. No pussy footing around a problem, sidling up to its edges or scurrying around in the hope of finding a hole in a fence. No, it was a case of smash right in and knock up against it; feel its prickly texture and then sneak up behind it, take it by surprise and tackle it to the ground.

Over the course of a typical unblocking session – never less than a full day – I would eventually spy a glimmer of light from behind the wall. A chink would open, a door ajar. Once I saw this evidence, it was sufficient for me to make further progress. I then had the measure of the block. I understood it. I knew where it hailed from and had a pretty good idea of what I needed to change in my approach to future work. Only then was I able to relax and ease off the obsessional accelerator pedal.

Did I fail to knock down some of my blocks? You betcha. Did it matter? Yes, it did. There are many I have yet to tackle. I've made a list of them. I've got them in my sights. They sit at the back of my notebook, waiting patiently. Incidentally, do treat yourself to a fancy practice journal. You've seen them: quality paper, beautiful cover, a place for your pencil, a marker ribbon. Love your journal. After six months you won't be able to live without it. Make a note, every day, of whatever it was that you did to nudge the progress dial towards positive territory. Crucially, you will be able to look back and rediscover the exercises you found most helpful and those you found most taxing. Moreover, you will see patterns in your work, routines repeated just because you can (easy pickings), and exercises you are avoiding (necessary evils).

My own practice notebook was, and still is, a godsend. The daily record allows me to see the steps I have NOT taken. It prompts me to be creative and to design unblocking exercises of my own, remedies honed to whatever obstruction or hurdle I am currently facing. As I am pulled along by the perpetual forward motion of the bumpy escalator I am riding, I need that support. The infernal contraption is always throwing up new blocks. My notebook is one antidote; a joy, not a chore. I will never tire of the small pleasure of returning to a page where previously I had scrawled the word 'Impossible!' only to discover, months or years later, I can legitimately use my eraser to rub out that particular block. Yes, I did eventually find it possible to find any chord, in each of the standard jazz voicings, almost at will, just like my teacher. It wasn't yet 'music', but it sure felt good. Today, my knowledge of harmony and my dexterity with voice leading are still far from perfect, but I consider each a cornerstone of my time on the escalator.

7

THE FOURTH

In which I demonstrate an experiment that anyone can perform. It helps explain the pattern of black and white notes on the piano keyboard, and why the 4th is special indeed.

Not the fourth lesson, but the 4th note of the major scale; in other words, F in the key of C; A♭ in the key of E♭; C in the key of G, and so on. Let me explain. It would be helpful if, during this chapter, you have a piano to hand so that you can play and hear what I heard.

The experiment was prompted by my penfriend. Writing to me, he asked, 'Why, on the piano specifically, is there such an odd pattern of black and white notes?' He still asks this question every so often even though I have explained the reason to him several times. My answer has never wholly satisfied him. And, to be honest, I've never been 100 percent sure. Let's start with the basics.

The white notes sketch out the scale of C major; at least they do if you start on C. Start from A and its a different scale entirely: A natural minor. More on this, and other 'modes', later in our journey. For now, let's keep things simple. We are going to look at the structure of the C major scale.

The twelve notes of the keyboard from C to C (one octave) are evenly divided into smallish musical intervals called semitones, also called half steps or half-tones. The major scale uses just seven of the twelve:

C D E F G A B C

Look closely at the keyboard. You will see that the intervals between these consecutive white notes are uneven. Most are separated by a whole step. But there's a half step between E and F, and again between B and C – my penfriend's question was 'why?' When he plays (or sings) the scale, he believes he is hearing seven *evenly spaced* rising notes. Not so. It's an aural illusion. The reasons are, 1) he is not listening closely enough, and 2) he has become so familiar with the scale from the music he's heard during his lifetime that it sounds to him as if it *were* a line of evenly spaced frequencies. Not so. So where do the unevenly spaced notes come from? How were they selected? Indeed, *were* they selected?

If you have ever pondered this question or questions like it, you may now be wanting to explain that early keyboard instruments were 'tuned' to a single key and could therefore only play harmoniously in that key. You will no doubt go on to explain how J. S. Bach suggested tweaking note intervals so that they were more evenly spaced (well-tempered), and you'll therefore conclude that today's standard piano tuning is an approximation. In other words: on a modern piano, all key signatures are roughly in tune, but no one key is accurately in tune. All this is true, but irrelevant to what we are about to explore here, so let's not confuse ourselves with the history of piano manufacturing and invention. The subtle tuning adjustments that Bach instigated allowed him to write works such as *The Well-Tempered Clavier* but won't help illuminate the correct answer to my penfriend's naïve question. What we need instead is pre-school physics.

Take a string, stretch it out and then pluck it. Stretch it until it sounds like a C on the piano. The string is vibrating along its length. The tone you hear most prominently is called the fundamental, but you are hearing far more than one note. The string is also vibrating in halves, just less so. It is also vibrating in thirds, quarters and fifths, again with a reduced amplitude as we move through the series. I stress: this is really happening and is NOT an illusion. The string is vibrating in smaller and smaller divisions all the way up to the notes we cannot hear because they are either too quiet, too high, or not vibrating at all – the result of the physical characteristics of a string of a certain thickness. These auxiliary vibrations are called the 'harmonic series', also referred to as 'partials' or 'overtones'. Every string of the piano acts the same way. It is what gives each struck note its richness.

Did you find a piano? A real one? You will need one. I will show you how one string causes sympathetic vibrations in others; so-called 'resonance'. A cheap electronic keyboard will not help in this demonstration. A more expensive one may. The very best digital pianos and synthesisers sound more realistic because they contain sophisticated electronics and algorithms that simulate the way a real string vibrates; either separately or against others.

Here we go.

Play C on the piano an octave below middle C. All the overtones are there in that one string. Let's prove it. Let the piano quieten down and then, ever so slowly, press and hold the lower C such that its string is 'open' (no hammer on it, free to vibrate) but *not* sounding. Then, hard and fast (staccato) hit middle C. Hear how it stops abruptly, but the lower C 'rings' as if it *were* middle C. It actually is. You are hearing the lower C 'ring' in halves: as if the string were in two parts. The lower C contains within itself the C an octave above!

Let's repeat that. Wait until the piano is quiet again and hold down the lower C as before. Then hit the G above middle C. It stops sounding immediately, but listen carefully and you will continue to hear it playing in the open lower C string. Huh. Shall we go on?

Hold down the lower C as before and then hit the C two octaves above. Hear how the lower C rings as the upper C. At this point, you will need good hearing because the vibrations of the lower string are now vanishingly weak. I have performed this party trick many times, and it never ceases to amaze me. I am always pleasantly surprised when I hit the E two octaves above middle C and can hear it, albeit faintly, in the lower C string. Yes, I do have excellent hearing.

The notes of the piano keyboard, therefore, correspond to the overtones: the divisions of physical strings. This is why certain notes played together sound pleasant: what musicians call 'consonance' (as opposed to dissonance). The lower C and middle C sound similar because they are, in a real sense, the same note. Ditto G and C: they also sound good together because G is the second partial hidden in the series from C.

Let's play the complete series.

Play the lower C, then the C an octave above, then the G above that, then the C above that. Carry on … the E above that, then the G above that, then the B♭ then the C above that, then the D, then the E, then the F♯, then the G, then the A, then the B♭, then the B, and, just a semitone further, the high C. Phew. Play all these notes in sequence while holding down the sustain pedal. They will pile up, sounding together. Feels consonant? Yes, it does. You have just played all the partials of the bass C.

Here are the relationships:

Note	*Division of the string*	*Note number in scale*	*Interval formed*
C2 (C below middle C)	1	1	Root
C3 (middle C)	1/2	1	Octave (8th)
G3	1/3	5	5th
C4	1/4	1	2 octaves
E4	1/5	3	3rd or 10th
G4	1/6	5	5th
B♭4	1/7	Not in C major	Flat 7th
C5	1/8	1	Root
D5	1/9	2	2nd or 9th
E5	1/10	3	3rd or 10th
F♯5	1/11	Not in C major	Sharp 4th, 11th
G5	1/12	5	5th
A5	1/13	6	6th or 13th
B♭5	1/14	Not in C major, but in C minor	Minor 7th
B5	1/15	7	Major 7th
C6	1/16	1	3 octaves

What lies beyond C6? We could carry on dividing the original string into more and more segments, and so obtain higher and higher frequencies. But look closely … why does the B appear so late in the series? And where is F? We have F♯, but no F. Why?

What's happening is that the B is 'far away' from the fundamental, harmonically speaking. F is missing, it never appears in the series; if it did, the string would be divided so many times that F would be impossibly high in pitch, effectively absent. At least for a human, not a dog. Try folding a page of a broadsheet newspaper in half more than ten times and you'll soon get the idea.

It is the relative volume of partials in a single tone that largely determines the timbre of different instruments. The column of air in a brass instrument acts the same way. As do the metal bars of a xylophone. It is the comparative mix of partials that give each its character: a guitar is plucked; a piano string is hit by a hammer; air is blown through an oboe. Everything about the design of an instrument affects its partials and therefore its timbre. And this is why 'instrumentation' – the arrangement of diverse instruments in a band, quartet or orchestra – is so complicated for composers. But I digress.

Now the surprise. Have you spotted it?

In the regular C major scale, the B *is* right there, up close and personal, sitting right next to C, separated by only a single semitone. And F is the 4th note of the C scale, not F♯. Why?

The C major scale is mostly, though not entirely, formed by 'folding down' the partials of C so they 'fit' inside a single octave. This is achieved by dividing their frequency by two, i.e. dropping one or more octaves. Look at the sequence: as we go up the scale we are collecting all the main notes of C major, C G E A D. These are the first notes encountered in the harmonic series and are the tones most closely related to the root of the scale, C. The B, however, is way up the series, and the F never appears. This must imply something about how the C major scale 'sounds'. And it does. If you have enough patience, let's continue this experiment.

Open your ears.

Play the C scale in order, just one octave ... C D E F G A B C. Familiar? Now try this. Play the B by itself. Does it sound 'in' the scale? Or does it feel out of place, needing to 'go' somewhere? Yup, sure does. The B just begs to have a C played as the next note. It's what musicians call 'resolution'. That B, you see, is 'unstable' once the composer has established C as the root of the scale *in the mind of the listener*. Play the B, and it *feels like* the next note must be C, an aural law of nature. Do you hear it? If not, play the scale again. Then play the B again. Feel the way it pulls the ear *towards* the C.

Now let's listen to F. Play the scale again. All sounds neat and cosy, doesn't it? Now hit F again. Whoa! Feels very out of place. Sounds like it doesn't belong there? Hit it again. It sounds unrelated to the other tones. Do you hear it? You should, if your ear is accustomed to hearing music. The effect is real, not imagined. Even though F is 'in' the scale and sounds perfectly natural when we sing the scale, F is harmonically unrelated to the other notes. It, like the B, wants to resolve or 'move' somewhere. Where? Up to the G or down to an E. Try it. Play the scale. Then play F and then G. Play F again and then E.

If you cannot discern the resolution effect of the F, the 4th of the scale, try playing pairs of notes: intervals instead of single tones. Play C and G together, the interval of a fifth. Play C and E together, a third. Play C and A together, a sixth. Play C and D together (the D an octave above, remember) a ninth. All these intervals sound consonant. But now play C and F together. Sounds odd, right? Yes. Discordant. That F is clearly out of place, yet it's right there, nuzzling into the fourth position of the major scale that everyone, even my penfriend, can sing:

do re mi fa so la ti do (major)

The F and the B, in the C scale, serve a specific purpose. They break the neat maths of partials. They were chosen deliberately, to create 'tension', a sense of movement. Once you hear it, you will always hear it. Sing F, and it seems natural to sing G or E, almost inevitable. Sing B and surely C must follow. It is as if we have discovered a law of music.

If you are still with me, well done. Now for an epiphany.

If you studied music theory at school, you will no doubt have been told about the so-called 'dominant' chord, the 5th of the scale. In C that's the G7 chord. Look at the notes of this chord ... G B D F ... it contains both the B and the F. The G is the bass note, the first harmonic in the C series (other than the octave), and therefore having a strong relationship with the root. The D is likewise related .... but the F and B? We now know they 'pull' towards notes like C, E and G ... suddenly it all makes sense. This is *why* the dominant 7th chord 'resolves' to C. It's called a 'perfect cadence'. Every child has played one. Every child who has completed a theory exam has been tested on cadences. But few know why they work. The dominant chord often precedes the root chord towards the end of a piece. The two chords played one after the other create a sense of completeness. The dominant chord can also appear at the end of a section of music, where it creates a sense of 'hanging there', ready for the next phrase to begin. Do you see why? Such cadences pervade all classical music and all tonal music from any era. It's nothing more than high-school physics.

I accept that musicians don't give a damn about the science of string vibration, but I maintain that the aural experiment described above is one that everyone should experience. I've performed this magic several times. It always elicits a 'wow' from friends and family; even those with no interest in the theory of music. And for a child or an adult returning to the piano late in life, the exercise is more than a 'wow' – it serves an essential purpose. Hearing the harmonic series, understanding how the B, and specifically the F, lie *inside* the major scale but *outside* the harmony provides a palpable jolt of ear training. And none of this is limited to C major: the same is true of all major scales. In E♭, for example, the two 'outsiders' are Ab (the 4th) and D (the 7th, the leading note). It did not surprise me one bit when I discovered that the musical prodigy Jacob Collier is often heard singing up and down the harmonic series, avoiding these dissonances, as he explores the farthest reaches of jazz harmony and explains the concept of 'negative harmony'. Look it up.

So where does this leave my penfriend's original question about the odd-looking pattern of black and white notes? Well, the white keys are laid out conveniently for C major. The black keys are those we need to fill out the harmonic series. As we do, the pattern emerges automatically: two black notes, then three black notes, then two black notes, then three black notes, etc. There is no black note between E and F, nor between B and C, because there is no partial frequency between them; at least, none a human could hear. So there is my answer to my penfriend's question: the white notes on the piano *are* the major scale to which we have become accustomed. The unevenly spaced B and F were chosen to create tension and release in tonal music. Without these two mathematical renegades, there would be no cadences, just a consonant series hanging in the air with little sense of movement. No dissonance. In effect, there would be no music. So let's make some.

8

THE CIRCLE

In which I discover that the physical proximity of piano keys and their harmonic distance are very different things. And that the devil's interval reveals an aural illusion, encoding an irrational infinite sequence.

Sorry about all this theory, it is not to everyone's taste, I admit. If you wish, feel free to skip. I promise we'll get to the more 'creative' period of my time on the escalator anon. That's the way of it for most musicians: from the science to the art. Mind you, I am a theory groupie and have always harboured a desire to compose.

I no longer remember when I first encountered the ubiquitous 'circle of fifths'. It may have been as early as week three, certainly no later than week six. My teacher handed me a sheet of A4 with a circle drawn on it. Set out around its circumference were the twelve notes of the Western musical scale. Read the circle clockwise (or as I have it below, left to right) and the intervals formed between adjacent tones are the so-called 'perfect fifths'. Try this on the keyboard. Play *up* from C:

C → G → D → A → E → B → F♯ → D♭ → A♭ → E♭ → B♭ → F

Read the circle anti-clockwise (right to left) and the intervals formed are also fifths, but only if we play *down* from C:

G ← D ← A ← E ← B ← F♯ ← D♭ ← A♭ ← E♭ ← B♭ ← F ← C

Play any of those intervals up the keyboard and, hey presto, the fifth is now a fourth. And vice versa. Magic. Which is why the circle of fifths is also called the circle of fourths! Yes. C → G *up the keyboard* is a fifth. C → G *down the keyboard* is a fourth. C → F *down* is a fifth. C → F *up* is a fourth. I found this utterly confusing.

So which is correct: circle of fifths or circle of fourths? Both. Which is most commonly used? Well, a Google search for the former returns five hundred and twenty-seven thousand results, while the latter four hundred and fifty-five thousand. Roughly even-stevens. Interesting. Despite the symmetry of the circle, I expected the fifths to score a few more. The reason will soon be apparent. All musical intervals, the ratio of their frequencies, have a mirror image: the interval's 'inversion'. Knowing how to use this difference turns out to be extremely useful to composers.

A fifth is formed between C and G if C is in the bass. If G is the bass, then C is a fourth above: two distinct but related (by inversion) intervals. And when composing a bassline, say, or a melody for that matter, the distinction matters – a lot. The circle turns out to be a visual device that illustrates the harmonic relationship between the twelve keys, their corresponding signatures and associated scales, major or minor.

Children, it seems to me, are first taught the C major scale because it uses only the 'easy' white notes. The child is then introduced to G major, which adds one sharp: F♯. They are then presented with F major, which introduces one flat: B♭. G is a 5th above C. F is a 5th below C. Each new scale, separated by a fifth, introduces just one new note, F♯ in G and B♭ in F, etc. The same is true for any key. The two scales either side of a root, anywhere on the circle, differ by only one note – sharp or flat. And only by one semitone. By contrast, look at the physical position of F and G on the piano keyboard in relation to C.

Lying in the middle of the octave, G is as far as it can be from C, physically. Yet as we have seen, it is as close to C as it can be, harmonically. By contrast, the notes D♭ (C♯) and B (C♭) are snug up against C, a semitone apart. But they are miles apart, harmonically speaking.

Look at the circle. G and F lie either side of C, a fifth apart. D♭ and B are on the opposite side of the clock face. The circle is therefore describing the *harmonic distance* between keys and *not* their proximity or distance on the keyboard. Let's hear this in practice.

Play each of the following major scales, C, F, G, D♭ and B ... Can you hear that these scales sound either close to C or far away? You can? Good. Yet these scales consist of precisely the same pattern of tones and semitones. Weird, eh? Do you hear it? When you do, it will be a sign of your improving ear.

Perhaps you are already a theory super-whiz. Maybe you already use the circle as a practising musician. Whether by instinct or from maths, the circle matters. Musical compositions move through these mathematical relationships to form the beautiful harmonies we perceive, consciously or unconsciously. The circle is an encoding of those progressions. And the mystery does not end here.

There are details of music theory that are nigh on impossible to explain using text alone, combining as they do, hand, ear and keyboard. So, piano to the ready! Let's befuddle ourselves with more theory.

To recap: walking around the circle in a *clockwise* direction yields fifths: C → G, G → D, D → A, and so on. Walking around the circle in an anti-clockwise direction *also* gives us fifths: C *down* → F, F *down* → B♭, B♭ *down* → E♭, and so on. Yet some musicians report that, to their ear, moving anti-clockwise makes more musical sense. Others claim there is no difference. Clearly, there *is* a difference. It's to do with the movement of the bass note. Am I confusing you? I do hope so. It took me a while to work out what the devil was happening. Let's spell it out.

If you move down a fourth or up a fifth, you are moving around the circle clockwise. If you down a fifth or up a fourth, you are moving anti-

-clockwise. But there is one interval where this does not apply. And it's at the heart of music.

The tritone, sometimes called the devil's interval, consists of three whole tones, for example, C → F♯ or F → B. The tritone splits the octave precisely in half. C-F♯ is the same interval (the same ratio of frequencies) as F♯-C. Unlike every other interval, the inversion of a tritone is, therefore, another tritone. Remember your maths, A x B = B x A. The musical tritone is commutative.

Listen to a tritone. Play a few. The tritone hangs in the air, floating, not wanting to go anywhere. At other times it reveals its nature clearly, exhibiting a strong magnetic attraction to one of two keys. It either wishes to 'resolve' to the major key a semitone above its upper note, or to the major key a semitone above its lower note.

Try this on the keyboard: play the interval F-B (notes together, not F followed by B) followed by a C major chord. Sounds 'right', yes? Now do this. Play F-B again but this time follow it with the F♯ (G♭) major chord. That also sounds 'right'? The interval F-B can resolve to either C or F♯ (G♭). It sits on the wall between the two keys, like Humpty Dumpty, undecided as to which way to fall. The tritone not only divides the octave in two but also forms a valid interval in its own right, perfectly poised between two entirely different key signatures. The tritone is a strange beast: ambiguous, ambivalent, paradoxical. When we hear it, it plays tricks on our mind; an aural illusion.

There is a twist in this tale. If we play a perfect cadence (a resolution) several times, our musical ear (brain) settles on the root note to the extent that it perceives the alternate resolution as VERY odd indeed. Try it by playing F-B to C over and over again. You are, literally, programming your brain (via a preliminary action) to expect the C major scale and to shun the F♯ major scale. But the F-C tritone, the devil's interval, is not so biased. It has no brain. You can equally well programme your mind to expect F♯ (G♭) and to shun C. Again, try it. Play F-C then F♯ (G♭).

If you heard the distinctions described in the last few paragraphs and didn't just accept my written explanation, you will have taken another valuable step forward in ear training. The tritone splits the scale down the middle. Every other interval has its inverse *in* the scale. The 5th has the 4th and vice versa. The 3rd has the 6th. The 2nd has the 7th. The tritone only has itself. It is neither entirely in, nor out of the prevailing scale. Where it feels it should be is governed solely by establishment of a root.

How does the brain pick up this signal?

When the brain absorbs a melody, it hears partials (frequencies) strongly related to the scale from which they were selected. Remember the overtone series from a previous lesson? The brain is hearing these relationships without knowing what they are: mathematics. And the most important of these is the harmonic association between scale notes and their root: the name of the scale itself. The fact is, the root is the root. Repeating the root note, or notes close to it, harmonically speaking, establishes it as the root – no matter in what order the notes of the melody are played.

I've been using the word 'half' to describe how the tritone splits the scale. Of course, the tritone is not 'half' an octave in an absolute sense. The tritone is not half a cake or half a mile or halfway between C and C. Rather, it is whatever it means to halve a 'multiplication by two'. This is all about ratios, remember. C to C, D to D, any octave: each is a doubling of the frequency of the string. What's half of a double? The tritone. What is that, mathematically speaking? Rather, it is whatever it means to halve a 'multiplication by two'. This is all about ratios, remember. C to C, D to D, any octave: each is a doubling of the frequency of the string. What's half of a double? The tritone. What is that, mathematically speaking?

Remember those vibrating strings in the last chapter? Come on ... back to those maths classes? Remember your square roots? $\sqrt{2} \times \sqrt{2} = 2$.

The musical tritone (three whole tones) is the square root of two (the octave). If I'm right, that's $\sqrt{2} = 1.4142135$ ... and all the rest of the digits. As any mathematician and school children know, $\sqrt{2}$ is an 'irrational' number. It cannot be written down. To do so would require an infinity of digits: endless non-repeating chaos. Truly random, without repetition or pattern. The same is true of all irrational numbers, the best known being pi π: the ratio of any circle's circumference to its diameter. It is believed that within such infinite, seemingly random sequences of digits can be found an encoding of everything ever written, including the complete works of Shakespeare. 'Random' does not imply noise. Assign digits to musical notes, and we would similarly find the complete works of Bach, Beethoven, Britten and all the rest. If this is true, it must also be the case that we could find – if we could write out the infinite sequence in practice – all works of music yet to be composed, good, bad and indifferent: a profound mystery indeed. Infinity. The tritone; colloquially known as the devil's interval (*Diabolus in Musica*). Irrational. Unresolved. QED.

Oh yes, why did I draw the circle as a line? It became my preferred way of visualising music and, as it turned out, helped me use what jazz musicians call 'stacking in fifths' (or fourths) when 'building chords'.

What has this to do with music? you ask.

Everything.

9

THE MUSICAL MIND

In which, by observing musicians, I note a correspondence between innate musical ability and high intelligence. Questioning my own unrealistic goals, I offer a psychological remedy.

Writing this book, endeavouring to spell out the theory I was gradually coming to understand, could create the entirely false impression that I am a musical genius, rapidly absorbing new concepts and using them to transform my music-making. Nothing could be further from the truth.

During the early weeks and months with my new teacher, it was a case of 'through a glass darkly'. I was glimpsing the beauty inherent in music in dribs and drabs – chinks of light at the end of a long dark tunnel. Learning to play an instrument at any age is tough. Doing so at sixty is not something to be undertaken lightly. The work required is significant. Dexterity and coordination are just the basics. The piano is a complex instrument, perhaps the most complex of all. Playing good music demands a robust intellectual focus: the brain must be fully engaged. Revisiting a few of the emails I sent to my penfriend during this period, I fear, now, they were a garbled mess. Yet writing them down, trying so hard to explain, helped me enormously.

It begs the question: is intelligence a key to making music? I think so. At least, I have not met an unintelligent musician in any genre. On the contrary, those musicians I have had the good fortune to spend time with, are super-bright. And like many smart people, they are delightful to be around. You see it in the twinkle of their eyes. Not all my musical heroes play complex concertos – many play what, to a classical aficionado, might seem trivial – but they bring to their genre a canny unification of mind, soul and body. You know it when you see it. It's a beautiful thing.

Long before this story began, I tripped over a virtually unknown (at the time) songwriter who, it seemed to me, was crafting heavenly indie-pop music. It is no exaggeration to claim that the first time I saw her sing live I was smitten. The gig was held in the upstairs room of a small local bar in the seaside town of Brighton, overlooking the often bleak English channel. To suggest this concert was 'niche' would be an understatement. I counted fifteen in the audience. Yet she sang like a songbird and there was not a blank face in the house. No one could prevent themselves from breaking out into broad and deeply felt smiles. I left the event elated, and, gushing, immediately called my penfriend to tell him about the experience. I had to share, I had no option and could almost hear what he must have been thinking at the other end of the line: 'Why did Howard just call me to tell me this?' Well, if you're reading this, dear penfriend, do you remember the telephone call? I assume you put it down to an expectant flush of excitement with the 'new to me' musical world in which I was immersed. Is that what you thought?

A couple of years later, now fully engaged with music – and holding onto the escalator for dear life – I was fortunate to have another chance to hear the same songwriter weave her magic. Her fame was spreading; she was playing to a larger audience, in London. The performance was equally exquisite as the one I remembered from Brighton. Determined to speak to her after the set, I wanted to understand something of her journey to becoming a musician. Did she study as a child? Did she take music A level or grades? Did she go to college to study composition? And where did she find the inspiration for her lyrics?

A somewhat giggly young woman on stage, our short conversation offstage was of an entirely different character, revealing a profound musical intelligence. As we chatted, I learnt she had no formal training but had been writing songs from the age of twelve. I found this surprising given the craft inherent in the glorious music that poured from her. And, not surprisingly, it appeared others were noticing. She has since made a career teaching other budding songwriters. She now flies the world, collaborating with other bands, as well as continuing to write and record new music of her own. Her fans are eagerly awaiting a second album; it's long overdue. If only she can find time away from helping everyone else to be a musician! Scanning her social media, it is clear she is having a blast as pop music guru, co-writer and creative whirlwind. What a life!

Chatting with her that night, and observing similar traits in other artists, I put a new task on my to-do list: to find out more about whatever people mean when they use the phrase 'musical intelligence'. And in that instant, self-doubt kicks in. Intelligence? What if I am lacking an essential ingredient that will forever prevent me from becoming a musician? Is there such a thing as innate musical talent? I shudder at the thought.

As a child, I gave up on piano lessons far too soon. Was it laziness, or the distraction of my other love, electronics and computing? I partly blame the unimaginative regime I was subjected to, the rote learning of set pieces, my childhood teacher's lack of empathy with my desire to understand theory ... but could there be another reason? Did I get stuck because I sensed I could never be a 'natural' musician?

At school, we were all acutely aware of friends who, seemingly without effort, streaked ahead to higher music grades, gave startlingly professional performances at end-of-term concerts and, in a few cases, exhibited a near virtuosic ability far beyond their years. I was NOT one of those. On reflection, I struggled to make progress much beyond grade four (or was it three? I no longer remember). Sight-reading was a continual challenge. Still is. And my 'hand independence' was weak, limiting me to pieces of only modest complexity. As I ponder this lack of childhood progress, fear wells up in the pit of my stomach even as I write. Am I destined to repeat the past? Will I waste precious years in later life in a futile effort to become the musician I never was and never can be? If I struggled as a teen, why do I believe I stand a chance as a mature adult?

I don't know how to say this without sounding arrogant, but when I approach a goal, any goal, I have a tendency to stubbornly refuse to accept defeat. My friends tell me I can be 'unrealistic' ... more than is good for me. I call it determination. Yet I don't believe I am naïve. I know I could fail in this journey. If it comes to that, I shall accept it. Yet if I had admitted the probability at the outset, I would never have started. So I push any fear of failure to the back of my mind and set off on the voyage, carefree, riding high upon the seas and hoping for a fair wind and a favourable tide. My penfriend's wife calls it 'driven'. Not that being 'driven' is particularly heroic. Much of the time I just feel exhausted.

My mind floats between two extremes, just as Satan's tritone lies at the unstable middle of the octave between two consonant harmonies. At one moment I am convinced it is the journey, and only the journey, that matters: the joy of learning, not an imagined end result which must be achieved at all costs by an artificially imposed deadline. A second later, in the twinkle of an eye, I find myself arguing that if not destined to be a concert pianist in five years, well, what's the point in trying. Worse, I persuade myself that the impossible goal is not only possible but entirely probable, even likely ... if (and only if) I work hard enough. To put in hours of practice each day, to work diligently through the theory and gain distinctions at every grade, to live and breathe music in each moment, then, surely, there is nothing whatsoever to stop me ...

As I flip-flop between these extreme mindsets, without resolution, I find I can nudge my way forward. Like an unstable note slipping to the tonic, a path opens. In my 'realistic' mood I am pleased with any modest progress I make. When 'unrealistic', I find new energy to push on, and with laser focus. It's a potent mix of attitudes, but hard for those not riding the roller coaster alongside me to grasp. I hear it in their language: 'Be realistic, Howard, then you won't be disappointed'. By which they mean, but won't say, 'Howard is being ridiculous and over-ambitious'. How I hate that thought – though offered with good intentions. Being 'realistic' is the mind-killer. Being 'realistic' is the principal, logical and sensible reason to stop right here, right now. Why bother with all the practice if to be 'realistic' is what is required? Acceptance of mediocrity is not in my nature. As John Lennon once said, 'If being an egomaniac means I believe in what I do and in my art or music, then in that respect you can call me that … I do believe in what I do, and I'll say it.'

So if and when I do fail to achieve my goal – an outcome which is as sure as day follows night – I shall not care a jot; water off a duck's back. But – and it's a big but – woe betide anyone or, more likely, anything that gets in the way. THAT would be a disappointment, on a stratospheric, earth-moving, planetary-wide scale. No, if I'm prevented from completing my journey to the max, it must be down to one thing and one thing only: a decision I take, without influence from friends, family or teachers, and having understood the limit of my musical intelligence. And I shall only come to accept any limit by pushing so hard it hurts. Psychology lesson over. Let's move on.

What next? A winter's day. I step into an unassuming shop on the wrong side of town and ask for a lesson. It seems an age away.

10
TWO-FIVE-ONE

In which a new demonstration fails. I learn the value of harmonic language, the function of chords, and how this can expand what I can say at the keyboard.

I often wrote to my penfriend the night before my next lesson, to explain to him, at great length, about the horrors I would likely face. Last week my teacher had announced we would be focussing on something called the 'diatonic cycle using 7th chords: major, minor and diminished'. Gosh. We would, he warned, be 'moving through the cycle using first, second and third chord inversions to create well-voiced changes'. My penfriend's reaction to this foreboding news was threefold:

'WTF.

'Didn't understand a word I'm afraid.

'Have a good lesson!'

Geez. Had he not been listening?

A few weeks prior, he and his lovely wife were over at ours for the weekend and, as is my wont, I subjected them to a music lesson. Sit up straight, stop talking, concentrate now ... I didn't say that, but it is how I felt, so eager was I to share the intriguing theory I was unearthing. Yes, I had become a musical nerd.

Sitting at the piano, I played them a C major scale – to keep those pesky black notes out of the way – and demonstrated how each triad, formed on each note of the scale, is of a different 'quality'. The triad on C is major, C-E-G. The triad on D is minor, D-F-A, and so on. This demonstration, which I felt perfectly explained the logic of music, did little to convince my friends. To them it was annoyingly confusing that a major scale contained a mix of major and minor *chords*, and one so-called diminished triad, on B (the seventh note in the C scale), comprising the notes B-D-F. My enthusiasm for such analysis only succeeded in further reinforcing their view that musical terminology and its notation were both irrational and impenetrable. My friend's reasoning, which I believe remains firm to this day, is that such conventions, including the curious arrangement of black and white notes and the seemingly arbitrary structure of scales and chords, is a real barrier to understanding.

'Surely it could be simpler?' he suggested. 'Has it simply evolved this way over time and is now in need of a thorough shake-out? Is anyone working on a solution?'

It's remarkable how mistaken an intelligent person can be.

My friend may dislike me for saying this, but it's the truth: the logic of scales, keys and chords arises naturally, as naturally as flowers grow in a garden or butterflies emerge from cocoons. Musical biology. To understand this, you have to *hear* music and not just study it academically. My teacher was right about that. And the best way of doing this, by far, is to play chord progressions. The most famous of which is undoubtedly the 2-5-1. According to my teacher, that is where every musician's harmonic vocabulary should be laser-focused and deeply rooted.

The chords formed on the notes of any scale are the Lego bricks of harmony. The notation 2-5-1 refers to a sequence of three chords. In C major they are D minor (on the 2nd), G dominant 7th (on the 5th) and C major (on the tonic). There are many ways to play and voice these chords: as triads (three-note chords), as 7^{ths} (four-note chords), and in numerous inversions and extensions. In each case, however, you'd still be playing the 2-5-1. It's that fundamental.

The 2-5-1 litters many genres. It pervades jazz. A jazz 'standard' can consist of little more than the endless repetition of 2-5-1 progressions (modulating between keys) over which a melody is woven and improvisation conjured. A jazz pianist can sit at the keyboard for hours, doodling away over 2-5-1s, and never get bored. They will often suspend their return to the tonic for minutes, repeating the 2-5-2-5-2-5 and then finishing off via the 5-1 to provide resolution and release of tension.

It took me a while to hear the 2-5-1 in my head. When I eventually did, I could recognise it in almost any musical context. Pop, jazz, classical, whatever I was listening to, I was able to spot the 2-5-1s buried in the mix Anticipating their arrival, I would hum, sing or voice them out loud in time to the rhythm of the piece … two-diddly-dum-five-diddly-dum-one-diddly-dum. It must have been irritating to be around me when this involuntary exclamation occurred, but I could not help myself. It became an instinctive reaction for me to mutter the words 'two' … 'five' … 'one' … under my breath whenever I heard the 'changes', I was that excited. The 2-5-1 was the first musical idiom I had firmly under my belt. It sounds so small, but it was a huge step forward. How did I get there? By playing 2-5-1s of course.

My teacher gave me a series of exercises in which I played 2-5-1s in every key. Being keen to ensure I was using good voice-leading, he insisted I use appropriate voicings. So, for example, I might play the 2-chord as 1357, followed by the 5-chord as 5713, followed by the 1-chord as 1357. Try it. It flows.

To help cement these chord shapes in my brain, my teacher also asked me to write out the progressions on stave paper – in every key, of course. He also recommended I chain changes of harmony together by modifying the quality of a chord. For example, to play 2-5-1 in C major, then drop the major chord to C minor. Treat *that* as the 2-chord in B♭ major and continue … C minor, F dominant 7th, B♭ major. Repeat. Drop the

B♭ major chord to minor and treat *that* as the 2-chord of the A♭ major scale. Get it? It's the circle. Oh my. The world seemed to open up. Suddenly I was playing music. And, over the following months, I learnt to play several other progressions at will, in any key. No sheet music required. Joy.

And the learning never eased up. My teacher continued to drop new musical terms into our flourishing conversation. He never held back, nor doubted my ability to learn. At the same time, he never assumed I would grasp a new concept immediately and was always ready to offer up gentle explanations when asked; unless it was one of my pesky mathematical 'theory' queries. To those, he often replied: 'Just try to hear it, Howard.'

This week he felt it was high time I heard about the concept of 'function' in harmony. There we were, playing a few chords, and he chimed in with, 'What role do you think the B♭ chord is now playing in the music?'

At first, I had no idea what he meant. Wasn't it enough that it was a B♭ major chord? Apparently not. Any chord can, he told me, 'play multiple roles depending on the prevailing key'.

I feel I should introduce another notation at this juncture. It will help, trust me. Up to now, I have been naming notes and chords using Arabic numerals. Going forward, that's going to be confusing. Let's distinguish the two by using Roman numerals for chord positions in the scale. Moreover, I shall use lower case Roman for minor chords and upper case Roman for major chords. Using this convention we have:

The ii-chord in the key of C (D minor) could be the iii-chord in B♭ or even the vi-chord in F. See how it works? The same chord but playing a different role, or function, in each key. So where I used 2-5-1 before, I shall now use ii-V7-I, meaning:

- Play a *minor* chord on the 2nd of the scale; and then:
- Play a *dominant* 7th chord on the 5th of the scale; and then:

- Play a *major* chord on the root of the scale.

Nice. Now we have a way to talk about scales and chords without confusion. But I shall still write 2-5-1 at times, depending on the context.

Week after week, I was learning more and more.

Minor scales, it turns out, have their own harmonic logic, mirroring that of the majors. The 3-chord in a major scale is iii, a minor chord. The 3-chord in a minor scale is III, a major chord. Every scale, major or minor (of which there are at least three types in common use: natural, melodic and harmonic) allows us to 'stack 3rds' and build chords on each of their seven notes. These alternate harmonies are the things that create variety in music. My teacher, naturally, encouraged me to practise 2-5-1s on minor scales as well as majors. I found this considerably more challenging. New shapes, new chords, new sounds; that's music.

Everything was, however, gradually clicking into place. To be a musician like my teacher, able to improvise at will, I needed to learn scales, build chords and craft harmonic progressions, and do so in any key. Combine this skill with a good ear, a few subtle inversions and smooth voice-leading, and I would be well on the way to entertaining myself and other for hours on end; and without ever seeing a page of sheet music.

I was learning that to expand one's harmonic vocabulary should be the primary goal of any aspiring musician. Working with my teacher, it took me a year to grok (understand intuitively) this, and I am still extending my musical language today. Language is a good analogy. The American jazz pianist, composer and educator Barry Harris once used the phrase 'the things I can *say* at the keyboard'. He was referring to the role or 'function' chords perform in a harmonic progression. Just like Harris, we musicians (it sounds so good to say that) all need to work on being able to *say* new things. Everyone, myself included, tends to fall back on a few addictive chord sequences that happen to appeal. Like drugs, they become a habit. Fighting this tendency is key to growth as a well-rounded musician. It starts with the 2-5-1 always, but the journey never ends. Evidence my anecdote of the singer-songwriter who now makes her living teaching others: while her compositions will, I suspect, always be recognisably hers, her work with other musicians will help them grow as artists. She is giving them a tool to express their voice; to play what they wish to say.

11

ON TECHNIQUE

In which I recall how a glass of water helped me as a child, and how, as an adult, I now play a quadrillion games with scales to thoroughly mess things up.

All this talk of chords and progressions and I've hardly said a word about what it means to physically move one's arms, hands and fingers around a keyboard.

Our lessons were short, a mere thirty minutes. I always arrived early, my teacher a minute or two late. He would burst into the room, larger than life, carrying his bass, a bulging backpack, and a bundle of paper (lead sheets, I expect) under one arm. He would then apologise profusely and comment on whatever I had been playing before he turned up. Uncanny. Our practice room was at the bottom of a long flight of stairs, ample time for him to pause and listen to my prep, usually a simple chord sequence. Had he been lurking outside, listening through the wall, feigning lateness? No. He would never play such a trick on me. He had a knack of immediately cluing in to whatever it was I was attempting. His subsequent advice was always relevant and helpful. But there were limits, even for this teacher: he did not teach technique.

He told me of his frustration with students who could not play evenly, hands together, fingers moving in sync. Fortunately, I did not disappoint him in that regard. I have a feeling that, despite uninspiring lessons as a child, I had been taught something. My adult teacher spotted it right away, a decades-old residue clinging to my late-middle-aged fingers.

'Your problem, Howard,' he said, 'is not that you cannot learn to play the piano. You will do that yourself and won't need me. To compose and improvise, however, you must develop your ear. Hear. Listen.'

Ten weeks in and I was only now beginning to appreciate what he meant. Of course, I was not ready to play Chopin, but for the music we were working on, coordination was no impediment, at least not yet. Lack of technique was not preventing my hands from moving to where they needed to be. It was instead an uncertainty of *where* they should move to: the problem was in my brain. At the tempo of the music he assigned, I was unable to think fast enough to determine the appropriate chord shapes and voice-leading to be ready for the next bar or beat.

But ... and it's a big but. Anyone who has ever set about learning to play the piano knows all too well that coordination can be, and almost always is, a huge issue. Adults coming to the keyboard late in life are often able to play simple music hands separate (HS) but struggle to bring their two hands together (HT) and perform the piece as written. Arm movement, hand positions, avoidance of unnecessary gestures, fingering ... all this and more must be mastered.

As a child, my teacher placed a glass of water on the back of my hand and insisted I play scales without spillage. This disturbing trial by fire happened more than once. Can you imagine? My memory is vague – this was a lifetime ago – but I also remember being asked to play five-finger exercises, hands together, ever so slowly, almost imperceptibly slow. Slower than a snail. This, I was assured, would help ensure that when the fingers of one hand pushed on a key, the equivalent fingers of the other hand would do the same at precisely the same moment and with precisely the same pressure, releasing both simultaneously. The interminable exercises must have had some value.

As a result of such childhood strictures, when I play a scale nowadays, even at speed, you cannot put a cigarette paper between left and right.

They work as one. If this is not the case for you, go get a real piano teacher a.s.a.p. No avoiding the basics. Playing any music, even the more straightforward stuff, without a modicum of technique is like trying to ride a bike without pedals. It won't work, and you will waste your time in the attempt. The traditional roll-up-your-sleeves and watch-those-fingers piano teacher is still very much in demand.

My own facility, while reasonable, is far from perfect even now. I regularly hit limits and discover rough edges in need of a good polish. One that everyone notices, is a tendency to remove my hands from the keyboard unnecessarily and to flick my wrist upwards between phrases or on specific beats or chords. Not only is this ugly for the audience (I wish) but it also destroys any chance of playing true legato and 'cantabile' style. My adult teacher could not help with such problems. Had I asked, he would have refused.

'Go find someone who is a stickler for such details,' he would say. 'Do a year on technique, Howard, if you feel you must.'

He was right. Self-learning keyboard skills is a dangerous occupation. The autodidact rarely becomes a concert pianist or even a competent amateur. Scan the web and you will find a slew of articles, blogs and videos purporting to teach the fundamentals. Read them all. Watch videos. But be realistic … muddling through alone – trial and error – will only embed bad habits. Trust me on this. Your parents taught you how to ride a bike and avoid falling off before you were allowed to head out at speed. Piano, or any musical instrument, is no different. Eradicating an ingrained habit or affectation later will be nigh on impossible.

It's not only concert pianists who need great technique: we all do. Watch any half-decent pianist, professional or amateur: *fluent* is the word. Professionals and good amateurs alike have learnt the correct finger positions for every scale and arpeggio. They know how to press and release keys and pedals to create a beautiful tone, line and emphasis. They use the weight of their arm to sustain dynamics and phrasing, and they know when to use 'gravity drops' and 'chord attacks'. They exhibit poise and posture, breathing to emphasise the emotional content of the music. They become one with their instrument. Not all of us need the coordination and skills of a concert pianist but everyone – no exceptions – should start with technique, if only to avoid injury (all too easy if unguided) and build strength. Virtuosity comes later.

I guess, at the outset of my adult journey, my own skills were that of a child at grade two. That's pretty basic. I have improved significantly since then, but I did not until much later (years) decide to take instruction from a traditional piano teacher. This was a mistake. But frankly, with everything else I was doing with my jazz teacher, I would have been overwhelmed. I was not ready for the luxury of having one teacher for theory, another for improvisation and another for technique. Wonderland Alice could do six impossible things before breakfast. Most of us cannot. What I did do was weave complementary styles of practice into my routine.

Suppose I was learning a scale. I would do all the things any piano student does: start slow, ensure the correct fingering (as written out in a respected scale book), hands apart then together, gradually building speed. I would then mess with the scale. Starting with one octave, then two, then four, I would play it legato and then staccato. I would play it starting at different points on the keyboard, high up or low down, stretching my arms. I would play it in different time signatures, emphasising every other note (duple time), every third note (triple time) or every fourth note (common time). I even tried to play on every fifth note, just to see what it sounded like. I noticed how, for example, if I played in triplets, I needed a three-octave span if my hands were to arrive back at the tonic on the beat. And I would always (try) to play in every key, forcing myself to transpose the pattern. Hypnotic. It was hard work, but I was learning.

Forgive me, I'm starting to sound like a music-practice saint. It was not like that, I assure you. I do, however, admit a tendency towards obsessive behaviour; a benefit when it comes to the piano. As an example, I once suspected the joints of my right hand were limiting the movement of my fingers. So, whenever I sat watching TV, I took the thumb of my left hand and pressed it into the crease of my right, digging deep, working the joint. I would then swap over and repeat the process. This massage would continue for the duration of whatever film I was watching. The manipulation helped, not just with coordination and dexterity, but to prevent injury: now that I was practising two to three hours a day, hand flexing avoided any stiffness that could have set in. Or was it a placebo effect? No matter. It worked.

'Rotation' proved elusive, at first. Look it up. It refers to the slight, almost imperceptible, circular (perhaps oval) movements of the wrist while performing; one essential technique among many. As is 'wrist flex'. I found YouTube videos helpful, but even the best tutorials could not unlock everything I needed. Once again, I improvised. Sitting at a table – hands relaxed, fingers curved – I rotated my wrists back and forth. As I did so, I moved my arms left and right, in the same or in opposing directions, to simulate how rotation would feel in practice. And I moved my hands forwards and backwards to emulate the required navigation between the white and black keys. Wrist rotation, left and right arm movements, sliding in and out … it must have looked ridiculous. Was it helping? I thought so. I hoped so.

Such games were not handed to me on a plate. My teacher never suggested them. No, I invented them, and they developed in variety and sophistication over time. Once I had a recipe, I would jot it down in my notebook for safekeeping. I often referred back to these notes and tried to bring whatever had worked previously to everything new that I was working on. I was turning practice into an enjoyable game. The mundane was transformed into a rewarding intellectual pursuit. My methods were far from scientific, and a traditional piano teacher would have been appalled. Yes, it was haphazard experimentation, but it was working.

My friend was over for the weekend. We had been chatting by email about the sheer number of scales that exist in music and the quadrillion ways they can be performed. I dragged him to the piano for a demonstration, building a sequence of notes into a crescendo of variations. As I shouted out the names of what I was doing, musical terms flying thick and fast, the absurd nature of the game became apparent. We ended up laughing our heads off. He found it bewildering and wondered how I could possibly remember so many patterns. How did I do it? I was probably using a similar technique to that employed by magicians able to read hidden sequences of cards from shuffled packs. I was applying game logic, not the individual moves.

An analogy that might appeal to my penfriend: a racing driver does not (cannot) memorise the precise sequence of teeny-weeny movements of his steering wheel when circuiting a racetrack. The driver has learnt to drive! He navigates the twists and turns of the layout and executes subtle manoeuvres as needed, in order to win the race. So it is with the piano.

As an adult, I was intellectualising my goal and devising tricks of my own. It kept me amused through hours of otherwise tedious repetition. Few children could or would do this of their own volition, but had my childhood teacher taught more games I might never have struggled with the weekly grind and might now be an accomplished pianist. But my halcyon years were lost in other pursuits, and I was now nearing sixty. Could I ever catch up? I had to believe I could.

12

MODES

In which self-doubt leads to a nonsensical conversation about fun. Surrounded by modes on all sides, I accept that an overwhelming combination of intervals demands that I not only hear but sing!

As the weeks rolled on, lesson after lesson, the magnitude of the voyage ahead loomed ever larger. Self-doubt became a regular feature of correspondence with my penfriend. The thought of leaving the escalator never entered my head, but I sure would have appreciated it if a mechanic could have turned up and oiled the machinery once in a while. New jolts, stops, fits and starts were occurring with increasing regularity.

Looking for encouragement, I wrote this to my friend:

'Hit a real impasse over the last few days ... cannot make headway on the stuff Teacher asked me to work on. I think it may be like this for several more weeks. Feels like a brick wall running for miles to left and right. Or is it a cul-de-sac? No way out or round – have to find a chink somewhere. And don't re-send me your idea of tunnelling underneath. I know you like analogies, but that one won't help. It's more like I need to knock out a brick along the way, but the problem is, which one? There are SO MANY. My teacher, and books I am studying, tell me I need to listen to hundreds of pieces, with the lead sheets in front of me. I am told I need to play whatever I can manage, fragments, a few bars, a sketch of the melody. If this is true, and I can only believe it is, I need to get organised on an industrial scale.'

A mountain of new musical concepts was rearing up in front of me. As

I dug in, more appeared – wave after wave, piling on top of each other, forever increasing the hurdles I faced. I was drowning and, I admit, overwhelmed and confused. One example: modes.

Take any major scale, say the most straightforward, C major … all white keys … we see a pattern of tones and semitones from C to C. But play the same notes beginning on G and we see a difference arising from the keyboard's apparent asymmetry. This new scale has a name … wait for it … Mixolydian mode. It's a scale (and a key signature) in its own right. It's not C major, and it's not G major (because that would contain F♯); it is … G Mixolydian. Guess what: this odd-sounding scale is used to sketch out (improvise) melody over the blues: dominant 7th chords. Using our new notation that's I7-IV7-V7. 'I'm in big school now,' I wrote to my friend. 'No more simple major and minor.'

How many modes? One for each note of the major scale. Start on D (the supertonic), and we hear another pattern, this time sounding 'minor'(ish) but with a twist. It's called D Dorian, containing the distinctive major 6th interval.

Each mode is built from the major scale's pattern of tones and semitones but begins at a different point in the sequence. You have to hear this: play D to D on the white notes. Now play G to G. Now play F to F … that's Lydian mode. Every one of the twelve major scales has buried within it seven additional modes. Twelve by seven equals eighty-four scales. Combine this total with all of the ways I had been practising chords, and the combinations expand again, exponentially. Impossible. Overpowering. How to cope?

Look at F Lydian, F G A B C D E F … It's similar to F major except that instead of the semitone between the 3rd and the 4th there is a whole tone. It's as if the 4th has been raised to the sharp. And indeed it has. In F major, the B should be a B♭. In F Lydian it's B natural. The sharpened B is the adjustment we make to the fourth of the scale that creates the Lydian sound (or mode). When my teacher first explained this, here is what he did:

'Howard, play the first four notes of F Lydian over and over. That's right. Have you heard that before?'

And I had. At the movies! It's often used to create a sense of 'rushing around' – a musical cliché.

'Yes,' he confirmed. 'And did you know that the Beatles used Mixolydian in several of their best-known tunes? And Dorian. All these modes, these scales, and the chords formed from them – each has a role. Each evokes a different emotional response. Combine them into a progression and you can tell a story with music.' As he said this, I heard it: Lydian, in one of the greatest works of opera, *Peter Grimes* by Benjamin Britten, the *Sea Interludes*. Was my ear improving? Had my teacher heard of the work? No. But he had heard of Britten, thank goodness. Not his genre, however. Oh well, back to jazz.

As with Lydian, similar adjustments to the major scale allow us to construct any mode we like. To play in Dorian mode, for example, flatten the 3rd and the 7th. Play D E F G A B C D on the keyboard … see how the 3rd should be an F♯ and the 7th should be a C♯. Each is flattened to create the Dorian feel. And of course this works for any scale. Take E♭ major:

E♭ F G A♭ B♭ C D E♭

Sharpen the 4th and we get E♭ Lydian. Flatten the 3rd and the 7th and we get E♭ Dorian. Jazz musicians use modes all the time. It allows them to improvise melodies that 'work' over the chords of their harmony. They call this 'scale-chord theory'. The idea is simple enough; but executing it at the keyboard, with sufficient fluidity to make good music, was mind-bending. I struggled. Major and minor were falling under my fingers naturally. But now faced with six new modes (Dorian, Phrygian, Lydian, Mixolydian and Locrian), the pattern of black and white notes seemed more arbitrary than ever. Yet, as I began to practise the modes, as I had previously practised the classical scales, patterns were starting to fall under my hand. It was as if the early piano designers had discovered an arrangement that reveals everything we need to write diverse music, with all its bountiful harmonies and emotion. Clever. But knowing this does not make it any easier for a beginner pianist like me. BLOCKED.

Back to that email to my friend. I hit SEND and awaited his reply.

It arrived the next day. A multi-page letter:

'Hmm.

'This is why I never started learning piano, I guess. I've not heard you speak of Mixolydians before. Weren't they on *Doctor Who* last season? First off, Don't Panic! Most of this will come to you, some of it suddenly. In a way, you have more of a problem than me, because you already know a lot, and are grasping more all the time. So you are probably, subconsciously, thinking you should know more than you do and letting it worry you. Relax. You're doing this for fun, remember.

'I realise you couldn't have a black note for every white one for practical reasons because no one would know where the notes are. Indeed, it occurred to me at the weekend that the piano keyboard has the maximum number of black keys consistent with every white key being in a unique place and, therefore, identifiable. And once you have decided to delete one black note, you would tune the white notes so they can play major scales. I get all that. My problem is why can you delete one black note and make it all sound right. And what I realise now, from what you said before, is that the arrangement is not that special, because you can get correct-sounding sequences almost whatever you play. So, this must mean that the design of the piano keyboard has settled on the most convenient pattern and become a standard, rather like the QWERTY typists' keyboard. It works because everyone knows it, not because it's *right*. I am illuminated!'

He was wrong about that, of course, but let him continue:

'I think you need to relax a bit, just play with the exercise your teacher has given you and go back next week and discuss with him which bits you find most difficult. Firstly, you are paying him to help you have fun, and secondly, as a teacher, he needs to push you past your comfort limit to take you forward, doesn't he? What would you do if you had to suddenly start teaching someone you had never met before about software engineering? You'd make a best guess and give them exercises to gauge whether they were bored or out of their depth and then you'd zero in on what they needed to learn. I'm sure he is just doing the same and will be pleased to know you have reached your current limit so that he can work out what to teach you next. At least, that's what I'd do.'

My friend is so funny; in the nicest possible way, I must emphasise. But 'fun'? Relaxation? Really? Not many pianists would use that word when pushing hard on the accelerator pedal.

As I explained in my prelude, and to my friend and his wife face to face (and in several emails), I had stepped onto this particular escalator not to have fun but to pursue a vocation. I had not chosen this journey as a diverting pastime but to fill the last third of my life, post-retirement, with a new creative challenge, something at the extreme opposite end of the computer work and coding I was paid to deliver during my career. I consider my musical journey every bit as much 'work' as before, the difference being there is only one client: me. And I am a difficult client indeed, with demanding standards. Yet no matter how many times I explained this to my friends, they always came back to the same points: that I was 'doing it for pleasure' and 'must not take it too seriously' or burden myself with 'unrealistic' or 'overambitious goals'. Really? I had hoped that months of correspondence would deliver the message, but this particular nail sure took some hammering home. Even now, they (and others) can slip back into the language of post-retirement hobbies and pastimes.

So let's try again, shall we? To everyone who knows me:

Take note, dear friends. My voyage to music is NOT, and NEVER SHALL BE, a HOBBY. Nor is my intent FUN. So what is it? Rewarding? Yes. Intellectually satisfying? Also. A search for meaning in later life? Most definitely. A pleasure? Of course. What it is not is 'fun'. The pursuit of fun will never get me, or anyone else, off the musical starting blocks. Developing even a modicum of artistic ability takes HARD WORK. Trust me on this. Music is a SERIOUS pursuit.

Sermon over.

For example, take those tricksy modes; a.k.a. BLOCKS.

I met a young man at the shop, who was also seeing my teacher. I asked the student how he was getting on. Turned out he, like me, had recently been introduced to chord-scale theory.

'Frankly,' he said, 'he's losing me there.'

I knew precisely what he meant: BLOCKS. I never saw the boy again and often wondered whether it was indeed the modes that had tripped him off his escalator. But I cannot give up. Ever. My escalator would never allow it. I had no choice: I had to tackle modes. It was definitely not fun; it was a mountain to ascend. But like all mountains, there was a magnificent vista on the other side; ask any competent jazz musician. Learning when and how to use the seven modes in every key *is* the key to the door called improvisation. And the learning never ends. Are there modes of minor keys? Yes. Jazz musicians employ a raft of so-called jazz-oriented scales – modes derived from the classical minors – which play nicely alongside the more unusual chords they effortlessly pluck from the air. I wonder how many children learning to play the piano have heard such a glorious scale as the Lydian-dominant? It corresponds to the C7$^{\sharp 11}$ chord, with an added 9th and 13th. Lydian-dominant is the fourth mode of the 'ascending melodic minor' that every child has learnt by the end of grade three. If only their teachers had suggested starting on the 4th. What intriguing new harmony would the child have heard.

As I learnt, modes are the real stuff of music, not the scales we learn as children. How else could jazz musicians improvise melodies that float above such exquisite harmony? Jazz. It's the future.

So if modes are BLOCKS for you, get into whatever woodshed you can find and knock them down. Listen, really listen, to individual notes, to each scale and to every mode. Find the intervals which make 'just that sound'. Even a single tone is chock full of overtones! As we saw, play a C and you are also playing a G. And an E. And an A. And so on. Now play those notes together as a chord. By doing so, we emphasise partials that were present all along. I was beginning to understand how even the most straightforward note can paint an exquisite colour. The overtones of its constituent notes are vying for attention. There is a sense of motion, of moving towards or away from the tonic. C major only sounds 'right' after we play the dominant G-B-D because the partials of those three notes are sitting on the edge of their seat, waiting to resolve in the mind of the listener. Now imagine the bewitching zoo of jazz chords containing 7^{ths}, 9^{ths}, 11^{ths} and 13^{ths}. Go listen. The heady mix takes my breath away. I almost want to sing out loud.

13

THE THEORY EXAM

In which self-study leads me back to school, surrounded by children and revisiting the horrors of exam-hall formality.

A few months into my journey, it became abundantly clear that I needed to study music theory. Not physics, nor vibrating strings. No. I mean the topics which examination boards insist on if you are to progress to higher practical grades: details of notation, the technicalities of key signatures and of rhythms, scales, intervals and cadences. Of course, I had been picking up dribs and drabs from my teacher, but it turned out there was a ton of stuff he would not choose to teach and which, if he did, would waste our valuable lesson time. Those thirty minutes together were too precious to fritter away on details, technicalities he was sure I could teach myself. So, on his advice, I registered with a well-known and respected international examination board with a reputation for rigour. The next question was: which 'grade' to shoot for?

A flip through the curriculum convinced me there was no point in sitting grades one to three. Not only would doing so take at least a year – only being allowed to sit one grade every four months – but the content was child's play. I urge all adults, even those with zero musical knowledge, to start at grade four; no lower. Should I begin at five, I wondered? My board mandated a pass at grade five to then sit any practical examination beyond five. Such a rule was new to me. But since I intended to sit practicals all the way to grade eight – the base requirement to enter college or take a diploma – I would need to face grade five theory some time or other. As it turned out, I began with four. Why?

Many people who sit theory do so out of necessity, not because they are particularly interested in the subject. They do the minimum work to be allowed to sit advanced practicals. I, however, wanted to take the theory of music to degree level (at least). I'd always had a yen for composition. Why couldn't I shoot for the moon? I made it my goal to pass all such tests with 'distinction'. Nothing else would suffice. Anything less, I felt, was not really a pass at all, at least not in terms of the 'unrealistic' goal I had set. Yet I had to start somewhere, and I determined that grade four would form a modest refresher course. However, not wanting to waste any more time than was strictly necessary, I set about planning to sit one grade each term. Click, click online; and a few days later everything I felt I would need had arrived:

- The last three years' grade four and five specimen examination papers, and corresponding answer books.
- The official study guides from the board I had selected.
- A pack of grade five learning materials from a respected online teacher who specialised in preparing students for theory examinations.
- Grade one, two and three specimen papers (and answers) just to be sure I could pass these with full marks without needing to sit the exams themselves. (I found I could, presumably by virtue of residual childhood knowledge.)
- An index box with enough cards, of various colours, to make up a set of well-organised study notes. These would later prove invaluable.
- Several pads of blank stave paper. Of course.

These materials were set out at one end of our dining room table and the family were given strict instructions that nothing should be moved. Our dinner table, or at least a part of it, became my 'theory woodshed'. Every couple of days, immediately after work, I sat there to study. With no intention of settling for a 'pass' or a 'merit', and wanting to dot every 'i' and cross every 't', theory work became a further drain on my time. My card index gradually filled. Then, every couple of weeks, I would pick a past paper, set an alarm clock for two hours, and mark myself when finished. Each month saw progress, but even the grade four paper proved harder than I had imagined: details; hundreds of musical terms.

Have you ever known someone able to recall the names of thirty random objects despite having only a few seconds to commit them to memory? Well, I'm not one of them. I needed my card index and created a card for every musical concept I stumbled upon. At the end of this process, there were over three hundred cards in my deck, covering every conceivable aspect of theory from grades one to five, and maybe a few from six. My cards covered so many topics it would be impossible to list them all here. I had cards for tempo, for key signatures, for scales and accidentals, for rests and ties, note groupings, dynamics, phrasing marks and ornaments. I had cards for both simple and compound time, for intervals and transposition, for triads and other chord forms, including chord notation. I had cards for figured bass, for cadences, and for musical structures – lots of cards.

By self-marking the past papers against the answer book, it became clear that certain areas of the forthcoming examinations were going to be considerably harder than others. Even at grade five, the number of musical terms one is required to know (in Italian, French and German) is unsettling. I've never had a good memory for lists and could lose the chance of a 'distinction' merely by failing to answer a question such as 'Give the meaning of *acciaccatura*'.

The questions I found most straightforward were those that did not require rote learning. My favourites topics included 'filling in missing bar lines', 'naming chords and intervals', 'transposing and rewriting passages' (for other keys or for different instruments), 'making observations' about a piece by reading the score, 'writing out scales' and 'naming cadences'. It all seemed logical and approachable. But again, in testing myself I discovered it was all too easy to make silly mistakes or slips. A single ♯ (sharp) or ♭ (flat) sign out of place, for example, could spell disaster.

The parts of the specimen papers I found the most challenging were those where the student was required to exhibit 'musical' abilities. This included 'completing a melody', understanding the 'harmony underneath a melody', and so on. It quickly became apparent that if I could not 'hear' the notated music in my head, I would be at a severe disadvantage compared to those students who could. No singing or humming was allowed in the hall. I needed to add another thread of learning to my musical education: the ear training my teacher had emphasised. Without this, I figured, grades six to eight would be forever out of reach.

The day of the examination arrived. It was held at a local school, and frankly I did not know what to expect. Turning in to the school gate, I parked up. Next to me, on my passenger seat, was my precious card index. With twenty minutes to spare, I flipped through the box, refreshing my memory of the words and phrases I found the hardest to recall.

It was time.

I stepped out of the car, legs shaking (just for a moment) as I walked across the tarmac to join the queue of people waiting to enter the school. The atmosphere was orderly, expectant. The children, a zoo of ages, shapes and sizes, waited patiently in line. The majority were chatting with friends, a valuable distraction, perhaps, from the imminent plunge into the horrors of the examination. The younger children were mostly silent; maybe this was their first music test. Only then did I realise that I was the only adult present, other than parents accompanying their offspring.

The examination room was a large, austere school hall, also used for games judging by the layout of white lines on the floor. Desks and chairs were set out in neat rows and columns. Too neat. I counted eight to a row, twenty deep; one hundred and sixty places. Which, I wondered, was mine? On each table had been placed the examination paper and a single sheet of stave paper for 'workings out'. What? Only one! Surely I needed more? No. We were only required to bring our own pencil, pen and rubber. I held mine close. As I was led to the allotted desk, distant memories of term by term and year on year examinations came flooding back. School again.

Three stern and, in my judgement, overweeningly serious-looking adjudicators, sat at the front of the hall on a raised platform: the school's stage for theatrical events. One of these referees stood up to explain that, once the examination had begun, no one could leave the hall before the first ninety minutes, other than in an emergency. 'If, at that time, you have finished your paper, you are permitted to stand, bring your work to the front and leave quietly by the door at the back,' she explained.

As everyone trooped in and took their place, I looked around at my fellow students. Ah, there was one other adult present, but at least twenty years younger than me. I was the oldest applicant, by far. Everyone else was a child or a young person; seven to seventeen, I guessed. Something told me the desks had been arranged in grade order. The children's ages and numbers hinted that the majority were sitting grades three, four or five. Two teenagers had been assigned desks at the front. Grade six? A young woman who looked as if she may just have left sixth form and would soon be off to university was accompanied to a separate desk to one side. Grade seven? Or was it eight? Telling.

A prodigious clock on the back wall counted down the next two hours. The room was eerily silent. Sixty minutes in and one child was taken out, for reasons unknown. Other than this, everyone stayed the required ninety minutes. Three more children then left, having completed their work. At this time, I still had two questions remaining; and the pressure was mounting. And then … all done, with fifteen minutes to spare. However, I decided to stay to the bitter end, endlessly checking and rechecking details of my work, hunting down any small mistake, desperate for the 'distinction' I had promised myself.

Relieved when the ordeal was over, I was hot and more than a little flustered, which was crazy really, as these were tests for children, weren't they? I left the hall with a spring in my step – the flip side of the earlier wobble – and felt confident that I had done reasonably well but aware of how marks could be lost on the tiniest details.

Returning home, my wife asked how I had fared. I shrugged the question off with a non-committal, 'Oh, OK, I guess, but who knows?' And with that it was straight on to the next grade – no time to waste. And the card index filled again. A few weeks later, just as I felt on top of the grade five questions, my grade four results dropped onto our post mat, right on cue. With some trepidation, I gingerly opened the buff envelope. Inside was an embossed certificate (deliciously old-fashioned) stating a pass with distinction, achieving ninety-seven marks out of one hundred.

Three months later, I repeated the trick with a distinction at grade five, achieving ninety-two out of one hundred. Oh, how irritating. How had I dropped three marks? To this day, I wonder what detail I had missed. There could only be one reason: grade five must be harder than four! In which case, how much harder might grade six be? I made a mental note to ask my teacher when I next saw him. He told me – and I verified this by scanning online forums where such things are endlessly debated – that grade six theory is a significant step up, focusing almost entirely on those elements of musicality that allow one to read and write music 'in your head'. Curious about the challenges yet to come, I purchased the specimen papers, and sure enough it was true. Oh lord. My mind raced ... when to tackle six? There was certainly no chance of obtaining a distinction in just three months. Even six months seemed a stretch. In the end, I decided to give myself a year and promised to do a short aural training session every day. How that sorry story worked out is not something I like to dwell on.

All this theory. I needed a break. Time to get out and about.

MIDDLE EIGHT

'The beautiful thing about learning is that no one can take it away from you.'

B.B. King

14

POOKIN' DOOKIN'

In which I find value in gigs as education, invent a new word and improve my musicality no end – by following a different kind of circle.

In the first year of my adventure, or what my wife once called my 'musical malarkey', my enthusiasm knew no bounds. I was buying CDs like they were going out of fashion (which of course they were!). The shift encouraged by tech companies – from outside the mainstream music industry – towards streaming is a sorry story. Many independent musicians now struggle to make ends meet. The silver lining has been the growth in live music. Attending two or three concerts a month, and still inundating my penfriend with far too many emails, I needed to experience as much as possible and share every moment. Many of the emails I penned during this period were over-excited encouragements for my penfriend to jump onto YouTube or iTunes, or to offer him an invitation to join me at an upcoming gig. And he did join me, for a few at least, but travel to London was harder for him than for me. And yet ... how could he turn down the must-see events and musical delights I was turning up under every stone? Every artist I discovered was, of course, the 'best thing I have ever heard' and 'probably a breakthrough act' that would no doubt 'take the world by storm'. I sounded like a pre-teen desperate to see their pop idol live, hoping against hope to meet them after the show, grab an autograph, and concoct an artificial exchange of inane gushy compliments. And to a large extent this was precisely how I felt. I had become a teenager in my enthusiasm for new music, and I did not care a jot. To me, it was all so thrilling and wonderful. I was … reborn – yes, that's the right word. Why on earth had I not been attending concerts like this for the last forty years? Frankly, I have absolutely no idea. Perhaps there was a connection to the reason I had not returned to the piano years ago. Did my friend suspect a mid-life crisis, the musical equivalent of that eponymous signal of fading youth, the sports car? If so, he would be wrong on both counts. I'm not a petrolhead and have never been interested in expensive cars. And gigs were more than 'fun', although, I must admit it was fun to be around young people, and especially musicians. No, I was not looking for an escape from the march of time, hoping to turn back the clock, but rather a secret door: a passageway to a world which, up to this point, I had never imagined could be open to me.

For this late-returning pianist, every concert was a valuable learning experience as much as it was entertainment. I made a point of standing at the front of venues, as close to the stage as I could manage. Edutainment! Whether watching a guitarist or a keyboard player, I studied every detail, decoding their movements, straining to see the chords they were voicing, trying to understand how their fingers worked the strings or the keys. If I could have taken a microscope on stage, I would have done so. Everything these oh, so natural musicians did seemed effortless. The contrast with my own ability was stark. When *I* played the piano it felt awkward, uneven, lacking a distinct pulse and, frankly, decidedly unmusical. Uninspiring. What was to be done?

I was making good progress in theory, and my awareness of chord shapes was improving. But I was a mile from even the most basic of jobbing session players. My teacher, sensing my frustration, reminded me that 'becoming a musician is a lifetime of effort'. Frankly, I did not (or could not) buy it. First off, I did not have the luxury of a lifetime ahead of me. Well past mid-life, I needed to make substantial progress sooner rather than later. To my friends and family I referred to this as my 'window of opportunity'. My belief was that learning to play the piano beyond the age of sixty-five, let alone seventy – well, even I would regard that as an unrealistic goal. Yes, I was in a rush. Maybe not the best attitude, but what else could I do? Secondly, there was something 'fake' in my teacher's assertion about the necessity of a lifetime of practice. The musicians I witnessed at gigs had not been playing a lifetime, far from it; many were in their mid-twenties. If they could do it, I argued, why not me?

In an attempt to crack the code and, I hoped, improve what I had begun to call my 'virtuosity' (or lack of it), I left no stone unturned. Feverishly sourcing the Internet, I must have visited over a hundred blogs and read several hundred articles looking for answers. And not to ignore that old-fashioned idea, the bookshop, I became overly familiar with the stock of any bookseller I chanced upon who maintained any form of a half-decent 'music' section. I was not naïve enough to believe that reading a book could improve my skills in and of itself, but I needed a sense of how other musicians had approached their development.

As my bookshelf grew, it became painfully obvious that few volumes had been published that focused solely on 'performance', the term I used to refer to what I felt was 'lacking' in my practice. Had I underestimated the 'art' in music, qualities that could never be encoded in a book? There was no end of available sheet music, row upon row of collections of piano works, no doubt carefully curated. Few books, however, contained any detailed advice on how to play the music. For sure, I found good books on theory, from school-level texts to advanced degrees. Yet once again little on how to play and nothing that unpacked the mystery of performance. Exercise books were also in abundance, many with titles that seriously over-sold what they could deliver: *The Virtuoso Pianist In Sixty Exercises*, *Foundations of Piano Technique* and *101 Exercises For The Budding Pianist*.

Of course, I bought several of these, and more or less diligently worked my way through each. Repeating such exercises improved my dexterity at the keyboard no end, but not, it appeared, my 'musicality'. The key to the cabinet of wonders I witnessed on stage at gigs did not lie in books, as far as I could tell. Then one day I came across two that did seem to shed light on the matter. One was entitled *The Diatonic Cycle* and purported to offer 'essential exercises for all jazz, traditional and contemporary musicians'. The other was *The Path to Jazz Improvisation* and offered up 'lessons for all instrumentalists'. Could these provide the answer I sought?

The difference between these books and many others I skimmed lay in the fact that the exercises they illustrated were rooted in the all-important circle of fifths. This was important. It meant that at the same time as improving my physical facility I would also be taxing my aural chops – and therefore internalising the sequences of chords that lie at the heart of the vast majority of music.

One of these books offered three hundred exercises, one per page, each consisting of forty bars of music outlining a scale or mode in a specific key (major and minor) and did so using a variety of rhythmical variations. I won't call these 'arpeggios' (as found in 'classical' exercise books) because they were not. And likewise, I won't call them 'scales' because they were rhythmically diverse and did not start or end on the tonic. No, they were more than this, and they turned out to be useful. At least for me.

The C major drill in these books, for example, began on C and progressed through the major scale (also known as Ionian mode), then skipped to F and descended through the F Lydian scale, then ascended from B (Locrian), descended from E (Phrygian), ascended from A (Aeolian), descended from D (Dorian), and, lastly, ascended from G (Mixolydian). In each passage, the notes outlined the corresponding chord from scale-chord theory. The exercises therefore combined several valuable learnings in one: dexterity, the harmonic cycle, scales, arpeggios, modes and rhythm. I found this helpful, if somewhat daunting.

One of the books added an additional twist. Instead of strictly following the circle, it mixed in various chord progressions and cadences, including the all-important 2-5 and the 2-5-1. To top things off, it included a host of more esoteric scales with names I had never heard before, such as the pentatonic, the blues scale, the chromatic minor 7th, the whole-tone scale, the diminished scale, the bebop scale and the altered scale: a veritable goldmine.

Both of the authors were able to clearly explain the 'gravitational pull' in music that arises from the circle, how this relates to the overtone series (partials), to harmonic progression and the role of the tritone. Moreover, the books cited hundreds of jazz tunes that, if one cared and had time to listen, illustrated the use of each technique *in context*. Both books are, in their way, encyclopaedias of the jazz repertoire.

I had already sensed the gist of these ideas but been unable to reproduce them at the keyboard. Now, via these books, laid out clearly, it was blindingly obvious what to do. The gears of my mind were whirring and several questions that had been troubling me, and that my teacher had not explained, clicked into place. The authors had set out the language of jazz for all to see, in its countless permutations. By playing these exercises, I was absorbing the jazz language not only in my mind but also in my hands. And so it was that I learnt a word to describe this approach: POOK. Yes, the authors' comical term stands for the Polytonal Order of Keys. A silly name for a simple idea.

To POOK is to play an exercise, or indeed any improvised melody, through all keys (polytonally) in an order that gradually introduces each additional chromatic note: the tone that distinguishes one key from another and therefore one harmony from another. POOKin' works. It does. I have no doubt these exercises – dutifully followed, one for each day of the year, and completed with reasonable speed and accuracy – would significantly improve any player's musicianship and ear training. There is only one problem. The sheer number of permutations is intimidating. And this is why, despite embodying much promise, they now lie unopened on the top of my piano, teasing me to make a renewed attempt. They remind me of the oversized jigsaw puzzle of several thousand pieces, still in its original box because no one can quite bring themselves to place the first piece. To be fair, I did work through a good number of routines. But for now, my long days POOKin' and DOOKin' (the Diatonic Order of Keys, a term I could not resist coining) have served their purpose, at least for the time being.

To round off this segment of my tale, I must tell you how my teacher responded when I brought these books to his lesson and proudly showed him what I had been practising.

'Oh yes,' he said, 'No one uses those these days, perhaps other than jobbing jazzers.'

And with that I never opened them again.

15

ROCK SCHOOL

In which I am wary of time wasted in learning set pieces, fail to go to rock school, and so miss out on a simulated gig.

Where are we? Isn't this book supposed to be about playing a musical instrument and not just theorising? Shouldn't I now be playing 'pieces', not exercises? Probably. Did I want to? No.

Was it the memory of my past failure as a child pianist? Am I fearful that, despite a modest increase in the ability of my hands and fingers to traverse the keyboard, this will never translate into music that others would seek out and wish to listen to? Or is it just that I am lazy, a recognition of how long it takes to thoroughly learn a complex piece, to performance standard. Actually, it's none of these. The fact is, I've never been that interested in playing music written by someone else. My penfriend once suggested that by 'learning a few party pieces' I could then 'entertain people wherever a piano was nearby' and that this would be 'a wonderful thing'. And I have no doubt it would, but I fear I would then feel like the performing monkey I had no wish to be. Perhaps I would see things differently years later. For now, my passion lay elsewhere.

My teacher had not been clear on the matter. He had urged me to play more music (from lead sheets), and so develop a sense of what it means for a piece to 'come alive'. On other occasions he seemed ambivalent, satisfied that by gradually increasing my skills with chord progressions and voicings, this would – one day, quite suddenly – transmogrify to an entrancing improvisation. What to do? I did need a goal other than a deadline for the next theory exam.

Browsing a music shop, I spotted a series of books from an examination board which specialises in rock, jazz and contemporary. Curious, I bought volumes covering grades three, four and five. The music was set out in full (sheet music, not lead sheets) and included was a CD providing both a backing track and a lead singer to accompany the pianist. The idea is this: you turn up at the exam centre – taking your portable electronic instrument if you wish – and give a performance as close as possible to what you'd experience if you had joined a band for a real gig. Cool. I reckoned I should try it.

The pieces looked entertaining enough, and not too tricky. Yes, I would have to learn the music to reasonable accuracy, but pupils were allowed to improvise within limits and would 'not be marked down' for doing so. Missing the odd beat, or a note, or a chord change, would not matter as much as it would if I were playing Mozart: this was a 'pop' performance after all. I liked the idea of being stretched to deliver a 'performance'. This felt different from the precision required in a classical examination. I could imagine turning up for the exam with my keyboard – I still owned a couple of portables – plugging into their amplification, turning up the volume on the backing track and running off a pretty fine simulation of what would happen if I ever made it to Gig-land. Terrifying, but wonderful, and something I had dreamed of doing. And, to add icing to the cake, the board's grades required me to demonstrate 'session skills'. This involved listening to a previously unheard piece and 'playing it back' by ear; which is presumably what happens when band members are 'finding' each other and making sense of what's 'happening' (man). It sounded like 'rock school' was something I needed to experience, even if I doubted I could pull it off. At home, looking through the books/CDs I had just purchased, grade five appeared to be within my reach. The pieces were well known. I knew what they *should* sound like; always a good start.

All I had to do now was ... play them.

Over the next couple of weeks, I tried. I did; I promise. And I could, just about. But badly. Perhaps if I worked a bit harder and repeated the difficult passages more often, the magic would kick in and, hey presto! I'd be able to perform the songs fluidly. I'd then be able to stride into the exam confident in the knowledge that I could give a convincing rendition. Even, perhaps, mix in a spot of improvisation? And just as I had these positive thoughts, another reared up in front of me. Two more weeks of practising? Three weeks? A month or two! Lost time. What would I have achieved at the end? Party pieces. Rote learning. What then? On to my next showpiece? Another monkey.

Don't get me wrong. I have nothing but admiration for those who entertain others. But how long did they have to work at their music? I had read, via online forums, of classical students who, wishing to pass advanced grades, spent a year or more practising the required three set pieces and no others, attempting to perfect-the-hell-out-of-them and so gain a distinction. Would they, at the end of this process, be better musicians? I was not so sure. Nor was my teacher. He told me of several students he had worked with who 'could play the most exquisite grade eight music, but only those pieces. All their time and effort went into perfecting three performances'. Similarly, he told me of young people who could pass exam after exam but were never able to improvise a single line. Even I was now able to do that, albeit for short runs and simple chords. Of course, I do understand: building a repertoire of great music takes time, and there is abundant joy in playing pieces you adore, no doubt about it. It would be satisfying and rewarding, but boy does it take TIME; time I did not have.

The following story illustrates the point tenfold. My wife and I had attended a remarkable recital at a prestigious London music hall. A world-famous cellist was to play two complex classical works, accompanied by a full orchestra: cello concertos of the most challenging kind. That night, the virtuoso brought the house down. It was a wonder to behold. There was only one glitch for me; a big glitch. During the artist's pre-concert talk, he alluded to the considerable time he had spent studying, practising, memorising and rehearsing his performance. As he spoke, it sounded to my ears as if he were describing a quixotic, all-consuming and noble quest … an attempt to discover every nuance and hidden corner of the music.

'I find I am only able to learn one major new piece every two years,' the maestro proudly asserted.

His revelation hit me like a hammer blow. There was no way, ever, I would either want or be able to do that. Of course, his definition of 'learn a piece' and that of most mortals in the early stages of our musical journey are two very different things. But seriously, the same piece for two years! 'Just' to build repertoire? I can barely spend a few weeks with the same sheet music. Whether this reveals a fatal flaw in my character, a shortcoming that will eventually limit my ambition to become a musician, has yet to be seen. Still, unquestionably, I was aiming in precisely the *opposite direction* of this concert-level artist. I did not wish to spend days or weeks, let alone months, learning a small number of pieces to high precision. In truth, I did not particularly care to play anyone else's music or, if I had to, would like to believe I could crack a modest piece in a few days at most. Goodness, I was bored by the work required to sit the rock school exam-gig. I had not yet passed the sign on the escalator labelled 'impatient'.

The virtuoso cellist had clarified something for me. I knew it already, but his story brought it front and centre. I hoped to play music *at will*, not from a score, maybe from a lead sheet, without having to 'learn' anything: to improvise and create my own music freely, without being 'limited' by another person's transcription or composition. So I never did get to rock school, for, in reality, the pop and rock pieces offered little of interest. To play them over and over, I convinced myself, would prove tedious.

Am I making excuses for a lack of ability? I hope not. It's just that I was, still am and probably always will be, in a rush. Over a year into my journey and with *sixty* approaching head-on, wasting time on party pieces was an unnecessary luxury. And yet … I did need to move out of exercise water and into the flowing river that was music. And so, counter to the ridiculous statements I have made in this and previous chapters – and having a contrarian nature more often than is good for me – I set a new goal and labelled it my *Piece in a Day* challenge.

16

PIECE IN A DAY

In which Adagio observes that twelve practice steps, if applied rigorously over a day or two, allow me to play a new piece from scratch – and to a reasonable standard.

The idea was this: find a way to learn a brand-new piece, good enough to share with friends, in a single day. Start early in the morning. Practise until you drop.

As a child, I probably spent several weeks learning a new piece, I cannot remember clearly … but a single day? No way. Now, as an adult, I aspired to perform such a trick! And the standard of music I felt it would be worthwhile attempting to shoot down? A pukka, classical, grade five piece, of course.

Here is what I did.

I chose a well-known and rather beautiful prelude by Frédéric Chopin. Three minutes of music; tempo neither too fast nor too slow, a degree of rubato (subtle variation) expected. Perfect. The piece offered challenges, but not so many as to overwhelm. It demands a light touch and evenness of line to work as intended by the composer. When it does, it sounds lovely. When played badly, it's awful: plodding left-hand chords. For these and other technical reasons, it is hard to play well. Some claim it should be regarded as grade six, but I think that's overstating things. It's relatively simple, just a few notes, yet the music works well as a showpiece. Some maestros use it as an encore. I suspect there is a polite competition going on here, each artist attempting to outdo the other with controlled emotion and evenness of playing. The idea is to bring a hush to the audience, a sense of rapture in the hall. I had a mind to try.

To stand any chance of even half learning this piece in a day, I would need to approach the task with military precision.

Here is how I divided the time, and I suggest you do the same:

15 MINUTES

Study the sheet music carefully. Do you understand all the notation? Write down (yes, on paper) everything you can about the music. Here are some ideas:

In what key is the music written? Are there any accidentals? Why? What is the time signature? Do either of these change throughout the piece? At what tempo should it be played?

How many bars (measures) are there? Where do phrases begin and end? Does the music speed up (accelerando) or slow down (rallentando)? Where does it get louder (forte) or softer (piano)?

How does the melody line rise and fall? What do you notice about the pattern of notes? How are the motifs repeated? How are they being modified to create variety?

Where do cadences fall – in which bars and on which beats? Does the music modulate to a new key at any point? What is the overall structure? Where are the repeats?

Are there grace notes or other ornaments?

30 MINUTES

Now listen to three or four recordings of the piece (YouTube is a remarkable resource) while following along using the score. Include one great pianist and one rank amateur. Listen carefully. Concentrate. Make a note of what do you like and don't like about each performance.

Select the performance you would most like to emulate. Stick with this to the end of the day. Listen a second time, without the score, eyes closed. Soak it in. Imagine it is you playing.

15 MINUTES

Now, at the keyboard, warm up by playing a few scales, major and relative minor. Play in the key signature of the piece and in its related keys. Play hands separate (HS) and hands together (HT). Play in thirds, sixths and in contrary motion.

30 MINUTES

Ready? Play the right hand (RH) through, several times, carefully marking the passages you find particularly tricky. Practise those passages and those alone, a few times, no more.

30 MINUTES

Ditto, the left hand (LH).

As you locate challenging phrases or individually awkward measures, note them on the score. Practise these passages until they are as easy to play as the more accessible areas of the music. Play 'over' the boundaries – a few bars either side – moving between 'effortless' and 'demanding'. Focus your attention on those parts of the music where the phraseology, tempo, key or mood changes markedly. Look out for transitions.

15 MINUTES

As slowly as need be, play the whole piece through from beginning to end, hands together. Slow down to avoid too many blunders, trips or stalls. Keep moving forward through your mistakes. Aim to complete the whole piece, without error. Congratulate yourself.

45 MINUTES

Locate the hardest passage in the music. Focus only on it. Practise it obsessively. Only when you are confident with this, move to less complex phrases. If at any time you feel you are making more, not fewer, mistakes, stop at once. Over-practising is a danger.

BREAK

Take some time out. Do something different; get some fresh air.

I tended to pace around the room, wondering why my hands were so stubborn. Was it that I could not read the notes, or could not move to them when I did? Was I playing too fast? Were the rhythms confusing? Did I understand the harmony? It helped to think things through away from the keyboard: to reflect and intellectualise the problems. After all, we are intelligent adults, not children. What is stopping us? We can diagnose our problems if we focus on fixing them.

Slow down. Right down. For me, it helped to write out the chords of the harmony above the phrases of the music. It gave me a mental map.

30 MINUTES

Play the whole piece through once again. This time record yourself. A phone will do if you have nothing better to hand. Listen back carefully to your performance. Where are you weak? What is not working? Practise those parts only. Maximise the time you spend working on the hard stuff.

LUNCH

It's lunchtime already! Let off some steam. Sing to release tension. You are likely to be VERY tired. This is mental work. Give yourself a decent break, make a cup of tea, have a bite to eat (a sandwich, no more; we don't want to get sleepy as we are going to have to work hard throughout the afternoon). Stroke your cat. If necessary, take a power-nap; no more than ten minutes, though. There is still much to do.

Back to work.

Afternoon

It's now time to focus on dynamics and phrasing. As before, focus on the sections that trip you up or stop you in your tracks. Make another recording. Imagine you are a music critic. If you had played this music to your friends after a quiet dinner, would they have enjoyed it or would they, like you, be embarrassed? Be honest with yourself. How does your performance stack up against a professional?

Repeat.

Getting somewhere? Still having problems? Try singing the melody as you practise the right hand. Sing the bassline while playing hands together. If you can, sing the inner parts.

Do you have an electronic keyboard? Play with the sound turned off. Focus only on your arm, hands and finger movements. This may help you to memorise, and therefore internalise, the music.

How are things going? Can you play the piece now? Could I? I was still stuck at times and needed more practice time. And I was exhausted. I considered continuing into the evening but was finding it hard to concentrate for more than five or six hours at a stretch. It was clear by teatime that I was going to need a second day.

Day two

Do it all over again. By the end of the second twenty-four-hour period, I was playing the music without mistakes but was not entirely happy with the result. I let myself slip into a third day. (Later, I learnt that the brain needs time to absorb repetitive work and secure the muscle memory. It achieves this feat all by itself; no additional practice required, just elapsed time to allow for absorption. Which is why returning to difficult music some time after a period of intense practice, one is often surprised by the improvement.)

DAY THREE

Eager to crack the music once and for all, I woke early. Adagio was already ensconced in his basket. Our cat had sat with me throughout my ordeal of the last two days and I had spoken to him several times about my progress. Always responsive, if a little bored, he would look up as if with understanding and sympathy. I think he sensed my need for interaction and convinced myself he knew what I was going through. Had anyone else been in the house during these periods (my wife was at work), my conversations with a cat would have been signs of a growing insanity.

'Yes, Adagio, I know.' 'Absolutely, I shall.' And off I went to work on the hardest sections again; hands separately and hands together. By lunchtime, I had decided to cut my losses.

After a final (I hoped) recording, I cut a CD using my laptop. It sounded passable to my ears, but what would others think? Popping it into an envelope, I walked to the local post office, attached the required postage and sent it on its way: to my penfriend and his wife, of course. Yes, I could have sent them an MP3 file by email, but I wanted them to have the experience of opening a package and playing the physical CD on their (rather excellent) hi-fi system. This was the first 'real' music they had heard me play. My masterpiece needed the best chance of sounding good, and my friend's sound system would surely be that. Before this, the only 'performances' I had subjected them to were bland demonstrations of scales, chords, progressions and theory games. Now they had something meaningful to judge my progress by. I knew they liked the composer and would therefore know what to listen out for. I was about to be judged.

I received their reaction two days later:

'Dear Howard,

'Thank you for our parcel which arrived in the post yesterday. We played it on our system and were impressed. It must be hard to get the tempo, dynamics and articulation right. We guess this is why pianists practise for so long, to the point where fingers just fall into the correct place? To achieve the control you have so clearly demonstrated, you must know the piece so well that you could stop and restart after any note and not be lost.

'The fact that you can play this piece, to this standard, after just a couple of weeks, is remarkable. You should be justly proud of yourself. We do have this piece on our HMV "classic moods" album *Music of Peace and Serenity*. However, the recording has an orchestral accompaniment and the piano, which we love, is somewhat lost. Now we can hear it. Thank you so much. We will proudly add your recording to our collection. We trust and hope you will record more.

'Sending love, your appreciative friends.'

I was beaming, and wrote back immediately, telling them I had learnt the piece from scratch in just two and a half days. They were amazed. I had amazed myself. If I could do this, surely I could repeat the trick with other pieces of a similar grade? Maybe, in the course of the next few months, I should build a mini-repertoire of my own, enough to give a toy concert to a few of our friends? I reckoned I could. But never did.

As I write this, I am only too well aware that for some (perhaps all) of my readers, my attitude will come across as incomprehensible at best and an insult at worst. But I must be honest. Despite success with my *Piece In A Day* challenge, my mind was already racing towards a new tangent. There was just so much I had yet to learn about music that had nothing, zero, zilch to do with performing monkeys.

17

MY IMAGINARY PIANO

In which, encouraged by my unorthodox teacher, I learn to play the piano by not playing the piano.

As the relationship with my teacher deepened, the depth of his capability as a jazz musician continued to shock. For me, our time together was almost spiritual, a ritual I came to cherish. Had he ever met a student like me? I wondered. Had I inadvertently pulled him in a direction with which he was not entirely comfortable? Maybe. Was he nudging me back to a more conventional path, a path he had presumably taken with other pupils? Should he have protected me from myself? Yes. Never once, however, did he prevent me from exploring, finding my own way and making my own mistakes. And it was motivating.

By encouraging me to examine music from all angles, the learning mountain grew month by month. Determined to become thoroughly familiar with the keyboard – scales, every possible chord, their inversions and voicings – the workload was overwhelming. Ear training, theory, repertoire, improvisation, exercises, composition, sight-reading, the list went on and on, sprouting new leaves and branches in every direction: the mathematical term 'factorial' comes to mind. There was scant time to learn 'pieces', which was fortunate because, at this stage of my journey, I was not motivated to do so. My teacher tolerated a reluctance to dig into the meaty lead sheets he offered up each week, gently reminding me that 'unless you begin to play some music you may never understand the context for improvisation and composition'. Despite his gentle admonishment, however, I gradually wore him down and he grew accustomed to my way of working, with its brew of hesitant, amateurish, piecemeal investigation.

Was I a good pupil? My penfriend's wife thought so. She suspected I was 'an excellent pupil, always willing to do any set homework to the max'. She could not have been more wrong. I fear I dominated too many lessons with naïve questions, eager to extract more of the encyclopaedic knowledge my teacher so visibly demonstrated.

What were our lessons like? Mostly, we just chatted; he pointing me to concepts he felt I needed to study, me asking 'difficult' questions or veering off-road towards what to him must have appeared unrelated topics. If he suggested a book, however, I would always buy a copy and study it dutifully at home, saving face time for freewheeling exploration.

This unruly pattern continued. After a few months, my teacher rarely set any formal work and our time together dissolved into a hotchpotch of divergent conversations with no overall goal. Yet this was precisely what I needed to crack the factorial equation that was 'becoming a musician'.

The lack of a singular focus was entirely my fault, and I am sure he could have crafted a structured learning programme had I allowed him to. God knows, he tried. But he never knew in advance what I would throw at him next, and so gave up trying. My unusual chord sequences, usually made up the night before, were one example. He struggled to know how to respond to the more outlandish ones. But it was not all negative. Learning how to tap out complex rhythms was one area where we found common ground. But the next minute we were forking to more theoretical concepts such as 'what exactly *is* a tension?' or 'how do modes *really* work?' I was the nightmare student from hell. Our occasional attempts to create a lesson plan for the following term never did work out. Not once. No, my teacher was sufficiently experienced to take my haphazard questioning in real time. Together, we would trip off the escalator down some back alley to the nuggets of knowledge I so desperately sought. Mostly this consisted of picking a song, understanding its harmony and playing around with it to develop the idea. Our lessons were like jazz itself: spontaneous, unpredictable and richly layered. Just what I needed.

On hearing my description of a typical lesson, my penfriend was unimpressed. 'Have you ever thought about how your teacher must be feeling? I reckon he must be a bit of a saint.' And my teacher did appear to be just that. My tug-of-war approach would have frustrated others. But this teacher did not mind, reminding me that 'guiding an adult is unlike the way one directs a child'. You betcha. His sympathetic approach from the outset had initiated my journey to the piano. And it had done so without the baggage of learning to play from exacting sheet music. That was unusual enough, I suppose, but, as I was to find out, merely a taste of the weirdness to come. Have I spoken before about the games I played ruminating on chords and scales at night in bed? No? Well, I used chords as sleep therapy, hoping the semi-sleep period before deep relaxation would reinforce their shapes. I needed this augmentation. For me, practice at the keyboard was not enough to ingrain so many voicings within my sluggish adult brain. I told my teacher of these slumber experiments, and as a result the occasional homework he did assign took an unforeseen turn. A new type of exercise: not only was I given no lead sheet to play, but I was also barred from touching my piano!

Picture me in a darkened room, imagining the keyboard, eighty-eight keys arranged in their curious black and white pattern. Now I am pressing imaginary notes at random, naming imaginary intervals, playing imaginary chords – and their imaginary inversions – spelling out the names and tones of each. 'Try it,' my teacher suggested. 'If you ever get stuck, you can look, but not touch, your piano.'

Gee, thanks. Needs a hell of an imagination, I can assure you.

As I performed this ritual, a curious poem entered my feverish brain; a vision of the contour of my journey and its inevitable trajectory:

Learn to play the piano by playing from sheet music.

Learn to play the piano from a lead sheet; improvisation.

Learn to play the piano by imagining playing the piano – with or without imaginary music!

Learn to play the piano by not playing the piano.

Not playing the piano.

The irrefutable and undeniable outcome of *this* progression is that I can now be successful at playing the piano by not playing it. My success will come in leaps and bounds and can only improve in the future!

Such imagination games, pianistic séances if you will, worked wonders. I kid you not. Whenever I was bored (or simply dog-tired from the combination of day job and practice), I would grab a beer or brew up a soothing cup of tea, sink into the sofa (or lie down on the ground), fade the lighting and imagine I was playing … a little Beethoven?

These mental exercises grew ever more vivid as my imaginary practice chops matured. Initially, the dreaming took place in the room where our real piano stood idly by. Soon afterwards, I found I could conjure up scales and chords in more incongruous situations. Train or car journeys proved suitable venues for spectral performances. With concentration I could pick out a chord sequence at any time of the day or night, and in pretty much any environment. Floating off to Pianoland became second nature. Bedtime was glorious. I've always found it difficult to get to sleep, but dial up an imaginary piano – upright, grand, electronic, the choice is endless – choose an imaginary work from an imaginary book, and within a few bars I was snoring peacefully, dreaming of the progress I was making, spelling out the music while watching my imaginary hands perform. And yes, as with a real piano, I mind-played everything in every key. I was a pretty good imaginary pianist.

After writing to my penfriend with news of these newfound abilities, his reaction was subdued. What for me was a revelatory learning method was to him mumbo-jumbo. I should explain that he is not at all, let's say, spiritual. I would describe him as a rational atheist; a scientist with a big heart. The slightest whiff of the mystical gets his hackles up. As evidence, I present a story about how, during a house concert that my wife and I attended, we were invited to chant *om* for a child in the community who was suffering from a terminal illness. The remarkable manner in which we came to be part of this unusual event, I shall narrate later. For now, it is sufficient to explain that the evening holds a special significance for me during my time on the escalator. Although I have never asked my penfriend, I suspect that singing New Age prayers and chanting *om* to a nebulous life force 'out there' in the ether is not in my friend's nature.

My friend faces reality head on, not as we'd like it to be. A humanist and practical to the core, he would be deeply sympathetic for the sick child, but not for any superstition or belief in ritual. He would know precisely what to say and what not to say to the desperately worried parents, and is the most supportive friend in difficult times. But I am also sure he would have felt deeply uncomfortable at the house concert, unable to enter into the spirit of things. More likely, while we om'ed, he'd have been staring at his smartphone researching the latest scientifically sound medical breakthrough that might have a chance of helping the ailing infant. Yet I did enter into the spirit of the evening. Had my musical journey changed me? Were the bits and bytes of software engineering being pushed aside in favour of sensations and emotions: melody, harmony and artistry? The latter is not as easy to pin down as code and digital logic. Musical performance is neither 'provable' nor 'testable', dear penfriend. Surrounded by reciprocating souls, it seemed entirely natural to chant; the music that night *was* healing.

And with this change in my personality, my penfriend detected a corresponding shift in the tone and content of my emails. I was writing less of the mathematics of music theory and vibrating strings and more of the intangible qualities of performance. So, when I tried to describe my delight and 'feeling' during my imaginary pastimes, my penfriend flew back with, 'Oh, dear, how very New Age. Too Zen for me by far. Might be a good way how NOT to learn to play the piano. Will you be required to chant the notes as well?'

Joker friend. Well, yes, actually, he has a terrific sense of humour. But we'll come to his reaction to my first compositions later.

My fascination with mind play, a phase lasting no more than six months, had, I believe, a profound effect on my ability to learn. The deliberate and concerted imagining of practice became a daily habit. It fostered a degree of concentration on the keyboard's odd arrangement of notes that is difficult to achieve in everyday exercises and routines when you are also worrying about which finger to put where. Not only was 'ghost playing' a useful mental forcing factor, but it also increased the time I had for practice – a win-win. The constant distraction of my demanding career was still much in evidence, and I was pleased to find any approach that allowed me to grab extra time at the keyboard.

Prompted by my penfriend's scepticism of mind play, and hoping to find a connection to his scientific interest, I began to wonder whether there could be an *objective* basis for the efficacy of my imaginary instrument. Have there been any great imaginary pianists? Is there, out there on the pitch, a footballer who claims imaginary pre-match games helped him score goals at the end of the season? Does homoeopathy work? What about the 'laying on of hands'? Such mysteries may lie forever unresolved. I offer up only circumstantial evidence. But I'm convinced that I was, still am, and forever shall be, a better late-returning amateur for having discovered the delight of imaginary performance. Had my penfriend, so interested in the functioning of the brain, dismissed this diversion too readily? I fired off a quasi-scientific and carefully drafted question, sprinkled with a few faux transcendental sentiments, hoping to entice him to respond. It worked.

'Don't be daft, Howard,' he shot back, 'What you are describing is nothing more than "visualisation", a well-known and scientifically validated technique, nothing mystical there.

'Visualisation is practised in many fields, including sports, athletics, dance, coping with disability, even the achievement of business goals. I think what you are doing with piano work is called "process visualisation", envisioning the actions necessary to achieve an outcome you hope for. You might like to Google it. I think you will find it is taught as part of jazz training. Howard, you found this, you did not invent it.'

Well, that told me!

Today I play only in the real world, but who knows when I might be tempted to dream again, to enter a pleasant netherworld where I can rattle off a great concerto at a tempo limited only by my imagination, and with absolutely no performance anxiety.

Before my journey of three years was up, I would have my answer, and in the most unexpected fashion.

18
ON EDUCATION

In which disagreement over the importance of theory (again) leads to a realisation of how music evolves. Lacking a time machine, the only way forward is more study.

My penfriend sure seems to be taking a prominent role in my musical fable. Our correspondence was the starting point for my decision to document the journey; now I find myself sharing complete drafts! And most remarkable of all, my good friend is reading them. Thoroughly. He tells me my tale is 'coming on fine' and urges that I 'continue the stream of consciousness', 'watching out for too many commas' and 'reviewing the narrative' with the hindsight of where my journey *actually* ends'. Story arc. My penfriend, you see, by his very nature, is a 'consultant'. He loves 'clients'. As such – and I would expect nothing less – he is quick to speak his mind. My prose, he suggested, could be 'a little less self-satisfied'. And here I was thinking I had taken care to be humble. He has a point, though: where the heck is this book going? In his words: 'What is the overall thesis of your story?' Frankly, who knows! It's a journey. It had a beginning – a music shop on the wrong side of town – it clearly has a middle (writing the book), and it will no doubt have an end. Of course, I already know the final movement. It is imprinted on my soul, as indelible as any tattoo. As does my penfriend – on and off the page. Well aware of the dark days to come, it is only to be expected that he sought to guide me to some kind of 'right' answer, in writing as in life. He wants my time on the escalator to end well, if at all possible. Letting any 'client' run into the buffers is not in his nature. If a foreboding evil or inauspicious star can be avoided, he is compelled to act, to be the wise advisor he most clearly is. You see, he cares for me, as he does all his clients; and more than I realise. In any case, we'll get to all that messy stuff later. Goodness, I sound like I need a psychiatrist. My penfriend probably assumes that he is my doctor and not merely an interlocutor in my narrative. But I'd never open up to a bona fide head-doctor; ever. Stiff upper lip. Soldier on. No shrink required.

What next? Oh yes, on education in music; an excellent example of my penfriend's perseverance as advice-giver. Is formal education a prerequisite for success as a musician? To put it simply: do I need a degree in music? He thought not.

My penfriend often teased me, if that's the right word, with his understanding of the early days of jazz. He held a conviction (yes, that's not too strong a word) that musicians of that era had not found it necessary to put themselves through the education-ringer. They had no need, he was convinced, for the arcane details I was wittering on about in my emails. You know the type of thing: why a flat-III suspended-4th with an added 9th resolves to … well, you know. The implication of my friend's assertion was that I was, in effect, 'wasting my time on theory' and should just 'get on with the playing'. Was he right?

There is a misconception here, I believe, so let me bat this particular ball back. Listen, dear penfriend. Early jazz was born in the red-light district of New Orleans known as Storyville. Ragtime and blues were fusing into forms of music never heard before, characterised by 'blue' notes, 'call and response' vocals, poly-rhythms and improvisation. This was a profoundly cultural movement, woven into the pulse of everyday life. Jazz was something lived. It evolved through a mingling of influences that individual musicians brought to the table. One player would create a lick or a chord change, and others would gather around the piano, eager to learn, replicate and later evolve their own style. Thus, to take my penfriend's advice and avoid theory would require me to go back in time and live a similar existence. But I am here, in the present. What to do? Perhaps there are jazz collectives in our era, developing new forms of musical expression through a freewheeling exchange of ideas. If so, their understanding of musical structure must be, like those before them, built on the shoulders of giants. I have no more chance of being accepted into a pioneering jazz commune today than I could construct a 'Take Me Back To The Roaring Twenties' time machine.

I have no choice. Music theory allows me to understand the past and so develop in the present. Who knows, one day I might contribute to the development of a new musical form (though I seriously doubt this). If I did, it could only be built on a solid foundation of theory, just as early jazz musicians relied on their heritage. The same is true of all fields of creative or scientific endeavour. The thoughtful musician cannot buck a musical education. Any debate over the value of music theory is therefore quite futile, a moot point. Jazz musicians of the past may never have attended a college, but make no mistake: they built their own! Among them were the adventurers and pioneers who composed at a level far beyond mimicry or extrapolation. Their names have gone down in history: Charles Mingus, John Coltrane, Herbie Hancock, Miles Davis, Thelonius Monk. Watch them play or teach. Read their bios. Even as young men, they exhibited a depth of theoretical understanding and a higher musical IQ than we amateurs could acquire in a lifetime.

To perform to a high standard involves theory. To teach others requires a great deal of theory. To create a new musical form demands deep theory. The jazz greats were formidable theorists and methodologists. In fact, the vast majority of the world's leading musicians are well qualified, holding advanced diplomas, graduate degrees and postgraduate masters. Even in the world of popular music – which some, condescendingly in my view, dismiss as 'trivial' – the relevant music theory is taught and practised to degree level in all the best contemporary schools and conservatories. I am referring to institutions such as Trinity Laban, The Royal College of Music, Berklee and Juilliard.

I thought I had made my case. But would my penfriend give up?

Of course not.

'What about this guy?' he asked, pointing to a young musician, 'I cannot believe he studied what you are writing about.'

Well, there might be exceptions, but guess what? Most creative musicians do study theory. It's a simple fact. Perhaps my penfriend was getting too hung up on linguistics? Is the word 'theory' in musical life a misnomer? Maybe 'theory' exams should be renamed 'language' exams?

In science, a theory is a well-substantiated explanation of some aspect of the natural world. Science is based on a body of facts, repeatedly confirmed through observation and experiment. If music has 'theory', it is not in the sense of science. Understanding the pattern of tones of a musical scale, how to form a chord, how chords 'progress', and how melodies are woven on top, is more akin to what a gardener does when they tend and grow a beautiful display. Some knowledge of botany might creep in, but the science of botany is not their predominant focus.

The way I see it is this: music is an art form, and like all mature art, also a craft. Prose fiction, poetry, photography, painting, sculpture … theory cannot explain the wellspring of the creative process, but it can describe the intricacies and complexities of the act, before, during and after. Theory can and does characterise musical harmony and compositional patterns, including their effect on the listener. 'Theory' in music is a notation, a descriptive language allowing musicians to exchange ideas (music): entire symphonies or simple pop tunes.

The average pop star who typically has her music written for them by a seasoned pro uses only a teeny-weeny part of music's rich aural linguistics. Even a pop hack, however, will be familiar with some chords! And the few who aspire to escape the clutches of the money-men will choose to learn more, especially as they begin to collaborate with more experienced, battle-hardened session musicians. By contrast, the 'serious' composer of a great work of classical, romantic or contemporary music speaks the entirety of the musical language in all its forms and details. They are fluent in its myriad nuances. And this unique language (yes, I think it is unique) is still developing today. It is our accumulated musical heritage, and it is this that forms the body of 'theory' I speak of. Which explains why (to some ears) avant-garde or 'modern' music sounds like little more than noise, or, as my parents once described the music of Sir Michael Tippett, 'plinky-plonk music'. Travesty! His glorious music, some of the greatest ever conceived, is simply in a language my parents neither studied nor 'heard'. Their brains (penfriend take note) had not been shaped by the experience. We, however, decades on, have been infected and restyled by our musical furniture, whether we like it or not. Thus, to the modern ear, works previously dismissed as ugly vulgarity now sound ... how can I put it? Approximately conventional.

Music, it appears, has always been in prototype, forever a fomenting brew. Its form – the acceptable arrangement of its elements and structures – evolves over time and, for some listeners, more swiftly than *they* can change. Driven by the creative force of writers and composers of all eras, music races ahead. This, no doubt, is why so many of us get stuck in the past, preferring to listen to the music we grew up with. Music – at a point in time – permeates our being and soaks into our skin. It's hard to keep up with the shifting genres. Yet being a musician requires just that.

In many ways, therefore, the theory of music is analogous to a descriptive account of natural language. Notes, scales, modes, chords and cadences have a rough correspondence in verbs, nouns, prepositions, sentences, poetry and literary forms of speech and writing. Great novelists, like great musicians, know their canon.

Here's anecdotal evidence:

A singer-songwriter friend of mine – who you will later learn plays a prominent role in my journey to 'music' – unexpectedly turned up at one of the rare concerts my penfriend could also attend. After spotting each other, she came over and sat down between us. A song had just ended and I had made a (most likely inane) 'theory' observation, something about melodic intervals, the chords used and how the songwriter on stage had used them in some oh, so clever way; or so I thought. I fear I may have sounded a tad pretentious. Not really, though: I was just being me, trying my best to understand the music in front of us – and responding to the arrival of another musician who might be interested.

My songwriting friend turned to my penfriend and asked, 'Do you understand what Howard is talking about?'

'I have no idea,' he quipped, 'but he says those things quite often.'

'I know!' she replied.

And they giggled. At me. In the nicest possible way.

My penfriend has a flaw – just one. Very occasionally, he can be stubborn (firm) in his beliefs. The ailment reveals itself when he is seduced by the rational basis for his argument. When this happens, no alternative evidence can then shake him from his conviction. This is a hazard, no doubt, of a high intelligence and logic taken to extremes. Our ongoing disagreement about the role of 'theory' was one example. He never let up. It is littered throughout our correspondence. True to form, he would often remind me of his cheeky exchange with the singer-songwriter, reiterating his conviction that I was 'over-egging the theory side of the journey'.

Let's get this straight once and for all. I disagree profoundly.

Yes, of course, the pop singer who has their music written for them doesn't need theory. Or the musician who only manages to conjure up a pastiche or crude imitation of another artist's work; they may not need theory. Or the pumped-up 'five minutes of fame' media personality, only notable as a result of 1) a well-funded marketing promotion, or 2) their looks, or 3) some cute gimmick that distinguishes their tunes but which, when looked at in the cold light of day, is just that: a trick. Sure, *they* have no need for theory. But almost everyone else does. I do. You do. If we stand any chance of creating something beautiful, that is.

My anecdote has a twist.

A year later, the same songwriter friend and I were sitting in a fashionable café in the heart of London, sipping coffee (me a regular Americano, she something exotic). We were chatting about the trials and tribulations of being a creative artist in the niche area of the industry she occupies (though these days I reckon even mainstream musicians have a hard time of it). Surprise, surprise, she revealed that she does, in fact, hold a degree in music. Listening to her bewitching music, I am sure my penfriend would never have guessed. So what he took as confirmation of the non-essential nature of theory was dead wrong; in her case at least.

Creativity can be deceptive. The word sits uneasily with the rigour implied by the terminology of 'theory' in the mind of non-musicians. Perhaps this is why musicians play down their quals and play up the 'mystique' of the illusive phrase 'the creative artist'. Are they toying with the rest of us, hinting that their superhuman ability springs from some 'unfathomable and indescribable well' that resides 'at the core of their being'? The implication being that non-musicians, like my penfriend, could 'never understand or imagine its depth and beauty, let alone reach such a 'profound state of self-expression'. Clichés over.

So what had the singer-songwriter meant when she turned to my friend and teased, 'Do you understand what Howard is talking about?' It was no proof of his argument. She was simply being polite in front of my penfriend, so as not to exclude the outsider. We, the struggling musicians to be, know that without a healthy smattering of theory it is impossible to step off, let alone leap beyond, the starting block. While we will never reach the creative heights of the jazz greats, we are sure going to try. Count on it. Music theory is our toolbox, as in all artistic endeavour. So let's do some more, shall we? Why? So that we can be creative, of course.

Note to self: book next theory exam. Sermon over.

19

MOVING IN DIATONIC CIRCLES

In which I decode that most mysterious designation: diatonic harmony. And find that, by using modes, all kinds of marvellous music emerges, as if by magic.

Of all the concepts I encountered during my time on the escalator, the word 'diatonic' caused the most difficulty, until I finally realised how simple it could be.

There are twelve notes on the keyboard, C to C, black and white, each separated by a semitone. A musical scale is nothing more than a selection from this basket of twelve tones. The classical majors and minors (natural, harmonic and melodic) employ seven of the twelve:

do re mi fa so la ti do (major)
do re *me* fa so la ti do (melodic minor ascending)
do *te le* so fa *me* re do (melodic minor descending)
do re *me* fa so *le* ti do (harmonic minor)

That's solfège by the way. Look it up.

In jazz and blues, two notes are added and one taken away, forming the so-called octatonic scale. This then gets complicated … a zoo of outlandish scales with names that are impossible to remember. They include the Phrygian-♮6, the Dorian-♭2, the Lydian-augmented (♯5) the Locrian-♮2 and the Altered-dominant (also known as Super-Locrian mode). See what I mean? To my surprise, these esoteric scales were not invented by jazz musicians. Before the jazz era began, these unusual scales were used by the great composers of the early twentieth century, including Debussy, Ravel and Stravinsky.

At the polar opposite of the complexity spectrum, the whole-tone scale uses only six notes. Starting on C, they are C D E F♯ G♯ and A♯ (whole steps). And the pentatonic scale uses only five notes, those core frequencies which are consonant (sweet-sounding) among themselves in all combinations: the natural result of the physics of vibrating strings. Much folk music is written using this charming scale. The pentatonic tonal relationships are the simplest to compose in, and the easiest to listen to. Hence, I believe, the popularity of folk music, past and present. In C, the pentatonic scale is C D E G and A. The relative minor pentatonic, A C D E and G, is just as attractive. Try playing both in various keys.

All melodies are written using notes of a particular mode, but many tunes also include tones from outside the scale. This happens in three cases: 1) if the music moves to a new key (momentarily, temporarily or permanently), or 2) the composer steals notes from a related key, or 3) the piece introduces accidentals (notes outside the prevailing harmony).

The term 'diatonic', an adjective to describe an interval or harmony, is simply a way of saying that the notes played are the notes of the prevailing (established) scale without any chromatic (non-diatonic) alterations. Get it? If not, here's the simpler version: a diatonic melody uses only the notes of the key the piece is written in. Simple.

Now we are clear on that, let's talk about a new kind of circle: the diatonic circle of fifths.

You remember the regular circle, right? It progresses through the twelve tones of the modern piano in an order such that each successive interval is a perfect fifth from the last. From C, that's G up the keyboard and F down the keyboard. C-G is a perfect fifth. F-C is a perfect fifth. Keep going, and you end up back at C, having explored all twelve notes, black and white. Intriguing, is it not?

The 5th, you remember, is obtained by dividing a vibrating string in three. If it were divided in two, the interval formed would be the octave. So, strictly speaking, the physics 5th is larger than the physics octave. It's the 12th (7+5), the octave being, of course, the 8th.

Mathematically speaking, the 5th divides the string in the ratio 3:2. Of course, we cannot divide a string this way in practice. On a real piano, the 5th above C, the G, is 'tuned' to that interval. But the 5th above that, the 12th (an octave and a 5th) does sound in the partial series of the lower C. Remember the demonstration I described earlier. It might be worth hearing that again.

In any case, by repeatedly applying the 3:2 ratio to a root string, you end up back at the root, six octaves higher, after twelve repetitions. Those operations generate the twelve semitones, and the pattern is repeated up and down the keyboard. Isn't maths (and music) cool? Try it. Play the lowest (leftmost) C and work up the keyboard in fifths:

C	G	D	A	E	B	F♯ G♭	C♯ D♭	A♭	E♭	B♭	F
1	2	3	4	5	6	7	8	9	10	11	12

This is the traditional circle of fifths, whether played clockwise or anti-clockwise. It's all fifths up and all fourths down, each the inversion of the other.

The *diatonic* circle, by contrast, uses *only* the notes of the prevailing scale, whatever that scale happens to be. It too moves in 'fifths', but the number 'five' is interpreted differently. We *count notes* of the scale (ordinals) and *not* the tonal ratio of the intervals formed.

When speaking of the traditional circle of fifths, the intervals between notes are in all cases a perfect fifth (i.e. by the ratio of their frequencies). When speaking of the diatonic circle, we refer to *note positions* in the scale (counting fingers). Thus, in C major, the diatonic circle is:

C	G	D	A	E	B	F	C
1	2	3	4	5	6	7	8

Only notes of the scale are used. As a consequence, one of the intervals formed is not a perfect fifth. In C, it is the interval between B and F: the tritone. Two tones, four semitones. The devil's interval. It can be 'spelt' as a diminished fifth (a perfect fifth minus a semitone) or as an augmented fourth (a perfect fourth plus a semitone). In diatonic terminology, however, the tritone is still fifth (up the keyboard) or fourth (down the keyboard). Now do you see why I was initially confused?

Diatonic circles turn out to be incredibly useful. Take the C harmonic minor scale for example, C D E♭ F G A♭ B C. Its diatonic circle is:

C	G	D	A♭	E♭	B	F	C
1	2	3	4	5	6	7	8

Look closely, there are now two tritones in the circle, D-A♭ and B-F. This gives the minor scale a quality which some describe as 'sad' (as opposed to the 'happy' majors and 'bright' Lydian). The minor scale also contains one interval not found in any major, an augmented-fifth E♭-B. Interesting. Do other modes create new intervals? Let's look at D Dorian:

D	A	E	B	F	C	G	D
1	2	3	4	5	6	7	8

Once again we find B-F, the tritone, but the rest are now all perfect fifths, just as in C major and all the other major keys. Not so surprising, since Dorian mode, as we saw earlier, is just the notes of the major scale starting on the 2nd (the so-called supertonic). Nevertheless, chords formed on the Dorian scale, their progression and harmony, are immediately more engaging. Let's see why.

The diatonic circle, whether built from a major, minor or indeed any other mode, is talented. By constraining the intervals to those of the prevailing scale, entire pieces of music can be crafted. There being no obvious way to show this in a book, please step up to your keyboard. I am not going to provide a web link to the following music, partly because this is not a book that does this, but mostly because I want you to hear the harmonies yourself. Play a sequence of chords around the C major diatonic circle as follows:

CΔ | FΔ | B^0 | E– | A– | D– | GΔ | CΔ

Lovely, isn't it? And no, I don't mean the new symbols. They are short-cuts used by jazz musicians. Δ signifies major, – minor and ^{0} diminished. Jazz musicians, especially when improvising, are necessarily lazy. They need a quick way to capture musical ideas.

Play the progression. I hope you were using good voice-leading? I personally enjoy splitting the chords between the two hands using seventh (four-note) chords: play the 1st and 5th of each chord in the left hand and the 3rd and 7th of the chord in the right hand. When I first discovered this music, I played it endlessly, over and over again, listening to its intervals and wondering how many pieces 'out there' employ the same pattern (the same circle). My teacher's answer was: LOTS.

Now try the same circle logic but in C minor. Result: new music! How? Because new chords are formed and they appear in a new order.

The chord on the 3rd of the scale now happens to be an augmented triad, E♭+. The chord on the 4th of the scale, F major, is now F minor. Clever eh? *This* is why theory is vital. Circle malarkey is what musicians do. It is what jazz musicians do all of the time. They do know 'theory', dear penfriend, and understand the methods of progression and cadence, even if they do not go around bragging about it to all and sundry. After all, not everyone needs to write a book to be a musician – far from it. Writing a book was furthest from my mind as I stepped into the music shop and asked for a lesson. The idea of documenting my adventure in such detail only came about after two years of correspondence with my musically curious, detail-oriented, and oh, so rational penfriend. Nor would I ever have written a book had THING not come along and given me the time to do so. But now that I *am* writing this book, it is undoubtedly cementing my knowledge.

Back to circles. Diatonic progression is one small but essential recipe in the creation of music. It was the first I discovered (a.k.a. composed) all by myself, and all from theory. But I hope you see how it is possible to play similar games with circles in any key or mode, and so create other kinds of music. Notes, scales, chords, circles, progressions ... it's all coming together. Now the challenge is to put it into practice, at the keyboard. And let's not forget, we are looking to write music that someone might actually want to listen to. Yeah, really; you know the kind of thing, with a MEL-O-DY.

20

A PLEASANT DAY

In which I write a tune using the diatonic circle, discover there is as much science in melody as in harmony, and that only by fusing the two can music emerge. Am told I am now a musician: not true.

I hesitate to write a note on mel-o-dy because, quite frankly, melody was, and still is, the most mysterious aspect of music I encountered during my time on the escalator. I never did bottom it out.

We all know a great tune when we hear it. It grabs us by the throat and never lets go. We absorb good melodies so readily that, after only a couple of listens, we find ourselves humming, whistling or singing away to ourselves with gay abandon; often in the shower. Yet what we hear is more than the notes alone. How?

Sing or play a tune without its bass notes, to someone who has not heard the song before, and they may not 'get it' at first. Even the best tunes can sound like a random set of tones. Most of us need the accompanying harmony to make sense of a melody with which we are unfamiliar. I think we recall popular songs so readily because of how we first heard them: complete with their bass parts, accompaniment, and therefore chords. Melody and harmony are inextricably linked. Perhaps this is why it is so terribly hard to write a truly memorable song.

My teacher had little to say about the composition of melody, at least not from a theoretical point of view. But he surprised me when he suspected I had an ear for it. 'You write good melodies, Howard,' he said. Had he based this hunch on those occasions when he observed me improvising circles and twiddling about over the top with what I felt at the time was the aural equivalent of a child's scribble? Not exactly a random set of tones, but close enough. What had he heard that I had not?

I often asked my teacher if we could dedicate the week's lesson to studying a specific jazz tune or folk song that had caught my attention. He readily agreed, and, dialling it up on his computer, we listened together, each of us tempted to pick out its notes on the keyboard. It was a bit hit and miss, but I reckon I was guessing correctly about 75 per cent of the time. As the notes piled up, it did not take me long to find the key that songs were written in, and I was soon playing snatches of the melody. My ear was improving. This was, according to my teacher, the result of nothing more than having absorbed music for the last eighteen months. More tricky, of course, was how to write a distinctive line of my own. He offered no advice on this, beyond urging me to 'experiment and hear what works'. Hardly helpful. He did discuss 'rising' and 'falling' lines, 'smooth' and 'awkward' intervals, but I had the distinct feeling he had not taught melodic composition. In the absence of a repeatable recipe, I did what I always do, find the best book and read up.

To my surprise, there are few books on the topic of melody writing. A handful, if that. But I did find one that sounded semi-promising from its marketing blurb, and so ordered it online and eagerly awaited delivery. A few days later it dropped heavily to the floor. What I found in this tome was a revelation. My workload expanded again.

The art of tunesmithing, it turns out, is more scientific than you might imagine. It has its own field of theory. My new two-hundred-page manual was littered with melodic concepts, all of which were news to me and had never been mentioned by my teacher. They included such ideas as 'conjunct & disjoint melodic motion', 'stable & unstable tones', 'open & closed phrasing', 'pulse & meter', 'summative stress', 'masculine &

feminine endings', 'phrasal balance' and 'melodic contouring'. Yes, another dense forest of learning branches was fanning out for me to explore. Here was theory, once again: a never-ending merry-go-round of ideas, methods and idioms. No escape.

As well as many new technical terms, the book also described a raft of so-called 'song forms', including the importance of the central statement, the different verse forms, the refrain, chorus, primary and secondary bridges, pre-chorus and other structures of popular song. But one thing stood out as I read the book: more than half its pages were dedicated to … you guessed it … harmony! Yes, the book reiterated well-trodden territory: the content of the higher theory grades. I cannot, however, criticise this excellent new resource. It was the only text I found that put melody front and centre. It emphasised the relationship to the bass by presenting 'a unified theory' and the 'melody/bass relationship'. It pointed to many 'melodic/harmonic considerations' and suggested that writing a song should always 'start with the harmony'.

I never did read the book in detail, but from the sections I did study carefully, one thing became abundantly clear … never write a melody line alone: to write a compelling tune, we must compose as a unified whole; with the harmony. I simply had to try, but where to start?

Have you ever sat in front of a blank sheet of paper and had utterly no idea of where to begin? That intransigent canvas was 'songwriting' for me, eighteen months after I had stepped onto the escalator.

How to get started? I made one simplifying decision: strictly no lyrics. This was to be a tune, not a song. To include the enigmatic task of writing poetry at this stage would undoubtedly complicate the process. And so I gazed again at the keyboard, my mind a blank. Think! Key signature. Let's start in E♭. Play an E♭Δ7 (major 7th) chord. Good. Now where? 'Follow the circle' was all I could think of. Yet jumping straight to the 5th sounded wrong. Try the 2nd, F–7 (minor 7th). Good. Repeat that, E♭Δ7, F–7. Fine. Now the melody: dum dee dum dee dum. Sing it out. Repeat that idea over the next chord. Dum dee dum dee dum. Hey, this is working. I had started! Now where? And how to return to the tonic? 'Follow the circle' echoed in my mind. G–7, C–7, F–7, B♭7, E♭. Does the melody fit? Boy this is hard. Play it again. Change that note. Drop this one. Or raise it? That cadence B♭7 – how about B♭7^{sus4}? Better. Hey, I think I have a section of a real tune. Now what? The middle section. How to create contrast? Didn't my teacher tell me something about the 4th? Let's start with A♭Δ7, a fourth above the root. Follow the circle. That didn't work. Wait a mo. Follow the circle backwards? D–7$^{♭5}$, G–7, C7, F–7, B♭7^{sus}, E♭Δ7. Wow, that's really nice. Ha. How to finish that section? Of course, with a dominant 7th cadence – A7? Hmm … a bit corny. Add a sharp-4 to make an A7$^{♯11}$. Yes, that's better. What about the melody? Adapt it for the new harmony. Sing it again. Nice, but how to end this? Let's side-slip a semitone from A major to A♭ (that 4th again). Then a 2-5-1, F–7, B♭7^{sus}, E♭Δ7 to round it off … that works, but how to exit? I vaguely remembered something called a flat-7th? From the blues? Repeat the tonic thus, E♭Δ7, D♭Δ7, E♭Δ7, D♭Δ7 then …. my goodness, I am composing! The flat-7th is a slip to the parallel minor, so continue the pattern. G♭Δ7 (the flat-III), EΔ7 (the flat-II) and, huge relief, we find our way back home to the tonic: E♭Δ7. Repeat that, G♭Δ7, EΔ7, E♭Δ7. Add some variety towards the end. How about using the chord E♭Δ9 (introducing the 2nd of the scale)? Does that work with the melody? Yes. Not sure why, but it sounded great. Note to self: must understand what I just 'said', to use Barry Harris's analogy.

I had composed my first jazz tune, melody and harmony working in … harmony. It had taken four to six hours of painful head-scratching. Now what? Write it down lest I forget. Chord symbols were hurriedly strewn across a fresh sheet of stave paper. The bones of my melody were then added to the stave in enough detail to be able to recall the song the following day. I had my first rough and ready lead sheet. Nice. It was a musical sketch, no more, but like every example I encountered, sufficient for a competent musician to improvise from. Would *I* be able to play my own lead sheet, I wondered?

After a few moments of self-satisfied contemplation, I decided to try out a promising software tool I'd been experimenting with. Able to play back transcribed sequences using only the chord symbols and without the need to specify individual notes, the software could even 'improvise' its own drum parts. Chord by careful chord, I transferred my composition to the computer. As my tune came to life, it sounded … OK (ish). Not great, but good. I hit RECORD and, selecting a sax sample, played along to the harmony. And my melody came to life. I was suddenly a band. Satisfied, I turned up the volume and listened back to my creation. I cannot begin to describe how I felt. It reminded me of the occasions when, after weeks of coding and testing, my software system could do what the client had asked it to do. Wonderful. The act of creation: deeply satisfying, life-affirming, and a hundred other clichés.

The next day, I decided to delete the draft sax part and re-record it, this time more expressively. Goodness, what to call this piece? It sounded kinda lazy-lazy, so I named it … 'A Pleasant Day'. Later, I added the gentle ambience of children playing together in a school playground, a delightful soundscape I had downloaded as a WAV file. Weaving this into the mix, the combination of my music and the children's voices sounded cute. My creation was complete. Cut to CD and upload to SoundCloud. Ship to penfriend and wife. Wait for reactions.

An answer came back the next morning:

'You are a musician! We don't want to hear any more nonsense about how you're not progressing or that it's all too difficult. You have achieved the ability to conceive, compose and perform a delightful piece of music which would sound perfectly good at any mainstream concert.

'You've done this in less than two years, as an adult approaching sixty, while holding down a challenging job. So will you please now take a moment out to congratulate yourself and enjoy your music for goodness' sake. I'm really proud of you. Well done.'

Glowing with pride and with a wide grin on my face, I fell asleep that night with 'A Pleasant Day' spinning in my head, just like the circle of fifths it was.

Over the next few days, the tune was heard a lot around the house. It was hard to escape ... until, that was, we were all thoroughly sick and tired of hearing children make kiddy noises in the schoolyard and an overly breathy sax weave its naïve magic over my formulaic circling harmony. Time is a harsh judge. Even Adagio looked irritable. Had I imagined it, or was our cat leaving the house earlier than usual?

Weeks later, I told my penfriend about the software I had used to make the recording of 'A Pleasant Day'. 'The computer played the chord progressions,' I admitted. The embellishments it had added, the voice-leading and occasional flourishes, contributed to the quality of the final result. I could not have played those chords as elegantly. As a pianist, I was less than a computer! I was a cheat ... though the sax part I did play live, and rather well, though I say so myself. Via this unusual mix of my creativity and software automation, I had pulled off a minor miracle. I strongly suspected, however, it might be a one-trick pony. Clearly, if I was now 'a musician', as my penfriend claimed, I was still at base camp looking up at the peaks of a very high mountain indeed. Perhaps a crack at grade six theory would take me to the next elevation? Within minutes I had ordered specimen papers. And I signed up to a new online course in which a remote teacher would, at my pace, set tests, mark my results and give feedback, long before I entered the lion's den of the examination room. Once again, I was aiming for a distinction.

Listening back, two years later, I still like 'A Pleasant Day'. We songwriters can be precious about such things. The arrangement sounds surprisingly professional, but only I know how little that means. My penfriend was kind when he told me I was a musician. Nothing more.

21

GRADE SIX THEORY HIATUS

In which I discover there is only one goal on the path to becoming a musician. More than ever, I am questioning my musical intelligence.

As I may have mentioned, grade six theory does appear to be a giant leap forward. My award of a distinction in four and five was little more than the result of a few months' focused work. Grade five is the mandatory step for anyone wishing to sit higher-graded practical examinations. Beyond this milestone, the performer is free to ignore pesky theory altogether, if they so choose. Of course, I regard this as both a cop-out and a terrible idea if one wishes to become a well-rounded musician. But I do recognise that it is entirely possible to progress to the highest standards of virtuosity in any instrument without the need to sit more theory.

The reason that grades six to eight can prove challenging is because the majority of the theory paper is not based on rote learning or the mechanical transcription of musical passages. These higher grades directly test what I call 'musical intelligence'. And that's hard to bottle.

My online teacher for grade six theory was a lovely person. Our email correspondence was a joy. She always answered my awkward questions in full before sending me a new assignment. I would then print it out, sit quietly at the end of our dinner table (my theory woodshed), scribble all over the sheet in black pen, and then scan it into my computer and email back my work. She would mark my answers using the same criteria as the examination board, being familiar with every detail they expect. She is without doubt the leading remote teacher for graded theory, certainly in the UK and maybe also internationally ... evidence the fact that she publishes a rich resource website, offers well-structured books, and provides a subscription to a comprehensive database of self-help tutorials.

Her grade six workbook is a hefty, large-format tome of nearly two hundred pages. Divided into clear and meticulously documented sections, it covers all the required topics in depth: chord inversions, harmonic progressions, melodic decoration, harmonization of a melody, figured bass, composition, motifs and sequences, cadence, interpolation, tonality, modulation and 'how to read an orchestral score'. See what I mean when I claim grade six is a giant leap from five? Sure is. Anyone who has ever tried knows. Every teacher knows. The exam board knows. It's deliberate: grade six theory is a first landmark. Which is why few people bother to sit the exam. But if you can approach six, then seven and eight will be within your reach, the gap between them being no big deal, or so I've heard.

Looking through a smattering of past papers, I concluded it was not only desirable but absolutely essential that I pass grade six with distinction. If I could do this, I argued, seven and eight would fall within a year or two. That was important to me. The entrance criteria of any good music school require the applicant to have obtained grade eight in either theory *or* practical; rarely both are mandated. Returning to the piano at the age of sixty, and having achieved so little as a child, I was unsure if I'd ever be able to *play* to the standard required for a place at college. Maybe higher-level theory offered a way in, an entrance ticket. With this in mind, my aim was to pass grade six with distinction in six months, twice the time I had allowed myself for four and five. However, the goal proved a bridge too far. Feedback from my remote teacher indicated I might scrape a merit, but certainly not a distinction. Not good enough. Only a distinction award would convince me that I had absorbed the prerequisite skills to shoot for eight. As the date of the exam grew close, it was clear I had been unrealistic. I cancelled the exam sitting, lost the entrance fee, and gave myself another six months. But this created another problem. Extending my study over such a long period, I was already starting to forget details I had learnt earlier. Test sheets returned by my remote teacher contained the same kinds of mistakes I had made at the outset. It was a mental struggle that eventually overwhelmed me. The combination of a full-time job, a couple of hours of daily practice at the keyboard and the interventions of real life conspired against me. Grade six theory was dead in the water. Correspondence with my teacher dried up and she never heard from me again. I was to her, no doubt, one more distant pupil who had stepped up but was found wanting. I was bitterly disappointed.

As I sit here, typing this segment of my tale, all I feel is despair. According to a friend of ours, a professional musician, grades seven and eight filter out the 'non-musicians' among us: those who lack an innate musical intelligence; the no-hopers. Without six in the bag, there would be no grade seven. Without seven, no eight. Without that milestone, maybe no college! Even if I eventually chose not to go back to school – a cost-prohibitive move for many, of course – I feared I would never have the qualifications to do so in the first place.

During the very first lesson with my jazz teacher, I remember him asking what my ultimate goal actually was. A good question and one my penfriend occasionally probed. Well, I wanted to learn to play the piano, of course, silly him. But my teacher wanted details. There are many styles of music, as well as differences of emphasis between performance, theory and composition. As far as he knew, I may have wanted to become an accompanist or teacher. Teasing my dreams from me, he calmly suggested there was only one end state worth having: to attain a Master of Music qualification. I could not refute his assertion.

The Master of Music (M.M or M.Mus) is an academic title, the first postgraduate degree in music awarded by universities and conservatories. The course combines studies in theory and practice, the history of music (musicology), and allows for specialisation in performance, composition or conducting. It is typically two years of full-time study and prepares the student to be a professional musician. My teacher was correct, M.Mus was a useful abbreviation for my unrealistic aspirations. And as I met and interacted with more musicians, guess what … they had, or were working towards, their own graduate or postgraduate degree or diploma. That keyboard player in the hot group creating waves in the crowded electro-fusion landscape – turns out he has a doctorate in jazz composition. The 'girl with guitar' playing in the basement of a fashionable bar in London whose music you so love? Yup, she went to music college. The guy on the street busking his songs to all and sundry? Well, he's probably applying to music school right now. My first compositions, what did they mean?

Foothills my dear penfriend; no more than foothills. Sobering.

PRE CHORUS

'Such sweet compulsion doth in music lie.'

John Milton, *Arcades*

22

THE BLUE SNOWMAN

In which an idea lying dormant in my songwriting notebook comes to life in the most unexpected fashion. The escalator turns sharp left, towards Oxford Circus.

My journey had bifurcated. On the one hand, I was failing at higher theory. On the other, I had composed my first tune, and it was not half bad. I'd even managed to write it as a lead sheet. Now, instead of struggling to improvise from fake books, other musicians could play from mine! Flushed with this minor success, my journal began to fill with new compositional ideas. Many, however, were no more than outlines for songs I imagined I would one day complete but never have. Jotting down the song's title at the top of a new page, ever so neatly, an hour or so at the keyboard would eventually see me scribbling (and I do mean scribbling) the spelling of chords I had found. Blank pages were being consumed at an alarming rate. This, I hoped, would allow me to pick up again at a later date and complete the music. Many of these ideas, however, quickly became orphans. I had more song ideas than songs, and few had any lyrics. The backlog of unfinished work was expanding; I was dreaming of writing songs, not doing so. Advice from my jazz teacher was telling. 'The only thing that matters,' he repeated, 'is the end product.'

Something had to change.

Pleased with a melancholic chord progression for a song titled 'For My Friends', I spent a pleasant morning playing it through over and over, delighted with the descending chromatic bassline, and hoping for the inspiration that would lead me to a fitting accompaniment. With no 'theory' or recipe to follow for completing the tune, and with its nostalgic melody ringing in my head, I felt it was worth sharing. I flipped on my recorder. Two days later, the new composition was on SoundCloud. I had my second rough-and-ready song. The tone of an email to my penfriend signalled that I felt this was a super-special moment and that he and his wife should feel duty-bound to listen to my work.

It took three days (yes, THREE!) for them to reply.

'Rather nice. Thank you.'

Yeah. Right. Nothing more? Oh dear, I suspected this was about the time they had begun to ask awkward questions in private. Were they finding my over-exuberance and (far) too frequent emails a tad tiresome? Had I become the much feared high-maintenance friend? Probably. But what else could I do? I'd pushed so hard on the accelerator pedal over so many months. The goal of 'becoming a musician' was not coming as readily as I hoped.

What had I achieved? Two tunes, 'A Pleasant Day' and 'For My Friends', a modest improvement in my facility at the keyboard and a smattering of theory, insufficient even to sit grade six. I seemed to be making more progress writing email than composing or playing music. Was I destined to be a one-trick pony with a couple of minor successes and then nothing, evidence perhaps of the deficit of musical intelligence I feared? Should I have been tutored by a traditional piano teacher and learnt to play the instrument first, by following a formal syllabus? Were the methods I had 'invented', and which my teacher was (perhaps unwisely) allowing me to wallow in, holding me back? I felt they might be, and began to seriously question the effectiveness of my time on the escalator. And just as this terrifying spectre appeared, my life took an unexpected, but most welcome, turn of events.

I had become a fan of a Scottish singer-songwriter who, to my ear at least, was weaving a magical brew of indie-noir folk music. How I tripped over her body of work, I am not sure; browsing too many obscure websites and blogs, I suspect. One review caught my eye. Who is this? Nothing on iTunes. YouTube ... yes, a few videos here; home-made, by the look of them. Yet her songs, lyrics and personality were irresistible. The next few weeks heard me spinning her debut LP on repeat. It was inventive music. My wife and penfriend also became fans ... once I'd convinced them, of course, that here was 'surely the next Joni Mitchell'.

Though she rarely performed live, the Scottish songwriter had announced an unexpected gig at a lovely old church in an upmarket neighbourhood of London: the United Reform, Kensington. Unfortunately, neither my wife nor my penfriend could travel to town that evening. Unable to resist, I snapped up one ticket.

As I've admitted before, I prefer to be (must be) up close and personal at concerts, able to see every twist and turn of the artist's performance; the squeak of guitar strings, every movement of the keyboard player's hands. This evening, however, I arrived too early by far, even by my standards. The heavy wooden church doors were firmly locked. Unable to enter, and with light rain falling, I left the churchyard, found a nearby pub, ordered a beer and sat down, quietly anticipating the evening ahead.

After thirty minutes and unable to settle, I was back at the church, where a 'queue' had formed. Five people only. Over the next half an hour a few more souls turned up, and after what seemed an age we were ushered inside, where we were asked to stand and wait. The inner doors to the nave were not yet open, preventing me from rushing in and grabbing a pew at the front (ever so politely of course). Not that I would have needed to do so; I counted fewer than twenty people gathered in the foyer. Peeking through the inner door's thick glass towards the altar, the area in front of which I assumed would act as the stage, there was little or no activity. If the artist and her band had turned up, of which there was no evidence, they were certainly not in a hurry to get started.

Waiting patiently in the foyer, standing next to me, was a young woman. She seemed eager to chat. Exchanging pleasantries, she explained she was here to watch another musician, a young man. He was, apparently 'sharing the night' with the artist who had drawn my attention. The friendly young woman had not heard of the Scottish singer, and I had not heard of her musical hero. Enthusing about each other's reason for coming out tonight, we agreed we were in for a real treat.

As the inner doors opened, the young woman grabbed my arm and, in the excitable manner of youth, blurted out, 'Come on. Let's go. Seat at the front?' And we did; me in a drab raincoat, she a fashionable young thing wearing a style of clothing that only the young can wear.

The music that evening was delightful, and at times profoundly moving, as folk music can be. I enjoyed listening to the young man my unexpected concert companion had come to hear, and in the second half of the evening the fey Scottish songwriter blew us all away, especially when joined on stage by a local youth choir. Heavenly. Despite this, the young woman sitting with me, of whom I knew nothing, seemed at times to be curiously detached from the music, as much appearing to study it as to listen, or so it seemed to me. Between songs, she'd lean in close and, in a whisper, comment on some aspect of the performance, especially interested in my reaction to the music.

By the end of the evening, had someone observed the two of us sitting there chatting away, they'd have assumed we were the closest of friends and not, as we were, total strangers. She had, of course, introduced herself formally while we were waiting in the queue, but I'd not been able to pick out her name. Whether it was her accent or a particularly unusual name, I was too embarrassed to ask.

The gig ended with encores. As the concert-goers were leaving, my companion for the evening suggested we 'exchange handles'. (For anyone not familiar with this Y-generation ritual, it refers to the identities we create for ourselves on social media.) Despite being of a different generation entirely, I did use social media, extensively, the result of being required to 'maintain a web presence' by my employer, a large international consulting firm looking to impress their clients with the insight of their senior leadership team. I had a Twitter account and, surprisingly, thousands of followers. Handles exchanged, we said our goodbyes and left the church, heading off in opposite directions. I was sure neither of us imagined we would see each other again.

At home, a few days later, I chanced upon the young woman's Twitter handle on another music site. Curious, I decided to look her up. Ah, that strange name, now I knew why I had found it hard to pick out. My concert companion hailed from the Netherlands. Made sense.

The Dutch, I have noted, are some of the friendliest, most outgoing and delightfully open people you will have the good fortune to meet. Following a web link or two, the penny dropped. She was also a singer--songwriter, hence her interest in the detail of the performances. And now I recall … the moment when had she introduced herself … how she had spoken … Was it possible I was expected to have heard of her? If so, I apologise now and admit I had not.

Sitting at home, skipping through my concert companion's social feed, I suddenly felt foolish. Other than the Scottish songwriter who had caught my ear on YouTube and who I had been so excited to see live, I knew nothing of the indie-folk scene. The church could have been chock-full of emerging artists and talented songwriters; if only I had realised, I had so many questions I could have asked them. Now, sitting at home, and eager to learn more about the young woman's music, I followed her

Twitter handle to a website (one click). Wow … an unusual design, the homepage an equally original video: a hand-drawn animation.

A small stick figure, standing in the rain, is beckoning passers-by to 'Come Find Me'. His sad face … Walking alone, or driving a little car, a gloomy rain cloud follows him wherever he goes; that is until another character turns up and says … 'Hello!' Then the sun comes out, a toy cloud evaporates and a new relationship is formed, his forlorn expression replaced by a smile.

The animation was delightful. And another penny dropped. Was it my drab raincoat? Perhaps, like the stick figure in her beguiling video, I too was looking lonely that night. The young woman's approach was nothing more than acting out her philosophy in life: the simplicity of just saying 'Hello!' to strangers.

Over the next few days, unable to get the image of the little stick man out of my head, I returned to her website several times. The catchy melody that went along with the video I later found out was her signature tune, used to garner audience participation during her act. And it was then that a really crazy idea popped into my head.

In my journal, hiding among the ideas I had started but not progressed, was a sketch of an idea for a Christmas/New Year song. Wait, I need to get dates right before I go on. This was October 2014. That's right, I had planned to play 'The Blue Snowman' for friends and family during the upcoming 2015 festivities. My work on the unusual song was, however, far from complete. Some chords were in place, and a sketch of a promising melody, but a song it was not. Yet I had big ideas for my snowman. It would need strong lyrics; the story was far from straightforward. Did I have the skills to express the concept in words *and* music?

An extraterrestrial snowman, finding his way to earth, is 'blue' because he observes the problems of our age: fear, hate, poverty, and especially the environment: climate change and extinction. He has a solution; and a message of hope for all species. The problem is … he is melting, as all snowmen must. If he disappears before we, the ever increasing and ever more voracious and consuming humankind, hear his news, the world is lost. The race is on before Christmas ends and the New Year beckons us in. As we listen to the lyrics of the visiting alien's lament, we realise that even if his gift of kindness is understood, if it works out for us, he – our saviour, the snowman – will vanish from the world. All snowmen must die. His fate is sealed. Bittersweet. We grieve for him even as we find hope in his message.

Could this young woman, the singer-songwriter whose animation had touched my heart, bring my snowman to life? I had her Twitter handle. And so wrote this text:

'Look, this is insane. We hardly know each other, but here's the thing: I have this idea for a song squirrelled away in my journal. I am never going to complete it; I lack the skills. You should take it.

'All I have is a title, a few chords and the outline of a story. Nothing is set in stone. The concept is wide open to your interpretation.

'I found that animation of yours online, the little stick man and the rain cloud. It's lovely; it's perfect. You could bring the blue snowman … [explanation of the idea] … into the world in pictures, words and song. I just know you could.

'Do you like the idea? Is it workable? Do write.'

I signed off with '… sincerely, Howard'.

And hit SEND, not expecting a reply.

A few days later, a carefully written note appeared in my inbox.

Politely, it began, 'Good to hear from you. Generally, I rarely agree to collaborate. It always ends up being more work than expected. Right now, I am heads-down in the middle of the release of a new single, after which

I have to make progress on my debut album …'

But then she added, '… and yet, something about your story appeals to me. We should meet to discuss it, as soon as practicable.'

A month later we were sitting together in a café in central London, just off Oxford Street, sipping hot coffee, chatting about music and making decisions about what to do with 'The Blue Snowman'. As she spoke and listened respectively to my ideas, it was clear as crystal that here was an intelligent, creative and sincere person. Recognising that she had a profile and growing reputation and that I was a musical nobody, I clarified that I was gifting the idea to her and was not presumptuous enough to ask to step in as collaborator (even though that remote possibility thrilled me). I did offer to help but insisted that the direction, timing and outcome of any collaboration would be hers and hers alone. She was, and still is, a busy person, always on the move, running here and there, all over the map … deadlines for songs, single releases, gigs, video production, business management and all the other paraphernalia involved in that craziest-of-crazy vocations: carving an authentic niche in the overly commercial music industry. So while she was attracted to the project, I understood how it could also be a distraction. And I knew from my work in consulting that highly creative people need to own their own projects.

To my delight, she suggested that, at a minimum, we should meet every few weeks to discuss the concept, exchange ideas and decide exactly how and, crucially, when any collaboration might hatch. And we did. Our ad hoc liaisons continued in fits and starts over the subsequent months, and 'The Blue Snowman' grew in size and complexity as a result.

She was convinced, for example, that my promising but convoluted story could not be told in a single song or a few verses, at least not with any subtlety. It demanded an album of its own. The other-worldly snowman would arrive, unannounced, appearing suddenly in the middle of London, halting traffic and generally getting in the way. His message for humanity would be told through a series of tableaux. It would take place during the build-up to Christmas leading to New Year, each day dealing with a different aspect of his adventures on earth. There would be twelve songs, with full lyrics and reinforcing poetry. Each 'themed' day would be introduced by a single, emotionally charged message to the world: the antidote to a specific global ill. We made a list; unfortunately not a difficult task. There would be a CD (of course), a box set no doubt, and an accompanying picture book, for children and adults alike. Storylines, visual ideas and meaningful words were all carefully noted in our journals during our coffee-shop collaborations. During one such meeting, our table was littered with yellow Post-it notes; consulting habits die hard. The waiter looked surprised as we ordered more tea and cake.

In one imagined scene, for example, the snowman is visited by doctors in white coats who, in vain, apply scientific remedies and medical potions, hoping to prevent him melting. In another scene, religious leaders from every faith probe the unlikely visitor for philosophical and theological answers. Why is he here? What makes him tick? What is his message?

As our project grew in ambition, so did our understanding of the work involved. We knew what we wanted to achieve. We had tons of content. But the time was not right to start on such a complex collaboration. Had she done so, her own work – a forthcoming EP and debut LP – would have stopped dead in its tracks. That could not be permitted. Nor could I push ahead without her, even if I had wanted to, which I did not. We agreed the project was best put on the shelf, at least for the time being. And so for a while we stopped seeing each other. I missed our conversations greatly, not only because she was infectious to be around, but also because I hoped her creativity would infect me.

I found her answers to my questions about the songwriting process fascinating. Rarely spending more than a day or two shaping the initial musical idea for a song, she surprised me when she revealed that the bones of a tune could emerge in a few hours; less, if it was clear what the song was saying. One of her most accessible singles was written in just ten minutes. Composed during a workshop she had attended as a student, she distinguished such brief flashes of creativity from the meticulous, repetitive (and sometimes frustrating) hours and days in the studio to produce 'the finished product'. I immediately saw the truth of her statement in my own projects, so often started yet rarely completed.

'Why does it take so long to release a new album,' I asked?

'The addition of other instruments, the mixing and mastering, always take months, even if the work itself is only a few days of dedicated effort,' she replied. 'Much of the non-creative work consists of organising the ingredients. It takes time to assemble the team, persuade friends to help out, and so on. A cello part, for example, might be added remotely. It's easy to send a mix to a collaborator who's working in another country and who can use their own home studio to record an accompaniment. I then take their raw track, add it to the mix on my computer, and gradually my original vision for the song takes shape. When I feel that everything is gelling, I exchange a multi-track take with a mixing engineer, using an Internet file service. Over the next few weeks, we exchange subtle variations of each track until we are both happy with the result. I always try to get as close as possible to a near-final product. After that, it's sent off to the mastering engineer. He adjusts the feel and vibe of the album, to a brief I prepare, balancing each song against the others and optimising the sound for each of the different devices people now use to listen to music: CD, MP3 players, streaming, smartphones. I do not have the skills, or patience, for that type of technical work.'

None of what she explained would surprise a seasoned artist, but to me, a newbie, it was something of a revelation. When I quizzed her further about the final steps to cut a CD, she was at pains to emphasise that the technical processes could, if not controlled, destroy the original inspiration for the music.

'The spontaneity – the essence of performance – is so easily lost,' she revealed. 'I try whenever possible to record my parts live, in a single take, and oversee the whole process from that point forward, but ultimately some things are outside my control.'

It all sounded terribly complex. But whatever approach this songwriter used, the final result was exquisite. The more I listened to her sensitively produced songs – gentle, childlike in parts, sensitive to the many moods of life – the more my instinct to approach her with the snowman project was appropriate: he would be in safe hands. All I had done was sow a seed. It was her project now. I was nothing more than an interloper in her busy life. Yet the story of our collaboration cannot be allowed to end here.

With the release of new music, my unexpected concert companion, songwriter and animator, whom I now considered a friend, was giving regular performances of her beguiling music in the basement of a boutique cocktail bar in north London. I remember the first time I bought a ticket to one of her gigs – the excitement when I discovered that the venue was approached via an unassuming door, nestled away on an unassuming back street. Set around a large open square, hidden at the back of the buzzing high street, local people from all walks of life and creeds assembled to chat, drink beer, toss a can and wait in line for 'doors'. The area is still known for its vibrant, independent music scene; the place positively buzzed. This *would* be fun – a real adventure.

The tiny venue was niche as niche could be. I loved that. It was attracting emerging artists from every corner of the indie folk-pop scene. As the curator of the regular 'first Sunday of the month' slot, my friend introduced not one but two musicians. Each was given ample time to showcase their work, after which she would perform her set. How she managed to pull in so many artists, month after month, I have no idea. They were all so good! She was a strange-attractor, for sure, though when I once used this mathematical word to describe her (look it up), I suspect she felt it was me that was strange. Yet my use of the term was apt: my friend had a knack; the experiences she created were special.

Attended by guests of the featured musicians, a handful of the faithful and a few barstool regulars, the audiences she attracted were discerning. Her audience wanted to listen to the music. Rapt, contemplative and always enthusiastic, they appreciated the artistry. Believe me, this is not the case at all gigs. More often than not, and especially in public houses, musicians are required to perform with stoic perseverance ('the show must go on') against a distracting backdrop of clanking glasses, noise, chatter, or worse. The audiences (if you can call them that) hardly pay attention to what is played or sung. Dreadful. My friend's Sunday night slot, by contrast, was the polar opposite: you could hear a pin drop.

Hearing music live, among like-minded guests, was a joy. And the conversation during breaks, between artists and guests, was friendly and welcoming. Our lives were being enriched. We had the privilege of watching at first hand talents emerge. It would have been churlish not to buy every CD offered for sale during these delightful evenings. I bought them all, and each holds a special place in my collection and in my memory. I never wanted these gigs to end and would hang about at the end, desperate to be part of something I knew, in my heart, I could never be. The divide was stark: they were musicians, I was not. What did they do when the last hanger-on and groupie left the venue? I would never know. We lived south of the river, a not particularly 'creative' neighbourhood, and there was always the last train to catch and a home to return to.

I was excluded from the post-event chatter by the simple constraint of a railway timetable. Frustrating.

And what of *The Blue Snowman*?

She tells me he is always at the back of her mind, waiting, patiently expectant of his day in the sun before he, and the unusual collaboration which ushered him into the world, melt. Looking at the world today, I guess we need his message, more than ever. But for now, as I write these words, the time is not right for my unexpected friend to expend energy on what might turn out to be another obscure concept album, heard once and then forgotten. No. I must put all thoughts of our future collaboration to one side, at least for the time being. My own escalator is still moving forward, with or without me. I must jump back on. Sand, you see, is slipping through my hourglass.

23

LOSING TRACK

'Music was my refuge. I could crawl into the space between the notes and curl my back to loneliness.' – Maya Angelou

It was around this time, just as things were getting 'real', that my penfriend had to admit he was losing track of (or having difficulty understanding) the nuggets of theory I was still sending him weekly. Were my powers of explanation fading? Or, horror, should I have eased off the email pedal for a while? No way! I treasured our exchanges and told him so in no uncertain terms … by sending another email. I loved that he was curious about how music works, but I had to admit there were practical limits to the furtherance of our dialogue. After all, my friend was not learning to play the piano, I was. Was he paying attention? Had he ever walked upstairs (to where his wife kept a small electronic keyboard) and repeated the experiments I painstakingly described? I doubted he had, even with a single finger. His wife could have helped him find the notes, I was sure. While not a pianist, she dabbles and finds it fascinating; or, in her words, 'absorbing'. She has not, however, stepped onto an escalator (yet) … whatever kind it might turn out to be. Nevertheless, she has played a few simple pieces and could easily have helped my penfriend find the notes and follow along with my erudition. Am I being unfair?

Whenever our friends visited us, I was religious in my zeal to 'demonstrate', but those delightful weekends were too infrequent to build any shared understanding of the alligator I was wrestling. No. I had allowed my obsession to intrude on the lovely couple's precious time, and to a degree that was unfair, if not rude. I have a tendency to over 'share', and I was becoming a music bore: a muso. I needed to back off and accept that this journey was mine, not theirs. Yet despite continued overindulgence in email, my penfriend's patience knew no bounds and he continued to send thoughtful replies. His words were a constant source of support. I listened carefully to his take on the mountain range I was climbing, even if I could not always take his counsel on board. It is a testament to his character that my unreasonable behaviour had not led him to grow resentful and take a back seat when it came to my obsession and fixation, choosing to distance himself, or end the relationship.

'I know you are finding the process frustrating, Howard, but I am full of admiration for what you are doing,' he wrote. 'You must realise that acquiring a skill as complex as this, especially after childhood, when the brain is less plastic, can only be accomplished by putting in the almost superhuman effort you are demonstrating. Otherwise, you will not achieve anything close to that which you wish to achieve. Because music is partly intellectual and partly physical, you have to keep working at it until your brain "physically" changes. To allow it to do what I know you desperately want it to do, you are going to have to be patient. All great musicians had the advantage of building these skills when they were young. Their youthful brains could be moulded orders of magnitude more readily than yours.'

My friend knows more than most about the cortex. And his curiosity about the trajectory of my odyssey was, he told me, one way to gain insights into whatever might be happening in our brain when we listen to music. His most profound questions concerned how the mind 'hears'. Is our response to music innate or learned? It has been shown, he explained, that 'red is red and green is green to all those with good eyesight'. Do we 'hear' the same notes at the same pitch, as apparently we do with colour?

No research I was aware of, or he could find, has shown that C is C and D is D to all listeners. To such questions, all I could add was to point to the handful of books written on advanced music theory, probably not a great help with neuroscience. And yet ... he seemed genuinely interested in explanations of partials and the divisions of vibrating piano strings. Was there, he wondered, a similar mechanism in the inner ear and its connection to the mind? What was vibrating in sympathy?

'Why,' he asked, 'does a low C sound similar to C an octave higher? They sound almost identical. Why?' Good question. The two frequencies are related only by a mathematical ratio. Are these ratios 'built in' or learnt as a child exposed to 'tonal' music? Is harmony foundational or arbitrary, the result only of a convention in each culture? Are our brains pre-wired for sound? If so, which sounds? What is inherent in our physiology at birth that allows one person to become a great musician and another to struggle with the rudiments? And what, if that's the case, could the evolutionary reason be (in a Darwinian sense) for a 'musical intelligence'? We never bottomed out such matters, but as the riddles flowed it was cathartic to share my week-to-week progress, or lack thereof, and explain my premonitions and apprehension. From the stream of selfish shared meanderings, I hoped he could extract a few semi-scientific conclusions concerning the mental state of a musician. Mine at least!

I often found myself telling him how extremely hard I was finding the journey, and perhaps not only because of age? It had been equally challenging as a child. As a (very) late returning adult, among all of the anxieties I harboured, it was this fear that concerned me the most. Perhaps the goal I had set was not to be? On the other hand, had I ever practised diligently *and* effectively in my youth? My mother used to despair. An enthusiasm to tinker – to press notes in combination merely to see how they sounded together – far exceeded any discipline I could muster to learn a piece of written music to a decent standard; well enough to perform with subtlety and expression. Did sheet music just pass me by? Time has dimmed my memory: I shall never recall the exact circumstances that led me to give up on disciplined daily practice as a child. But I have a suspicion. And it's not pretty. Even now, I balk at the idea of spending months on a classical work I know has been played a million times before, by hundreds of pianists, and (the clincher) performed far more eloquently than I could ever hope to achieve! Apology: I know this statement (and previous remarks about monkeys) will be seen as an insult to budding pianists eagerly rehearsing their set pieces for an upcoming exam or practising a new work to build their repertoire. Yet I can only be honest: repeating the same music bores me. Perhaps I am just odd like that, wired for sound but not for practice, always looking for shortcuts. Do they exist? The traditionalists say no. I, the contrarian, am not so sure. Despite my avoidance of rote learning, my ability to improvise was improving. It was. Something was stirring in me. Where it could take me, however, was less clear. As you can see, it was not only my penfriend who was losing track.

Recently, hunting through some old files, I discovered a single sheet of stave paper and immediately recognised the handwriting. This was me, circa current age minus five decades! There was music here. I took the faded sheet to my adult piano teacher and picked out the notes for him, and was instantly catapulted back to my youth. The music was as fresh now as it had been then. However, the sixteen bars were barely more than a sketch, a few lines, plus some words (from a religious text). In contrast to my school chums, I had become entranced by the major works of choral music. I presume my 'composition' was part of a teenage pretension to write for choir and orchestra. Fat chance! But the music was good, stated on the sheet 'to be sung by a baritone voice'. However, the oratorio I had presumably imagined was not even a second date, let alone a fully consummated relationship. It was a flirtation with music, probably the result of a few days' experimentation, a fragment, the melody left hanging over decades. Why had I not continued to write?

If my childhood teacher had not spotted or could not spot my passion for theory and composition, who would? A child cannot reflect on their own development and initiate a change of direction. The role of 'teacher' remains paramount. Was my ill discipline the consequence of being dragged back to play someone else's music, to waste time (as I saw it but could never verbalise) in practice, practice, practice? Yes, I think so: a constant state of tension between that which I was motivated to do (experiment and explore) and that which I was told to do (rote learning). Did the energy required of the latter sap the life out of the former?

Now I see it. As an adult, I was reacting against my past, setting out to do the polar opposite of my childhood experience. Where the child learnt set pieces, I was avoiding them. Where the child is only allowed a new scale having perfected the previous one, adding each sharp and flat incrementally, I was looking for a generalised pattern that cut to the chase. And this approach, only viable for an adult (or rare child prodigy), was working for me, albeit painfully slowly. The great thing, I convinced myself, was that I hardly ever needed to repeat anything. The result, however – the output – would be regarded as superficial or worse by a classically training pianist. But at least I was writing, and it was liberating.

'Oh, how I long to perform longer and more sophisticated improvisations, and do so at will,' I wrote to my penfriend. 'I'd never have to practise. I'd already know the music. Joy!'

And so, for a while, I persisted in freewheeling mode. Exploring the keyboard instinctively – feeling its contours and quirks – I had finally begun to feel at ease with the instrument. Whenever I sat at the piano, there was rarely any 'them and us', nothing to get in the way of the music.

My penfriend was correct: I was making modest progress, and this success reinforced my commitment to what I imagined was the efficacy of my unusual therapies. I may well have been treading similar ground to legions of more capable musicians, but at least I had discovered the key to the medicine cabinet myself. That pleased me.

Still insisting I play in every key, major or minor as befitted the improvisation, I was able to ignore the fact that the time it took to do so was itself excessive. This form of repetition I found more acceptable than the the practice required to rehearse sheet music. Whenever I came across a new lick or chord sequence, I immediately performed it again, in each of the eleven other keys. As a result, I could now find scales and chords far more readily than in the past, and, as I played in those keys, I was making fewer mistakes, dodging the 'avoid notes' outside the prevailing tonic.

Scales were also proving easier to play at tempo, allowing me to test my readiness to sit higher-grade exams. I had not 'learnt' these scales as such, I simply knew them, as patterns. The majority I could play eyes closed. Playing 'in thirds' was more challenging but doable. 'Sixths' were noticeably harder. Arpeggios in both hands were still tricky. Minor modes, of all varieties, were too easily forgotten ... especially when played in contrary motion ... but the trend was clear: notes were falling under my fingers. As a result, I was also able to play several of the esoteric scales found in jazz, and could therefore recreate the unusual harmonic forms of contemporary music, including the genre called neo soul. The rich chords sounded great even if, theoretically speaking, I still did not fully understand how they 'functioned'.

Sight-reading was a struggle. I judged I was no more than grade two, or three at a pinch. This would have to change if I were ever to sit an advanced exam. The mountains in front of me continued to loom large. There was progress, but also new blocks.

My penfriend could not relate to my many mood swings. In one message I was heralding what must have seemed to him a minor success. In another, I was describing an immense difficulty which – in my heart – I knew he would never understand unless he could jump into my shoes as Mary Poppins had jumped into Bert's pavement art and the topsy-turvy cartoon world beyond. And at times it felt just like that. The language of my emails grew ever more hysterical, citing late nights and 'pits of despair'. My wife was encouraging, but I suspect she was also wondering why Howard was making such a big deal of things. Drama queens come to mind. Both our children had passed grade eight with distinction in at least one of the two instruments they studied. Compared to their rapid assimilation of music, I was a tortoise.

It is said that success breeds success. I am unsure whether this is true of the piano, the most demanding of instruments. As I was finding out, there is never a resting place from which we pianists can then coast. Once a new skill is mastered, it holds no more interest. The mind moves on, the next challenge is there, lying in wait. I was now spending an inordinate time at the keyboard to make any progress at all. Three hours a day, sometimes more, the complexity mounted asymptotically to the vertical … and I became filled with self-doubt. Would the effort ever pay off? Why is this not getting any easier? I muttered under my breath. Is the limiting factor my hands or my mind? Is it my DNA, or my age? Is my autodidactic approach letting me down? I'm not sure how, but I convinced myself that all blocks were 'of the mind' and that if I could develop the required rituals, any dragon could be slain. And so, day by day, exercise by exercise, my journal became the annotated timeline of my stepwise progress. Anchored by these notes, I somehow found the energy for the next few hours of practice.

The ritual went something like this:

Go to your music room. Stick an unnecessarily visible sign on the door announcing 'Woodshedding. No Interruptions. Except In Emergency'. Shut the door firmly. Pick up your notebook from where you should always leave it: on top of your piano. Reach for your pencil: the one with a rubber on the end. Write today's date at the end of the previous day's entry. Select an exercise. Note it down for future reference. Practise until your mind, or your hands, or both, ache, or until improvement is evident. Lastly, document how this felt: what worked and what did not.

Then, in LARGE letters, write out the NEXT thing to focus on if more PROGRESS is to be made. Draw a CLOUD round it. Add an EXCLAMATION mark! Underline in RED!

These ridiculous markers of my progression became steps on a ladder that I could refer back to if I ever slid down a snake. Struggling to find the enthusiasm to push on, I once again found myself describing the bloody skirmish in an email. Too painful to include here, I will leave my mental state to your imagination.

My penfriend agreed that only a mature adult could do what I was attempting. Nor would a child need to, of course, given their youthful mind. 'You are fighting biology,' he said. And then added, 'Is this overload wise, Howard?' Yet, there *was* progress. 'You are making up for lack of brain plasticity with excessive effort,' he asserted, reminding me that music is about 'far more than fingers': it is an 'intellectual quest'.

A recollection of his wife's experience was revealing. My penfriend explained how she had also tried to play the piano as a child. She was, like me, told to practise her scales and arpeggios. And she dutifully did what she was told. Her teacher assured her that if only she could persevere with the assigned work things would 'come more naturally' and she would soon enjoy all the skills needed to play beautifully. She never got this far, however. Her teacher (presumably a poor one) was unable to guide her to a holistic understanding of what is required to be a pianist.

According to my penfriend, I was 'coming at this from an entirely different direction', which was motivating me to 'create entirely new neural connections' so that I could do with my hands what my brain was telling them to do. The child starts in the fingers and hands, proceeds to the arms and shoulders and, years later, ends in the mind. Should it be precisely the opposite for adults? Mind first, then hands? My penfriend was prescribing a whole-body transformation as a prerequisite for success at the keyboard. Whether he is right, I have no clear idea. He was intellectualising my struggle, drawing on his knowledge of biology. Often, my only response to his theories was to throw up my hands in a metaphorical, 'Well, I don't know!' All I did know was that a great deal of effort was being expended. It was a slog. Whatever biological solutions were playing out in my physiology, I don't think they made a ha'p'orth of difference. But his advice kept coming. He reminded me of the business consultant parachuted in to fix the client's business. Can an external adviser ever really understand what his client is struggling with? There is such a thing as 'walking the walk'. My penfriend had never touched a keyboard; what could he know? He certainly did not understand what drove me.

Here is how it feels. There can be no progress in acquiring a complex skill, as a child or an adult, without a hunger to reach creative fulfilment. Only desire can summon the willpower that transcends the spadework required to secure the facility. This has nothing to do with biology, it lies in the realm of the psycho-physical. No practice regime – neurological, physical or intellectual – can foster a need that is absent.

After a particularly frustrating exchange of emails on the nature of biological reality and the vagaries of the human psyche, my friend admitted he would find it impossible to muster the energy I was demonstrating, if for no other reason than a lack of burning ambition. He told me, with some regret perhaps, that he was, if not jealous, then a little unsettled that he harboured no similar passion. He could think of no pastime that would lead him to focus on an activity to the exclusion of all else. He had no desire to acquire mastery in any field of endeavour other than to live well, do no harm, read widely and help others where and when practicable. And what could be more admirable? My penfriend was also honest enough to admit that if he did discover an all-consuming obsession, equivalent in strength to that which was consuming me, he doubted he would have the courage to invest the necessary time and attention, given the high probability of failure. Joking together as we often do, we gave this ailment a name: chronic pre-commitment syndrome. To which he suggested that perhaps I was predisposed to a mental virus at the opposite end of the spectrum: a carrier for obsessive impulsive over-commitment. The irony is, my friend does have a passion: reading. He once told me he'd like nothing more than to read all the books in the British Library. The difference between us, of course, is that he would regard that as unrealistic, whereas I would start right away!

Success in 'unrealistic' projects of any kind demands a willingness to experiment and investigate, to accept compromise, frustration and disappointment. Yes, I see this now. As a teen, spurred on by little but curiosity, I spent two years and nine thousand solder joints building and programming one of the first microprocessor-based computers, with no guarantee of success. The career this exploration spawned was littered with similar first-of-a-kind projects. Seen through such a lens, my pursuit of pianism is just another multi-year project. All of which begs the question: why, if the quest is so essential to my psyche – indispensable and central to my being – why did it not rear its ugly head long ago? Why didn't I return to music decades ago, if it means so much to me now?

Indeed. The question was first put by my penfriend's wife.

Flash forward. Holidays together. Norway. The four of us are out walking the hills overlooking Bergen: city of seven mountains. My wife is chatting with my penfriend, his wife and I are lagging behind, each enjoying a moment of privacy. As usual I am wittering on about music.

'If anything ever stood in the way of what you call my unrealistic goal, I would be unlikely to cope well,' I announced.

She, a well-adjusted and emotionally secure person, could not relate to my assertion. It made no sense to her, and I'm sure she dismissed it as hyperbole. Why was I placing so much emphasis on what for most people would be a gentle hobby, a pastime to occupy spare moments snatched from the more pressing matters of daily life? As we chatted together, I had the distinct impression she was (not so gently) reminding me to 'get things into perspective' and to consider others who had faced more serious disappointment. Desperate to explain, I continued:

'I have to be allowed to create. I've always needed to make things. You've seen my projects over the years. My career was creative, of course it was, but as the multi-year programmes grew ever more complex, the innovation suffered. Our delivery for the client was hamstrung by policy, bureaucracy and internal politics. I'm sick of all that. I need to spend the next phase of my life in a different mode.'

The answer did not satisfy her. Nor me. Was I making excuses?

I have never shared this before, until here in this book, but I had begun to question my motivation. From what was I escaping when I sat at the piano? Was it possible the obsessional musical expedition was an arte-fact, conjured up in later life in response to some unresolved problem in my past that lay buried, deep in my subconscious?

As quickly as the thought came into sharp focus, I closed it down, put the lid on the genie and looked for a less controversial answer. The simple fact was, I persuaded myself, I'd always been passionate about whatever I was engaged in. Frankly, I could be sweeping roads and still find a way to make it enjoyable, striving to do a better job each humdrum day. Some might describe me as a workaholic; others, a 'serial obsessive'. Yes, I think my penfriend once used that phrase. Yet music had been the constant and sustaining thread in my life, even if the bulk had been passive consumption. Just look at my bookshelves: filled with vinyl, hundreds of CDs and, today, gigabytes of downloads. With my career fading and the retirement train fast approaching, time was running out. It was plain for all to see. I could no more put my feet up and withdraw quietly to a gentle retreat than I could jump over a building. Having chosen to focus the entirety of my mind and body on music, focus I would. CREATE! Nothing must stop me. Music, I assured my friend's wife, was the next, and last, third of a productive life; health permitting. My die was cast. Unlike my penfriend who, amused – or likely irritated – by my next gushy email, could reply with a polite 'Hey, Howard, you lost me there' and immediately return to the book he was reading before my rude interruption, I could not. Music had become my life. I simply adored the stuff. Spending time at the keyboard was … healing. Yes, that's the right word: music the great healer, able to transport my mind and alter my mood like nothing else. Quite what needed to be healed, however, was less clear.

And as I write the concluding words to this chapter of my tale, I come close to the honest introspection I fear. What is it that makes music as sustaining for me as the air we breathe? I may get all misty-eyed and metaphysical here, something my uber-rational penfriend would certainly not relate to … I am struggling to find the right words. *Soul? Being? Purpose? Zen?* Stop it! Follow that thread and it could very well screw with my mind.

'Get back to the woodshed and practise your scales, Howard.'

Practice makes perfect. Takes your mind off things, I find.

24

LIFE INTERVENES

In which I find freedom in the midst of sadness. I hesitate, fearful that the escalator from which I cannot alight had been nothing but a distraction all along.

The last twelve months had been difficult. Father died at the age of ninety-three, his heart finally giving up the ghost. Mother could not cope, and her mild forgetfulness and occasional obsessions worsened. We tried to help her but, like so many other families, found we could not. She was unable to live with us and incapable of living alone. Left alone for one night, she boiled water in a plastic kettle, on the naked flame of her stove. After weeks of tortuous debate among the family, a decision was taken for her: she would move to the north of England, to a residential care home close to my brother's house and his young family. We hoped that being near younger grandchildren would grant her a new lease of life. And it did, for a while, but the inevitable progress of her illness took her life as well.

Coping with Mother's dementia was difficult for us all. I can hardly bear to imagine what it must have been like for her. Our bedside sessions helping her recall her past life were dominated by a single question.

'Where is my mother? Oh, when will she visit?'

Helpless, we tried to obscure the explanation, avoiding the evident truth. But however we answered, whatever words we used, it made no difference. Within a few minutes, Mum had forgotten and would repeat the question again. In her illness she had returned to childhood. She never did ask about her 'beloved Arthur', my father. Had those lifelong memories also been wiped from her memory? Or were the final weeks of his passing too painful for her to recall?

My brother and family, living near the care home, were able to spend considerably more time with Mum than I could, something for which I shall be eternally grateful. My family was based in London, working full time or away at university. The transition was painful. My wife and my sister in law were a constant source of comfort.

The situation at work did not help. My employer, a large U.S.-led IT services provider, was experiencing marketplace challenges. A new chief exec had been appointed by the board. Folks like me, from the previous leadership team, were sidelined as subordinates in the new scheme of things. Nothing we had created was left untouched and 'change' was the order of the day. It took its toll on many of us. Round after round of 'improvement initiatives' (each announced to a fanfare and given a fancy and often ridiculous corporate brand name) were accompanied by repeated waves of enforced redundancies to meet aggressive new 'cost targets' driven by the quarterly demands of the U.S. stock market. Thousands lost their jobs. The career I loved was drained of its joy. My interest in computing waned and my mind had turned elsewhere. Yet the executive role I held still dominated and severely limited the time I had for the piano. Desperate to find the time for practice, I took a (just about) portable keyboard with me on business trips, preferring to spend evenings alone in my hotel room than out drinking with colleagues.

During Dad's final weeks and my subsequent worries about Mum, I often found myself needing solitude. If I was not travelling, I would walk the streets for hours, late into the evening, trying to make sense of it all. The dark helped. It gave me a space to think about my parents; and my future. I often arrived home after midnight. My wife must have worried.

Three months after Mum passed, I decided to take redundancy. No longer able to stand the toxic atmosphere at the office, my mental health was suffering. As family and work distractions fell away, I was free to concentrate on music. The relief was palpable. What had been an avocation was now my vocation: piano. Locking myself in the woodshed more often and for more extended periods, my learning accelerated. With each new concept thrown at me by my teacher, my determination to become a musician increased. If only I could have played to Mum as I could now play. I remember her words of encouragement to me as a child, so clearly.

'Such a wonderful thing!' she would say.

And it is! To have joy in your life; to play the piano. And so, I shed my past in the computer industry. No looking back.

My penfriend had experienced a similar redundancy a few years before. He had not found it an easy time and warned I might also find post-work life a challenging period, citing feelings that come with the loss of status (we had both held senior roles), a reduced sense of purpose and a very different daily routine. But in truth I felt none of those things. I had mentally left the firm a long time before, the instant I had stepped onto the escalator and into the hands of my adult music teacher. My 'new life', as I pretentiously called it, would focus purely on the creative arts, and especially on music. I relished the fact it was so different. To write a song, to write a poem … to share them with friends … I craved being stretched in directions that might put the fear of God into some. Creativity. Putting yourself 'out there' for all to see. And now I had all the time in the world to fulfil my dream.

In the immediate aftermath of redundancy, I became obsessed with the piano to the point of madness. I was a steam engine freed of its governor, wheels and pistons running out of control, engine rattling itself to pieces. Something had to give.

Suddenly, I found my practice regime lapsing. Where I had previously spent hours at the keyboard, I was now skipping whole days, sometimes a whole week. Just as in childhood, my appetite for practice was drying up. As empty days turned into weeks, I began to worry. Had I been using the goal of 'becoming a musician' as an escape from my parents' illnesses and my struggles at work? Wasn't I now free? Wasn't that the meaning of 'retirement'? Why then had I not opened my theory books for months? Why was I not practising 24/7?

Fortunately, the ailment was temporary, most likely the result of 'simple exhaustion' according to my penfriend. By the start of summer I was bouncing back with what felt like renewed energy. My zest for the ride had returned and I was once again writing to my friend with updated, and absurdly ambitious, musical goals. As a result, mountains started to appear again, and a host of new blocks sprang up around me. Situation normal. Just as I like it.

A small example:

When your teacher tells you that everything you had learnt about chords is wrong and they can be played without their root, or with the 5th replaced by a 6th, and often the 3rd just gets in the way and can be omitted, well … All those shapes I had neatly filed away under my fingers and in my muscle memory? What of them? They began to dissolve in front of my eyes. So a C major chord, for example, might consist only of the notes A, D and B … no C, no E or even G. And they could be played, I was assured, in any order whatsoever. These 'rootless chords' nevertheless required me to 'hear the root' in my mind, if I were to improvise.

I remember one lesson distinctly. I was to use two kinds of rootless voicings: the 3579 and the 7935. I was handed a lead sheet so sparse that, no matter how hard I tried to 'play' it, I could hear no harmony or music of any kind. Even when played by my teacher, the tune made no sense. As he notched up the volume of my musical education, it was becoming harder and harder to keep up with him.

'Try this, Howard,' he would say. 'Play the blues section using the rootless chords I showed you last week. Throw in a minor-7th chord on the supertonic and an altered chord on the submediant. Don't forget … use good voice-leading.'

My mind exploded.

I admitted I was struggling, and in response he suggested that 'the first year or two was inevitably going to be tough'. Yes, hitting a brick wall every few days is tough.

Somewhat disheartened, the week's practice was erratic. I told my penfriend of these frustrations, and he wrote, 'Oh dear, that does sound complicated, even though I don't understand a word of it! I suggest you just sit back and enjoy the ride.' But this particular ride was a roller coaster, and I never did like thrills. Once again, something had to give.

You know you need a sledgehammer when no other tool will do. I needed the musical equivalent. I was now facing hurdles that only brute force could crack. I fired back a quick note to my friend asserting that 'This coming weekend I'm going to the woodshed for two whole days, more if required, no interruptions. I must. I am going to make a great deal of noise, and it is going to be rather repetitive. Wish me luck.'

Never one to leave it there, the joker tossed back, 'Isn't your wife the one who will need the hammer?'

I went to bed early, slept like a log and woke at the crack of dawn. By the end of the first day I was exhausted but seeing a little improvement. Glimmers of light had crept into my playing. Sunday cemented the progress. My friend asked how my weekend had been. I told him it had 'been tough,' and that I 'ran out of steam' during Saturday afternoon but had managed a 'full seven-till-nine session' on Sunday. Yes, fourteen hours. I reassured him that I knew this was crazy but asked that he not try to lecture me. Taking the hint, he simply asked how my wife was after the 'solitary marathon' and suggested I 'take her out to dinner a.s.a.p.', adding, 'We should come over to see you if only to give you a reason NOT to spend the weekend in whatever the woodshed actually is!' I agreed completely, and a firm date was put in the diary. It should be a strictly 'no music' weekend, he insisted, perhaps a walk and a film, adding, 'and it's been too long since we have played with Adagio'. He loves cats. But unbeknown to my friends, I had begun to prepare another merry--go-round of keyboard demonstrations, some riveting aspect of theory no doubt. I was sure both he and his wife would find it fascinating.

25

SIX STRINGS

My penfriend asks two naïve questions. I write an essay in reply. It does not help.

My personal interest in the guitar is mostly aesthetic. I had recently spent a pleasant weekend renovating, polishing and re-stringing our instruments. We'd always had acoustic guitars lying around the house, but these days they stood idle. Sad really, but there it is, I could not afford time away from the keyboard to learn a second instrument. Our son chose to play the drums; our daughter the cello and piano. My wife sings, and was once an excellent flautist. She played guitar as a child, mainly folk music, which is how we came by so many instruments.

When our children were teens, I brought home an electric guitar and a small practice amp to add to our collection of unused instruments, hoping they would give it a try. The new six-string was a subtle glinting mauve, my daughter's favourite. Despite the colour, she never touched it, preferring to stick with the cello. My son was curious about the electric, but percussion was his love. When he experimented with the electric guitar he was hitting a drum. Who knows, maybe one day they, or I, will pick up one of our many guitars and start to learn. To motivate me, however, it would have to be a *fretless* bass, the five-string variety. Like the cello, I love the sound of bending notes in higher registers and am drawn to the beauty of such instruments, the wood used – ash, rosewood, maple – and to the craft of the luthier. However, constructing a quality bass, it turns out, is a surprisingly complex process, but for an engineer with pretensions to be a musician, a whole lot easier than learning to play the piano.

If keyboards do not work out for me, perhaps I should build that fretless … in a different kind of woodshed.

What prompted this diversion? Ah yes, a new email.

'I was beginning to wonder,' my penfriend asked, 'if I could more easily learn to play our keyboard by learning chords the way one learns guitar? Do you think it might be quicker or more natural for me?

'And while you are at it, I'm still not sure I get why, if a piano is tuned such that a scale which sounds right to the ear (because the intervals are harmonics of the root), it also requires two semitone intervals? Remind me again: why twelve key signatures and twelve semitones to the octave?'

Geez. I thought we'd covered this months ago. It was clear I was going to have to put the kettle on, brew up a strong cup of tea and give some serious thought to how to phrase a reply. Indeed, how does one approach such a question? Earlier explanations had failed. Yet naïve questions are always useful.

Where to start?

When a non-musician sings a major scale, they believe they are singing a series of equally spaced tones. They are not. Clear your throat, record yourself … do re me fa so la ti do. Now grab an oscilloscope and measure the frequencies. What! No scope to hand? What kind of home do you live in? A smartphone app will do.

The pattern of tones of the major scale proceeds in fits and starts: tone-tone-semitone, tone-tone-tone-semitone. It only sounds smooth to the untrained ear because we have heard the scale many times before, in so much music and throughout history. Sing it again. Focus on the intervals me-fa and ti-do … do they feel closer together than the others? Do you hear it? The F (fa) and the B (ti), remote in the harmonic series of the root (mathematically speaking), fall unevenly when 'folded down' to fit inside the octave from C. By contrast, the twelve semitones in every octave are equally spaced. Sing all twelve, up and down the keyboard, and you will hear what it is like for the ratios to be identical. It's called the chromatic scale. The modern piano, tuned in this manner, provides a 'bag' of twelve notes that we draw upon to approximate any key, scale or mode.

Next step.

Dear penfriend, if you were singing from C, please now move to D. Play its major scale. It sounds just like C, right? No? Did you forget the two sharps, C♯ and F♯? This is not Dorian mode, you know. Got it now? Good. The C and D scales sound the same, don't they? But both are approximations to the mathematically precise tuning as determined by the physics. In fact, all twelve major scales on the modern piano are approximations. Come on, you are good with spreadsheets and formulae, have a go at calculating the ratios and you will see why. Tables of fractional numbers illustrating this are scattered all over the web. Look them up. It's a numbers thing.

If the piano were perfectly tuned to a specific key, say E, the piano tuner would still have to decide where to place the remaining 'accidentals', and her choices might not be the best in the context of other keys. Try to play an E-tuned piano in, say, A or B, and even simple diatonic melodies without accidentals will sound Chas 'n' Dave. Very. And if we continue this process, moving beyond the perfectly tuned key (around the circle of fifths), the tuning errors pile up like rounding errors in the accountant's spreadsheet. This would create subtle but significant harmonic shifts when notes were played together as chords, leading to what might be called 'aural ambiguity'. Music played on such an instrument would confuse the listener; without realising it, they would lose track of the root and, therefore, also the key in which the piece was written. Harmony would be compromised. Worse, when the musician modulated to a new key, the transition would feel awkward, aurally speaking. The resolution of one chord to another, the sense of movement from key to key, would be less effective. Tension and release, the heart of music, could be lost.

The earliest keyboard instruments were tuned to a single key and they sounded wonderful in that key. But their tuning limited the sophistication of the music that could be performed. Composers of the time were, as a result, restricted to scale notes of the 'in-tune' key. Hence, music that modulated, or which employed (stole) tones from related modes, was rarely written or performed. No Bach, no Beethoven, no Delius, no soul music, no jazz, no R&B. Terrible! Without equal temperament (approximated tuning), the Western music tradition may never have emerged, at least not in the form we understand it today. But once the full power of twelve semitones was unleashed, composers had more options. *The Well-Tempered Clavier*, a collection of preludes and fugues by Johann Sebastian Bach in all twenty-four major and minor keys, was written in part to demonstrate the harmonic possibilities of the approximated tuning scheme. Bach would have been familiar with many tuning systems, and, as an organist, would have played instruments tuned to a 'meantone' system, another approximated tuning system obtained by slightly compromising the fifths (ratio of 3:2) to improve the thirds (5:4).

I emailed my thesis to my penfriend, hoping it would answer his original question. He shot back with a quip: 'I suspect that aural ambiguity is a terrible thing!' Via poking fun at me, I believe he hopes to improve my character. Unlikely. In any case, I cannot judge whether he ever fully understood why the modern keyboard is the way it is. I'm pretty sure he smelt a rat and guessed that I'd invented 'aural ambiguity' to appear more intelligent than I am or as a ruse to fool him into thinking I really did have an advanced understanding of piano tuning (which I do not). My friend can see through me, always. He is a tough nut to crack. So I shot back another message, asking him to think about what a 'key' actually was. We'd been using the term willy-nilly for over a year. Did he understand? It was back to his question: 'Why twelve?'

Tone-tone-semitone, tone-tone-tone-semitone … that's a scale. Place it on a starting note, a tonic, and that's a key. Move it up a semitone. Why is this a different key? The intervals are the same, but the notes are different. Sure, some tones are shared among the keys, but each key is distinct, even if they vary by only one note! The bags of notes that comprise C major and G major, for example, are distinguished only by the F in C, and the F♯ in G. Would this still be the case if the pattern of tones and semitones were different? Maybe. Let's try.

Consider the whole-tone scale: no semitone intervals. There are only *two* of these scales (keys) on the keyboard. Try it. Start on a note and proceed in whole tones. The pattern repeats after one octave. Now begin on the next semitone. Result: another key, different notes. Now on the next semitone. Whoops … it's repeating the first scale no matter where we are. QED. Only *two* whole-tone scales, yet *twelve* major scales. Chord patterns work the same way.

Play a diminished chord on C, comprising C E♭ G♭ and A. Now move it up a semitone: D♭ E G B♭. Move it up again: D F A♭ B. And again: E♭ G♭ A C. Oh look … an 'inversion' of the first chord. Same notes, different order. Get it? There are only *three* diminished chords possible on the keyboard. Why? Because a scale (or chord) of *four* equally spaced notes can create only *three* positions on the keyboard that don't overlap. Try it with your fingers, dear intelligent penfriend, on a real keyboard, and you will see it right away. Twelve divided by four equals three, right?

Let's round off this epiphany with a final question: how many chromatic scales are there on the keyboard? One, silly. Twelve = twelve.

Did my verbose essay answer my friend's naïve, but useful, question:

'Why twelve, Howard?'

I'm not sure it did.

So, back to my friend's equally naïve question:

'... could I more easily play the piano by learning chords the way one learns guitar? Do you think it might be more natural for me?'

Well, both instruments employ the same twelve semitones (otherwise they could never form a band). The guitar's frets are its semitones. And both play notes together as chords (harmony) and in sequence (melody). Why then would he think the guitar would be 'easier' to learn? Perhaps he felt, with just six strings, there would be fewer ways to make a mistake? Or, with only six strings, music written for guitar could never be as challenging as for the piano? Or maybe he was thinking about guitar 'tabs', tablature notation, cute diagrams which show the correct position of each finger on the fretboard for each of a zillion chords playable on the guitar? No, he would be wrong in all cases.

Tablature notation would be of no use to a pianist. How on earth would tabs work across the keyboard's eighty-eighty notes? No simple diagram will help there. How would it be possible to depict the fluid flow of the pianist's arms, hands and fingers as they spread, divide and duplicate the notes of chords to create voicings? Impossible. No, the simple fact is that the two instruments are as chalk and cheese. Each brings their own beauty and complexity to musical performance.

A simple triad, played on the piano, sounds dull; childlike. The same chord played on the guitar is rich in harmonic detail. The guitar breathes in a different way to the piano. Its body resonates. Strings not plucked still vibrate, there being no dampers. This is not true of the piano unless unplayed notes are held down (hammer held away from the piano string). And we know what free vibration means, don't we, dear penfriend? Harmonics, all the way up to the upper partials ... tones that musicians call 'extensions' or 'colours'. Resonance occurs in the piano, of course, but it is less pronounced than on the guitar. In this respect, therefore, obtaining a beautiful sound on the guitar is more accessible than on the piano. And perhaps this is why the ubiquitous guitar is the number one most popular instrument for the budding musician to pick up and strum. But how one plays each instrument is also chalk and cheese.

If a pianist jumped from chord to chord as if 'strumming' a guitar, the sound would be terrible and the movement awkward. The piano is a 'linear' instrument, its keys laid out in a line. Thus, 'voice-leading' is vital: finding ways to move from chord to chord while minimising unnecessary leaps and jumps. The strings of a guitar are close together and closer to the hand. The frets are aligned. The guitarist's fingers do not need to move as far; watch any good guitarist. Would the guitarist's technique transfer to the piano? Nope.

So there it is. I tried my best to answer my penfriend's question, but I suspect I merely added to his confusion. Wasn't it about time he *picked up* a guitar or *sat down* at a piano? He could then put flesh to strings or keys, but I resisted the temptation to send a final message suggesting this. Our text-based exchange had run out of steam: he was asking questions that demanded practical demonstration; I was running out of ways to explain. For a while, therefore, our correspondence dried up. I think we were both relieved. For my part, I fear I send far too much email, most likely the result of living in a multinational corporation for the majority of my working life. Inundated with hundreds of 'urgent' messages each day, and expected to instantly respond with a semi-intelligent answer from 'the expert', electronic communication has always been a natural medium for me. I tend to assume it's the same for everyone. Wrong again. Nothing could be further from the truth. I have other friends who take days or weeks to reply to an email, but drop them an Instagram or WhatsApp message and an answer pops back immediately: always-on social media. In any case, our lapse of communication via old-fashioned email gave us both a space in which to breathe. I certainly needed it because, on the front line of the escalator, things were not going well. Not at all.

26

LAWNS

In which I fly out of my body, evaluate my progress, find it wanting and face the willies, almost, but not wholly succumbing to chronic pre-commitment syndrome.

My attempt to play 'Lawns' by the American jazz composer and pianist Carla Bley – in her fluid, elegant manner – proved a sobering experience. Many musicians have tried. Few get close.

Our children were home for the weekend. I had been practising Carla's famous tune for a week or so, working from a sparse handwritten lead sheet I had found on the Internet, penned by the composer herself. To my knowledge, her glorious music had never been published, and certainly not in her unique arrangement. I thought it might be 'fun' – that irritating word my friend never stops using to describe the purpose of my journey – for our son to join me on drums and our daughter to improvise a cello part. After a hesitant start, we managed to get through it, and it was … fun. It was also revealing.

Our von Trapp family rendition of Carla's bewitching music brought to the surface all kinds of anxiety. Endeavouring to play the tune, with its odd syncopated rhythm – two melody notes on the fourth beat, stretched over the bar line to create a quiet pulse – is difficult to describe and harder to perform. No matter what I tried, I did it 'all wrong', according to my 'band' members. After repeated attempts, our kids grew tetchy and began to lecture me. 'Dad, you are not keeping time!' They had no idea how far such gentle jibes were causing me to question my time on the escalator and the limited progress I had made as a musician.

With 'Lawns', I was pushing further into the creative space of free-wheeling improvisation. The horror of failure, of being judged for what you cannot do, was rising. I saw it plainly: I was not a 'natural'. Yes, I could play (ish) when alone, in the dead of night or before the rest of the house woke, but things quickly fell apart when I performed in front of, or with, others. 'Performance' was presumably another piece of the journey-pie I needed to eat if I were to 'put myself out there' without fear.

Dear reader, if you are attempting or contemplating a journey in any way comparable to mine, there will come a time in your development when the blocks in front of you grow so vivid, so plain to see, that you will gasp at their effrontery. Standing there, bold as brass, quietly confident of their ability to stop you in your tracks, you almost sense they are gloating. When this happens, no teacher will be able to help. Books, manuals, self-help guides … these will be equally useless. You will be on your own, facing the abyss: your nemesis. You open the pages, pick an exercise – perhaps a series of progressions through a chromatic descent – and you know even before you start that it's never going to happen. Ever.

Blocks. Blocked.

Everyone comes up against them. It's an individual thing. One person may hit the buffers at grade three, another at five, or seven, or eight. And don't think there won't be blocks as we late returning amateur pianists head down the road to Diploma-land – if we get that far. As sure as night follows day, there will be blocks. They do not vanish overnight. They will be there in the morning, patiently waiting to prevent further progress. Everyone has such limits, and I desperately needed to know mine. A few musicians, let's call *them* 'naturals' (less than one per cent of those who try?) eventually find a way to navigate such obstacles. How?

Here is what it feels like: I contemplate my hands. I ask, 'Why won't they do what I need them to do? What is it, precisely, that prevents the movement?' I close my eyes. I imagine playing as I should be able to, and feel a flurry of imagined motion but no logic, nothing to grasp hold of. I step out of myself, floating, a spectral player examining my maladroitness from every angle. I fly around the piano watching myself play, developing my senses, studying every detail. I see what my alter ego is struggling with. And gradually, ever so slowly, I learn how to copy my ethereal self.

Such acts of self-awareness transcend all traditionally taught 'piano practice'. It required, for me, a Zen-like power of concentration. Focus. Slow right down. (The second hand of the clock is now minutes.) Look closely. Can you see the shape of your hand on the keyboard? Move your fingers from chord to chord. Ever so slowly now. Watch how they move. Imagine writing a novel about the experience. How would you describe this? Now do that again, this time stepping back from the keyboard to enjoy a bird's eye view. As you play, watch in overview and study the choreography of your arms, hands and fingers.

What did you learn?

An analogy, a science demonstration: push your fingers through the sticky black viscous liquid of a non-Newtonian fluid. Do it slowly enough, feeling your way, and it *is* possible. Yet punch the surface, and the rare substance absorbs the blow, solidifying as if it were instant-setting concrete. Musical blocks are just like that. Only you can grab hold of their fluid form and work it with your fingers. No one can do it for you, no teacher, no penfriend. And this was me, wrestling with Carla Bley's delightful but infuriating 'Lawns'. Every time I tried to feel my way through her treacle, it would abruptly congeal. I could almost hear Carla laughing. Except that she never would.

I discussed the dilemma with my teacher. Listening to a YouTube recording of Carla playing 'Lawns', he felt that while the piece sounded straightforward enough, naïve even, its form belied an inner complexity.

He urged me to listen to the passages where she broke into freewheeling improvisation. Wonderful. My teacher's take? It would take (me) weeks, perhaps months, to perfect such passages, and by that time I would be (in his words) 'perfectly sick and tired of the tune, of Carla and her style' – music I loved so much. Why should I subject myself to that? Again the old question jumped to the front of my mind. Why scripted repetition? Surely there must be another way to learn? Or had I, as my penfriend so often pointed out, set my goals too high in a futile attempt to progress at a velocity beyond my middle-aged brain? Was I, he asked, 'creating unnecessary frustration' for myself, a racing car driver who always takes the same corner too fast and repeatedly spins off the track? And was I, as my friend also tried (gently but firmly) to highlight, 'boiling the ocean': tackling too many learning paths in parallel such that none could adequately develop? Theory, ear training, harmony, melody, scales, exercises, improvisation, sight-reading ... was it all just too much? Did I have to accept that I needed more time? More years?

Time! Again, my fear ... Could I become the musician I wanted to be, to go to college and obtain an M.Mus if I was still learning the rudiments at sixty-five? At seventy? Was this even possible? I needed to be a musician right here, right now. I could not wait ten years! If that was the length of the escalator on which I found myself, perhaps I *should* give up now and succumb to the chronic malady my friend claimed prevented him from embarking on any project likely to necessitate sustained dedicated effort. The thought gave me the willies. No way, José. I could no more give up on my dream than I could stop breathing.

I needed options.

27

A PARTING OF WAYS

'How lucky I am to have something that makes saying goodbye so hard.' – A.A. Milne, *Winnie-the-Pooh*

It had been two years to the day since I had walked into the modest music shop that had attracted my attention while out shopping. A week later, I was sitting down for my first lesson with a talented jazz musician who became my friend and mentor. His almost superhuman ear invariably amazed me. We would dial up a song on the Internet, music he had never heard before, and within minutes he was playing it. Not just the bones of the piece, mind you, but the full essence of the music: all its details, perfect bassline and harmony. And, as I have probably mentioned too often, he was also able to explain the musical influences that led to its composition, in which era and from which genre. He could often point to specific songs or individual musicians that had inspired the piece. I kid you not. As you can imagine, it was with great sadness that I decided I must end my lessons with him.

My blocks and general lack of progress, as I saw it, were such that I judged there was nothing more I could learn from this teacher, given the sorry state of my ability (or should I say inability?) to play at a sufficient level. Our time together, so helpful at first, was now proving ineffective. He was racing ahead; I was lagging. Sometimes I could not even find the chords he asked me to voice. I'd be fumbling around, taking an inordinate time to do the simplest things, steps that should have been spontaneous. I was unable to keep up with the flow of his instruction. Worse, in a week or two of practice, I could not 'play' the latest lead sheet he gave me, at least not with any degree of confidence.

Something had to change. Again.

I wrote to my friend about the situation:

'I am about to do something I might regret,' I announced loudly. 'Whoa. Hard to write this. My teacher is so lovely. But I need to do things differently now. Not sure how it'll work it out. Wish me luck. STOP.'

I sounded like a ticker-tape telegram from the 1940s.

My theory was this: I needed more time with my teacher, on a less frequent basis. The weekly thirty-minute dose was unproductive. I needed more like four hours, total immersion in a relaxed environment, say once a month at my home. However, his work and family life did not permit anything close to this.

We parted on good terms, agreeing that, as an adult, my lessons had to be just what they needed to be, no more, no less, and not limited by what he could provide. I would need to significantly develop my improvisation skills before I could enter into the spirit of his tuition.

'Sure,' he said, 'When you feel you are ready, come back and see me. My door is always open.'

The final thirty minutes with my teacher were bittersweet. I knew how special he was and how fortunate I had been to meet him. As we parted, I thanked him for the considerable help and inspiration he had given me and handed him a small gift: a modest bottle of wine.

His last words were these: 'You know, Howard, you know more than you think you know and can do more than you realise.'

He may or may not have been right. The simple fact was that the balance of our work together was out of kilter. He was providing too much, I too little.

It was difficult to leave our practice room that day, and sadly we have not seen each other since. Upstairs in reception I informed the staff of my decision and paid the final fee due. They were surprised but understanding. To this day, I am unsure whether I did the right thing. I also fear that my teacher, not wishing to injure my feelings, was, in those last moments, probably thinking, 'Hey-ho, another who dreamed of being a pianist but failed to stay the course.' Yet I know he would not think that. He was the nicest guy you could ever hope to meet. Personality alone, however, was not enough to sustain our weekly regime. I needed to get off his style of escalator and onto a new highway. Precisely what this might be I had no clear idea, but unless I jumped ship now, I judged, it might never happen.

I told my penfriend of the decision the following day. He was his usual understanding self.

'Yes, I see that,' he said. 'I think your re-boot should be to start making music with others, rather than putting that day off with more exercises and theory.'

Easy for him to say. Harder for me to do.

I had to admit it, despite the disappointments, I enjoyed the continual challenges and the occasional blocks. The struggle is important to me. Let me explain. Suppose I had in front of me a stack of grade six sheet music, a thousand beautiful pieces, all within my ability to perform with a few weeks' practice. Surely I could then play to my heart's content for the rest of my life and never repeat a single piece! Would I be content? No. I'd eventually be bored silly. Piling up accessible music was never going to cut it, even if this was what my childhood teacher and parents had in mind. That's not me. A fresh start was required. But where, how and when?

My penfriend advised that, in all probability, I needed a good rest. Apparently, I'd been 'overdoing it', and should take a few weeks off.

'You are clearly overtired,' he theorised, 'and probably stuck in a rut;

musically speaking. Why not try something new after Christmas?'

Then came the following words:

'A word of warning is in order; if you don't mind?' he wrote. 'You have travelled a substantial distance already and achieved a good deal. You may not see it, but you have. It would not be wise to set a new, unrealistically distant goal and then treat it as a fixed destination and pre-condition for success, because, if you do, you will become disheartened and miss the whole point of why you started this journey.

'If you want to be a class jazz musician, you must realise that most people who set out down that road don't make it, which is why we celebrate those who do! Be kind to yourself. Be pleased with what you have accomplished so far and relish any further advancement.

'I am counselling caution because it would be oh, so easy to give up now and miss the joy of being a reasonable musician by worrying you will never be a greater one. There will always be a higher standard to achieve. Take a break. Relax dear boy. Do.

'So looking forward to seeing you both on Sunday, beer and hugs. Us.'

It was good advice, but not easy to hear.

Faced with this reality, all I could think of was 'Hell. No way. That's not how this ends.' A new strategy was already hatching in my mind. And yes, much beer would be needed.

Over a year ago, I had purchased several books on jazz improvisation, hoping they could unlock new skills. And they had, at first. But I eventually found them overwhelming, and they now lay dusty on top of my piano, hardly touched, rarely opened. Eighteen months on, perhaps these books could come to my rescue. Was I now ready? I committed to studying a chapter per week. Why could I not succeed? After all, had I signed up with a 'traditional' piano teacher, where would I be now? Playing a few set pieces, no doubt reasonably well, but what else? Would I have been able to compose 'A Pleasant Day'? Would I have hatched the crazy idea for a *Blue Snowman*? Would I have been able to play a little Chopin 'In a Day'? It was my jazz teacher who had inspired these baby steps, not rote learning. And under his instruction my ear had greatly improved. Whenever a song struck up on the television, I would jump up, rush to the piano and pick out the melody, and, where possible, a sketch of the harmony. Not always, but more often than not – and much to the amazement of my family – I found that I could.

Something 'musical' was stirring in me. The decision to withdraw from weekly lessons was, I now realised, a good one … my teacher's unique injection of wisdom had run its course. For now, at least.

A new chapter was opening. I sensed it on the wind.

CHORUS

'For the first time, he heard something that he knew to be music. He heard people singing. Behind him, across vast distances of space and time, from the place he had left, he thought he heard music too. But perhaps, it was only an echo.'

Lois Lowry, *The Giver*

28

REHARMONIZE ME

In which, struggling to find myself, I give not one but two public performances, of a kind.

As a metaphor for how I was feeling, reharmonization is not bad. Jazz musicians do it all the time. Keep the melody, change the harmony. Hey presto, fresh music. Ever listened to Eva Cassidy as she sings 'Autumn Leaves'? That's it, right there. Exquisite.

Think of reharmonization as the musical equivalent of new paint on a vintage car; not lipstick on a pig. Reharmonization gives colour and life to well-known tunes by changing the underlying harmony. As a result, the intervals between their bass notes and inner parts shift in ways that create delicate and glorious effects. Even a simple melody can be transformed. And always for the better. And that was how I came to wonder: what if I *had* continued to see my teacher? Could he have reharmonized me?

It had been several months since I had said goodbye to the shop on the wrong side of town. Adrift without a lifeboat, I was treading more than a little water. Had my teacher been a lesser musician, the voyage to my imagined post-retirement future may well have failed as spectacularly as it had in childhood. The jazz teacher I had decided to leave was, in large part, the catalyst for my time on the escalator.

Flashback to evidence.

I remember my first 'reharm', as jazzers call them. How could I forget? My assignment for the week was to reharmonize the classic song 'Over The Rainbow'. Encouraging me to trust my instincts, he said, 'Look, Howard, you now know everything you need to do this. Just do it.' And I did. And the result was not half bad.

I had shifted the piece from C major to A minor (the relative). That's not so unusual, but the way I had used the minor key 'functionally' was somewhat original, and my teacher agreed. Excited, I uploaded my work to SoundCloud and once again field-tested it with my penfriend, sending him several takes I had recorded throughout the day.

My friend replied that, to his ears, take #1 had 'lost it' halfway through the piece and, as a result, sounded more like 'lounge music, sooorrrrry'. Now you really don't need to hear THAT from a close friend. But he was more complimentary about take #2, writing, 'If we had been told this was an experienced musician messing with the song, we would have believed it. You are doing well at so many levels. We thought it was a proper download when you sent it. We are impressed!' Well, I did think it contained a couple of creative moments.

I had played this variation without a score or lead sheet. It felt great, just as I imagined improvisation could be: a musician 'doing that musician thing'. But the work to get there had been exhausting, an entire day of experimentation. I now understood why children learn to sight-read set pieces note for note, each phrase inscribed with military precision on sheet music. Rote. It's easier.

The next day, refreshed and basking in the glory of my first successful reharm, I wrote to my penfriend to thank him for his kind words. Brimming with self-confidence, I asserted that I must now 'push to higher grades' and 'study more theory' so that I could be 'deliberate when I compose'. However cute it was, the last thing I wanted was for my rendition of 'Over The Rainbow' to be the one-trick pony I feared.

Over the next couple of weeks, and desperate to find the inspiration to reharmonize other tunes, I rarely stopped playing my version of the famous theme. I could see how it worked. I could *hear* how it worked. But

I was unsure I ever fully understood how, from a 'theoretical' perspective, I had achieved the result. Decoding its logic, I became so proficient in accurately reproducing the improvisation that I became convinced I could play it to anyone, at any time, note-perfect. It had become my unwritten lead sheet, my first real 'party piece'. I even gave it a new name: 'Under The Rainbow'. I thought this was oh, so very clever and undoubtedly the kind of thing a proper jazz musician would do. And as I basked in my greatness, a crazy thought sneaked up behind me and planted itself firmly in my mind. Where, I wondered, could I perform this masterpiece for others to hear? The answer came in an instant: street pianos.

The area near St Pancras International rail station, close to where my employer had their central London office, had recently undergone significant renovation. Several large shopping centres had opened; all fancy glass and wide-open spaces. Plonked in the middle was a creaky old upright 'For Use By Members Of The Public'. The best shopping-centre pianists attracted quite a crowd, as did the elderly and children, no matter how well, or (more often than not) how badly, they could play. How could I resist? Returning to my old stomping ground, I stepped up to the white piano, sat down, and played ... 'Under The Rainbow'.

The piece sounded thin in the vast open retail space, and the honky-tonk effect of the poorly maintained instrument did nothing to reveal the subtlety of my harmony, but I enjoyed the experience of performing 'live' and hoped for an audience. Several passers-by glanced sideways but walked quickly on. None stopped. Clearly, I had more work to do. I may not have attracted an audience, but I did not mind. This was neither a grand piano nor a grand stage, but I had given my first public performance. It felt wonderful.

A second opportunity to perform came two weeks later.

Whenever I am in London and have time to kill, I often succumb to the temptation to visit a specific shop. The name is unimportant. Suffice to say, it sells keyboards, of all shapes and sizes. Gazing longingly at whatever new synthesiser is on offer, I always make a point of asking the assistant about the latest music gear and hot trends in the development of electronic music. I then ask to borrow a pair of headphones and sit for a while, fiddling with knobs and making sounds; a private bliss. It's one way I can return to my teenage years. On this occasion, the shop was relatively quiet. A young guy was doing the same, hovering over a high-tech analogue synth, looking intense. On the other side of the aisle, an older gentleman was giving a demonstration of what looked like an expensive eighty-eight-key stage piano. And at the far end of the shop, two young people, snuggled together, boyfriend and girlfriend, were browsing racks of sheet music. I decided to go for it.

Unplugging the headphones I had been using to listen to the keyboard that had caught my attention, its stereo output reverted to a pair of large monitor speakers hung on the wall. My shop-wide sound system was live. Gingerly, ever so quietly, I began to play my piece, its well-known melody floating over my unusual 'minor descending' harmony. So sweet. The electric piano sample I had chosen sounded delicious. The improvisation rang out throughout the shop, instantly recognisable but somehow different as a result of my reharm. For two minutes I kept my head down and just played. It felt like a lifetime. Hesitating, I lifted my hands from the keys and looked up. Everyone had stopped what they were doing. To my surprise, there was a little polite clapping. The shopkeeper spontaneously came forward and said, 'Man, that was really beautiful; and different.' In his forties, wearing jeans, with raggedy hair and sporting an unkempt, ruffled appearance, he knew what I had done with the music. He knew jazz. Even his clothes said it.

Nostalgia over. Back to reality.

And there it was again, the debilitating thought … the reality of how little I had achieved. Having stood down from lessons, I was on my own, with no teacher to guide me. It was disconcerting, but also curiously empowering. Whether this was the trigger for what happened next, I have no clear memory, but at that precise moment, at five forty-four on the afternoon of November 14th, 2015, I wrote … 'I've an idea for a book.' And pressed SEND.

I did try more reharms. None came as readily as the first, but a rather lovely (I think) rendition of the carol 'In The Bleak Midwinter' can be found hiding away among my notebooks. Who knows, one day I might bring a few of these jottings to life as recordings, but for now they are little more than baubles, trifles along the trail of the escalator as it races ever on. For having left the teacher who had inspired me to develop these skills, I was still struggling with the big kahuna itself, how to reboot and reharmonize *me*.

29

UNDER MY NOSE

In which I stop fiddling with trifles, recall how I once failed to understand how C-C♯ can be consonant and, responding to an unexpected invitation from the custodian of my snowman, decide to head in a new direction.

With no upcoming lesson to fret about, I now had more space in which to consider how to adjust the escalator to smooth out the bumps I had been experiencing. Whether I could ever control the unruly machine, however, I was unsure. With no desire to jump back on, I was enjoying a period in which I felt less driven, free to explore, without the stifling practice regime I had inflicted upon myself. Freedom! Goodness, there were even days when I permitted myself to do nothing at all. Doodling at the piano as I had as a young man fiddled with my synthesisers was a welcome distraction from the unremitting pressure of 'the next lesson'. But oh, the distracting knobs, dials and multitudinous parameters of those machines. To those of you who did *not* become obsessed with electronic instruments in the 80s and 90s, a word of warning. Do you have any idea how much time can be squandered finding a critical value buried deep down in the poorly designed and often impenetrable 'menu systems'? There I go again … time wasted. How I dread counting the years lost in failing to become a musician. But hey, mustn't look back. Soldier on.

Idly flicking through my 'Real Book' – close to five hundred lead sheets, half a century's worth of music – I wondered how many variations must be 'out there'. Tens of thousands? More? Worked and reworked by so many musicians, the ingredients of a brew that is still evolving today. Just as my teacher had shown me, there are patterns in music, repeated from song to song, a veritable treasure trove of recipes that I hoped would one day allow me to cook up some delicious suppers at the keyboard. Yet surprisingly, and despite the jazz tradition and its emphasis on adaptation, it is hard to find anything genuinely new. Odd. My teacher found this frustrating. His instant recall of so much past music, his ability to see similarities between songs and across eras, compounded the problem.

'These days,' he sighed, 'most new "releases" are just same-old, same-old. No inspiration there.'

One lesson, I recall, proved the exception to the rule. I remember my teacher's excitement, eager for me to understand his discovery. Apparently, a group of forward-looking jazz musicians were now treating the augmented-octave as consonant! What? C against C♯? F against F♯. How? Really? He demonstrated the harmonic effect as part of a labyrinthine chord progression. I could make no sense of it. 'Come on, Howard, listen,' he urged. But no, I had not yet 'heard' enough modern jazz for my ears to adjust to the shock of the new; the acquired taste of these tones simply made no sense. My palate was insufficiently refined. And to hammer the point home, when I did bring music to the lesson that *I* considered original, my teacher soon put paid to the idea. For him, it was all old hat. But, not wishing to squash my enthusiasm, he reminded me that it is not always the harmony that gives music its character.

'Do not underestimate the power of arrangement,' he said.

And he was right.

While able to play pretty much anything I introduced, and purely by ear, note-perfect, the effect he achieved on the piano was often very different from that of the recorded music, with its thick layers of sound, backing instruments and effects. There was a particular folk song that intrigued us both. I had managed to work out the majority of the notes and could play the tune reasonably well, but, for the life of me, I could not emulate the way I heard it on the LP. My teacher listened carefully, was immediately able to play it by ear, and then explained a possible reason for my confusion. The inner 'circle' of tones was divided between two instruments: clarinet and cello. He played the phrase a second time, adjusting the voicings, but to my ears it still felt wrong. Was it something about the way the clarinet pitched against the cello? He thought the music was 'a perfect example of a beautiful motif crafted from words, melody, harmony and instrumentation'. He was impressed by the arrangement.

'I write music myself, did I mention that?' he said.

I had been vaguely aware that he did more than play bass and piano but had no idea he had won competitions for his work. As a composer, he also taught students to use digital audio software (DAW) to shape and record their arrangements. My mind whirled again. And here I was skirting base camp, rarely straying out of the foothills, struggling to keep up with the tempo of the songs I tried to play, flailing around finding the right chords … and with the oh, so important voice-leading. So much to learn, so little time.

Well, no point reminiscing about past lessons. For better or worse I had abandoned the rudder that was my ex-teacher. To keep things moving, I had begun to dip into the 'Learn Jazz' books I had purchased nearly two years ago but not yet used. So now – in addition to scales, modes, chords and voice-leading – I was reading about playing in fourths, stacking in fifths, tritone substitution, upper structure extensions, approach and avoid notes, and more … What to focus on? I hardly knew where to begin.

When I shared such vexations with my penfriend, he usually responded with something like, 'Well, you could just try to enjoy the ride and have some fun.' Oh yes, easy for him to say. Now, more than ever, it was abundantly clear that to be the musician I wanted to be, I would need an amalgam of all the skills my teacher had demonstrated during our time together: technique, theory, harmony, composition, arranging. Drop any single element and the house of cards might fall. Advice from my penfriend to 'reduce the workload' and 'focus on one or two key aspects' was hardly helpful. No, it would have to be full steam ahead on all fronts – a leap of faith. I just hoped that one day everything would snap into focus and I would emerge whole: a musician! Naïve, of course, but what choice did I have?

I worked like a man possessed, which had the fortunate side-effect (for my penfriend) that I was no longer initiating as much email traffic. Having not heard from me for a while, I was delighted when I received an unsolicited note from him. My friend was convinced that to achieve my overall goal I needed to play music with other musicians. What could I say? I agreed it might be 'fun' but explained that finding someone with whom to collaborate was far from straightforward. The only other musician I knew lived in France, a professional cellist; and despite being a good friend, she was not someone who would choose to spend time jamming with me, a rank amateur at best. And I was hardly going to go down the pub, sit at the Old Joanna and strike up with a band, was I? I also had the terrible (and terrifying) feeling that even if I did manage to find the odd bloke or two who might be interested in making some noise, I might not choose to play with them. Look, I'm not saying my ability would be in any way better than theirs, but spending time with a few chaps my age for beer, skittles and man-chat did not appeal, not one jot. On top of those obstacles, the genres of music to which I was drawn (folk-pop/jazz/neo-soul) were not amenable to a 'bash-about'. As for my teacher, well, his band (a proficient modern jazz outfit) were hardly going to be interested in me, were they? And there was one more reason why I remained suspicious of any advice to 'play music with others'.

My penfriend had always been curious how any pianist could spend so much time alone, and never care a jot about whether others were listening. His suggestion was that I build a modest repertoire of well-known pieces to 'entertain friends and family'. It was a perfectly reasonable idea. Yet for me, spending time alone with my instrument was an entirely satisfactory pursuit, rather like fishing for trout. I could sit for hours in the semi-dark of a quiet room, dreaming up chords, experimenting with voicings and weaving some kind of a melody over the harmony. I did not need a band. Adagio was all the company I needed. It was enough to see whether I could create something interesting; no one to judge me, no metronome or other players to mark time with.

Most pianists – amateur or professional – will tell you the same: playing the piano is one of the most engaging and absorbing activities imaginable. It can also be, as the French-Georgian pianist Khatia Buniatishvili once observed, 'The blackest instrument, a symbol of musical solitude.' And this dichotomy – the solitary versus the social – was precisely where my escalator had come to an abrupt halt: the gulf between joy and abject frustration. Sometimes, when I play late at night, free of interruption, the walls around me disappear, the stars come out and I am transported to another world. And just as quickly I am jolted back to reality: I am nothing; I am not a pianist; all my work has been in vain.

There it is again, the big kahuna … where to GO with all this?

And then it struck me. The answer was right there under my nose all along. Silly, silly me. Songwriting! Words *and* music. Poetry *and* melody, plus a sprinkling of harmony. It was the logical next step beyond my thin solo-piano improvisation. But how? And almost like magic, a new message announced itself in my inbox. And not from my penfriend.

My unexpected concert companion, to whom I had entrusted a certain snowman, had announced a crowd-funding campaign to support the cost of studio time and mastering of a new album. And staring me in the face was an enticing offer, one option on the sliding scale of 'pledges'. In addition to the usual bunch of goodies – advance downloads, physical CD, hand-drawn lyric sheet, tickets to the launch show – was the very thing I needed: two hours with the artist to 'help complete any song you are working on'. Could I? Should I? My notebook was chock full of unfinished tunes. How could I resist? Impetuous as ever, I signed up there and then, click-click ... and immediately worried whether I had just made an abject fool of myself. Had she intended the offer to be taken up by her contemporaries and associates? You know, real musicians. Not me.

My unexpected friend wrote the next day with a straightforward, 'How wonderful! And how are you? It's been too long.' She knew of my piano journey. We'd chatted about it over coffee in London while brainstorming the snowman project. While a couple of hours' songwriting was hardly the same as a multi-year collaboration on the concept album our snowman demanded, needs must. Never look a gift horse in the mouth. Now I had the task of finding somewhere for us to meet. We'd need a piano. She would bring her guitar and voice. She lived north of London, I south. I promised to find a halfway house.

Scouring web ads for practice rooms in central London, I found a slew of possibilities, from high-tech studios to dingy rock rehearsal rooms. Many were either too grandiose, too seedy, or in the wrong part of town. I eventually fixed on a piano dealership in WC1. It offered three rooms downstairs (why am I always finding myself in basements?) the largest of which could accommodate up to fifty people. Each room was soundproofed, air-conditioned and claimed to be among the quietest in London. From the website, I saw that one featured a large grand piano.

The space was light and airy. Perfect. A date was agreed, a forthcoming Wednesday, the day of the week when my newly appointed songwriting tutor was usually in central London for other reasons.

I often wonder whether, had the pledge campaign not popped into my inbox, I would have been proactive enough, or had sufficient courage, to ask my unexpected friend for a songwriting class? And I thought back to the question put by my penfriend's wife: her confusion concerning the apparent contradiction between my claim of a lifelong desire to play the piano and the reality of what 'returning adults' call their 'gap' or in my case a 'chasm'. Forty years. Decades of either avoiding or not thinking to act on the uncomplicated impulse to walk into a music shop and ask for a lesson.

No more! 'If I am to be a musician, I must act as a musician.'

Musicians create their own luck. Starting now.

30

A GROWING EXCITEMENT

'If you cannot teach me to fly, teach me to sing.' – J.M. Barrie, *Peter Pan*

In the days leading up to the songwriting lesson, I can hardly describe my sense of anticipation and excitement. This will no doubt sound ridiculous, but I was placing a mark in the sand, a point of transition from piano-nobody to musician. In less than a week I would be in a studio, working with a real songwriter, making music. It felt as if I were crossing a chasm; a musical rite of passage.

My imagination was running ahead of itself.

We've all seen that scene in the old movie … Two people are sharing a piano stool, one working the lyrics, the other picking out chords or doodling a melody line, each working intensely on their contribution to whatever it is they are cooking. And suddenly a spark occurs, knowing smiles all around, the duo are now playing and singing a section of their just-hatched creation, and then … pencil grabbed, hastily writing it down on the lead sheet, words and notation capturing whatever had just 'clicked', only to stop again, hesitate, eyes wide, searching for their next idea, reaching down into whatever wellspring of creativity they can unearth, thoughts coming to life: a song that will one day be performed to the delight of many. It must have been this way, I realised, for the great songwriting partnerships of the past, George and Ira Gershwin, Rogers and Hammerstein, Lerner and Loewe … And I was to have a songwriting lesson! My entry in a future fake book?

Stop. I am way ahead of myself.

Yet I could not contain my delirium and zeal. I was to write a song (WRITE A SONG!) with a professional tunesmith and marvellous vocalist. She would give me a glimpse of a fascinating world that had seemed, to this point, wholly out of reach, an alien 'other place' that 'people like me' would never and could never access. What had begun as a regimented, austere, theory-bloated solitary quest to play the piano was about to change. No rote learning. No repetitive exercises.

The air quivered. The scene changed.

Even before my first songwriting tutorial – a term that hardly captures what was to transpire over the coming months – I knew there would be a second and a third and … It was as my penfriend had observed: collaboration is the centre of music. And the thought terrified me. But I loved it. Creativity. Raw. Exposed. My lesson in the craft would not only be beautiful, revealing, it would be … something else. Even if no music emerged from the collaboration, the experience would act as a signal, a trigger … a defining element, yes, to steer me through the final third of my life (assuming the good Lord – chance, providence, fate, call it what you will – afforded a fair wind and a favourable tide). I had found my purpose, my soul, my being … all the clichés. I now understood why I had stepped onto the escalator two years ago, and simultaneously discovered why, over forty-five years (FORTY-FIVE YEARS), I had never done so before. I now knew the solution to the riddle that had confused my penfriend's wife. And it shocked me to my core.

I rushed off a note to my penfriend to tell him of this unforeseen, though most welcome, turn of events. With his usual quick mind and razor wit, my friend fired back, 'May I offer one piece of advice? That any song you write just happens to end up in her key, not yours!'

I promised him it would.

31
SONGWRITING

In which I send a gushy email, am treated to an intimate private concert, and so receive a fire hose of knowledge about the process called songwriting. I commit to write a first song.

The day of my tutorial. No reason to be nervous, but I was. Very. It was not that we were strangers. Far from it; we had met several times in London to brainstorm *The Blue Snowman*. I had watched her play live in London and chatted together during breaks. We had become friends. Listening to her tales of what it was like to work in the independent music industry, I sensed she lived on a knife-edge, her delicate creativity finely balanced; that she could, at any moment, fall off, as a flower so easily crushed.

Was she on a similar bumpy escalator to my own? I occasionally wrote to her with words of encouragement, especially during those periods when she was releasing new music, putting herself 'out there'. Listening to her songs, I tried to explain how they affected me. And, I was intensely curious to understand more of her methods. There was mystery in her work. What was it about the voicings she used or the way she strummed the guitar that afforded her music its charm? It felt as if there was more going on under the hood than was apparent from a theoretical dissection of her harmony. Was she aware of this? I needed to know. She tried to answer, but I think she found my questions too analytical, too cold. In any case, she always thanked me for sending my thoughts and appeared genuine in her appreciation of my interest.

During the release of my friend's second album, I wrote a particularly gushy email. Recalling how her earliest songs had so enchanted me, her latest work was taking things to an entirely new level. I shall share my impressions here in this book because I believe they reveal much about what it means to be a songwriter.

'How does one describe a flower? Or a garden?' I wrote in one email. 'Such things cannot be described so easily. They just *are*. And so it is with your work. The words, melody and harmony are one; your songs speak to me directly and honestly; they bear repeated listening.

'There is a quiet beauty about them. Your songs do not shout. They invite the listener into your soul. The music arrives newborn, newly minted, each and every time.'

I urged her not to underestimate her talent. In each song, whether whimsical or reflective, raw with emotion or naïve as a child, her audience was being given the truth, no artifice – just her heart, mind and opinions … precisely as she saw the world. The gentle nuances of her guitar work and the beguiling melodies, woven among the sincere lyrics, said it all.

'You are your music,' I asserted.

Was this what it meant to write a song?

Could I emulate her integrity and her creativity? And the jarring words of my penfriend echoed once again: 'You must be realistic, Howard.' Wrong, wrong, wrong. Be unrealistic and write fearlessly. How else can one human soul create a work of art that another would choose to listen to, time and again? And as if in response, a new email announced its presence; and not from my penfriend.

'You have helped me more than you realise, Howard,' she wrote. 'It is important to have champions in this crazy industry.' And as I read those words, I was humbled. Yes, this was also the role my penfriend had played for me. His gentle encouragement and quiet questioning … it had helped me move off the gentler slopes and onto the black runs. Now, more than ever, I was taking the step that I hoped led to a higher peak: my first songwriting class. It made me smile. My penfriend's knowledge of muscle memory, tendons and brain plasticity might be useful to a budding pianist but was of no use at all to a songwriter!

As I travelled to London that day, I was more than a little apprehensive. Yet I had no reason to be. Any concern had nothing to do with my tutor and everything to do with me. It was a fear of being asked to be creative, of permitting a willingness to fail. I could not 'practise' writing a song as I had practised scales, arpeggios and chord voicings. Nor was the originality required of the songwriter in any way similar to the 'innovation' expected in my career. As a consultant and software engineer, failure was rarely tolerated. Songwriting was different. Utterly. The tunesmith, it seemed to me, was predicated on the necessity of pushing oneself beyond the edge of sure-fire success, to the chaotic space where defeat was a more likely outcome. If there was going to be a first song, and a second and a third … these were anxieties I would need to overcome. Half-completed tunes can hide away in notebooks, but songs? That would be a cop-out. Songs demand an audience. How else can they acquire their meaning?

I arrived at the venue early. Too early. Waiting for my friend and tutor while browsing the showroom, the shop assistant stepped over and inquired whether I was looking to buy a new piano. I replied that I might be. She showed me a range of models, uprights and grands, and I promised to get back to her. But I never did. Our piano at home is adequate, if uninspiring. One day I must replace it.

My tutor turned up looking precisely the way she often does: floppy coat, layers, guitar case, equally floppy bag slung over her shoulder and carrying a reusable paper cup filled with one of her more unusual beverages. The shop assistant looked alarmed. Liquid near our shiny pianos?

No way! To avoid any embarrassment, we stepped outside so that my friend could finish her hot drink. And then it was all systems go. Songwriting! What a thing. Whatever was going to happen?

Ushered down a flight of stairs to the basement studio I had booked, we found the room empty but locked. The shop keeper explained it would open automatically, at two o'clock. And it did.

The room was spacious, the piano gorgeous. My tutor busied herself, unpacking and tuning her guitar. I sat down and played a single minor-7th chord in second inversion. Wonderful.

The situation was unusual for both of us. My friend had never given a songwriting class before, and I had never attended one. Glancing at each other, we giggled. We knew which part the other was supposed to play in this drama, but we had no script. She probably had as much to learn about teaching as I had to learn about songwriting. Yet she proved an effective tutor.

Pulling a chair close to the piano, she sat down, guitar on her lap, strings at the ready. To me, her instrument had always seemed integral to her character, defining her personality. On the few occasions we had met without her guitar, she appeared naked, exposed, perhaps even vulnerable. Here, however, everything seemed right. We looked at each other and for a second or two neither of us knew how to begin.

I broke the silence with a simple request:

'I want to write a love song for my wife,' I announced.

And we were off.

To get things rolling, I suggested she sing a few of her songs and talk to me about them: how they came to be written, what they consisted of (musically speaking), and how I might learn to do the same.

The first song she played was one of her earliest. It can be found on her debut EP and is an exquisitely beautiful tale of two people who, frightened to get close to each other for fear of seeing what's on the inside, nevertheless contact, releasing a cloud of imaginary fireflies. The insects encircle the couple and weave their magic into the midnight air.

Over the next two hours, I was given what can only be described as a private concert for an audience of one. Performing many of my personal favourites from my friend's first album, I watched, spellbound, as she deconstructed the lyrical, melodic and harmonic ideas behind her process. Having come with no ready-made exercises or tutorial material from which we could work, I had no choice but to take my own notes in an attempt to capture the jet of knowledge that poured from her. It was hard to keep up with her stream of consciousness.

'Sorry, I know this is a lot to take on board,' she explained seriously and somewhat apologetically.

'No', I said, 'No problem, carry on, keep going. I am learning.'

And I was.

You may have picked up by now that I am both arrogant and foolish enough to believe I can learn something new merely by studying how another person does it. Innate talent is overrated as a concept. If you put in enough work, most people can do pretty much anything they want to in life. We each make choices about where we expend our time and effort. To acquire a significant skill, in any field of endeavour, takes hard graft. The input–output equation is a tough mistress: it's all about the passion. The work required to meet an unrealistic goal may be immense, painful even, but it will be worth the price if the outcome is more than just a way to pass the time of day. Hobbies are one thing, deep-seated needs another. I needed to play the piano and to compose. I felt this calling not as the ethereal, self-actualisation tip of a Maslow hierarchy, but rather at its broad base: music as essential as food, water, rest and safety. And this, my first songwriting lesson, was confirmation if ever there was.

Here is what I learnt during those seminal two hours:

- No book can teach me to be a songwriter. The best way to learn is to listen to as many songs as possible. And to spend time with other musicians.
- A song resembles a gemstone. There are surface details and sparkles, but also inner structures and nuances. File, polish and chip away at the song until it dazzles.
- When I write, start with my message. The sentiment must be genuine and heartfelt, never contrived; the lyrics devoid of all artifice.
- I must pinpoint the conceptual centre of my song. By observing the world around me, I will discover the metaphors that my audience can relate to and which allow them to understand what I am saying.
- The core of my song should be an immediately understandable gesture, to the point of being intriguing. It should prompt the listener to dig in and look for answers to the unanswered questions it suggests.
- My song centre must be expressible in no more than a few words. Sometimes a single word, or a word-pair, is all that is required.
- To develop as a songwriter, I should read more poetry. Songwriters are poets, of a kind.
- When listening to the songs of other writers, I should look out for – and 'hear' – the structure of their music: how it develops and what devices they use to reinforce their message.
- Try not to make things any harder than necessary. Writing a song by starting with the music, and then bolting-on the lyrics (or vice versa), can be debilitating: a deadlock where one or the other dominates. Words and music can emerge as one, fully formed, as a colourful butterfly from its cocoon (if a bit ruffled at first).

All this, in one lesson; it was remarkable. But there was more.

I also learnt:

- To be aware of the listeners' propensity to get bored. A song needs its surprises, and they should come earlier rather than later.
- Hooks are important. For a song to be popular, its hook should appear within the first fifty seconds, ideally sooner.
- The chorus should be crafted in relationship to its role in the unfolding story, as told through each verse; musically and lyrically.
- A lyric can employ either end-of-line rhymes or inner rhymes – between phrases. A rhyming dictionary may be a useful tool to have to hand when stuck for words.
- Technical work (recording, mixing, mastering and so on) must never be allowed to get in the way of the flow of the writing. Sing and play. Play and sing.
- Not to let the lyrics dominate. Leave room for the music to breathe; and vice versa.
- As the song moves into the studio, do not underestimate the need for thorough preparation. Do not waste valuable (and expensive) studio time. The session musicians and/or backing vocalists need a solid foundation on which to build if the collaboration is to be successful.

And finally:

- That music must provide space for the listener to reflect on what they heard. The vocalist also needs to breathe, as do the lyrics. The inclusion of a sparse section creates a contrast with regular verses and chorus. This, I was told, will pay dividends in the mix.

Fire hose over.

With some relief, my tutor advised that I 'keep things simple at first'.

'Write short songs, even if trite or cheesy,' she said, and 'keep practising your writing. The more songs, the merrier.' I was reassured that 'traditional song forms are fine', but I should 'feel free to experiment', there being 'much room for creativity'.

It was a lot to take in.

In the final minutes of the lesson, we touched on harmony. My tutor knew of my interest in jazz, its subtleties and complexities. Guessing correctly, she advised against using too many chords.

'A good song can be built from just two chords,' she claimed, assuring me I would be able to create variation by using inversions. 'Two or three contrasting sections should be enough.' As she spoke, I recalled how my jazz teacher had taught me to improvise by transposing to different points in the diatonic scale, for example, the 3rd, 5th, 7th or 9th.

Offering a final piece of advice, she revealed that some of her songs had benefited from the inclusion of a 'pre-chorus', and suggested I listen out for the device when playing her CDs.

'It's a difficult trick to pull off, however. Wait until you are proficient with the basic song forms,' she urged.

All too soon the lesson was over and we were ushered from the studio by the over-zealous shop assistant. It took me only a few seconds to realise there had to be a second, and a third, and a fourth, songwriting class. I asked whether this was possible for her. 'Yes,' she said. It was. We decided to meet no more frequently than every fourth week, this being a reasonable time for a budding songwriter to make some progress. After all, tunesmithing was nothing like scale practice or repetitive five-finger exercises: a good song takes time to bake. She predicted there would be periods, months even, when a song would lie dormant, waiting for the right time to hatch. 'Songs need nurturing,' she explained.

My goodness. For someone who had never taught songwriting before, I had certainly received my money's worth! In teaching mode, my tutor was thoughtful, focused and insightful. We were both on a journey of discovery, unable to control the escalator that carried us. As unexpected friends, we nevertheless needed to formalise the arrangement and agree on a fee for my tuition. That proved simple enough; the going rate for a piano lesson. Commerce out of the way, our collaboration began in earnest. Out was music theory, in was creativity: I was to be a storyteller. And with that, we left. Neither of us was sure we would use that practice room again, however. The space was great, the piano divine, but the cost a little high and the locked door a tad too stuffy for our taste.

A month later, I was on the train to London again.

Lesson two. A new venue. And this time I came prepared with the seeds of my first song; literally.

32

AS TREES WE STAND

'People ask me how I make music. I tell them I just step into it. It's like stepping into a river and joining the flow. Every moment in the river has its song.' – Michael Jackson

My friend, custodian of snowmen and songwriting tutor had suggested in an email that our next lesson should focus on 'finding my song centre'. We should try, she said 'to reveal the hidden meaning buried in your writing'. My homework for the month was to write! Furiously and often. And she did not mean chords.

'Write about anything and everything,' she insisted. 'Look around. Observe people, places and emotions to find inspiration. Be authentic. Study what you write closely. Find its essence. If you can, try to express your message in no more than four words.'

She recommended I obtain a songwriting journal.

'Keep it with you at all times. Make writing a daily habit,' she urged.

I did what I was told. Now, with two notebooks, one for creative writing and one to record daily practice, I felt like a real musician.

A month later we met in a different part of town, another piano showroom. Set out on the ground floor were several expensive-looking – forever beyond reach – grand pianos. Their names said it all: Fazioli, Grotrian-Steinweg, Steinway. Set further back were the uprights, mainly Bechsteins and Kawais. Guessing from our attire that we were not here to buy a new piano, the smartly dressed salesman directed us down a flight of stairs. My habit of taking music lessons in basements was certainly being ingrained. This basement was huge: hundreds of square feet, row upon row of 'for sale' uprights, each hoping to find a new home.

Two men, one elderly, one young (the apprentice?) were busy at work in a side room, a spacious and well-equipped workshop. Here, pianos of all shapes and sizes were being dismembered, renovated and reassembled. As a child, how I would have loved to tinker here, fascinated as I had been with the mechanism of our family piano, the front panel of which I had so often removed, distracting me from practice. Watching these skilled men at work, it would have been so natural for me to join them: no apprenticeship required. But I was here to write a song, not to fix up piano actions. And with that thought, everything clicked into place.

I was standing between two lives. The world of the analogue piano maker was that of the engineer. His technology may not have been digital, as dominated my career in the software industry, but it was a technology nonetheless: ask Steinway or Fazioli. And then it hit me. My goodness, I had been here before. Edgware Road, over forty years ago: the cluster of electronics shops I had frequented as a young man (now long gone) and which had inspired my love of computing. Standing here, in the piano showroom, I was straddling two lifetimes: the world of my youth and that of my future as a musician. And once again the escalator pulled me forward, away from my engineering past which, I suspected strongly, would have been a far more comfortable and considerably less exacting retirement pastime (for me) than any genre of songwriting or piano technique. Confused by the opposing poles of these two magnets, and marvelling at the coincidence, the physical presence of my friend and tutor pulled me back to the present. No, there was no confusion. I was here to become something *other* than my previous self. Yes, that was it. And in an instant we were hunting around for our allocated practice room. A computer monitor strung up on the far wall listed those available: who had booked them, for when and for how long. My name appeared on the screen: room thirteen, two hours, two o'clock. Behind the door we could hear someone playing – gloriously; the comparison with my meagre efforts stark. And there it was again, the thing I wanted to be able to do: make music. All further thought of my engineering past was forgotten.

At our allotted time, the door opened and the young pianist left in a rush, a cloth bag slung over one shoulder and carrying a pile of music books under both arms. She looked like a student hurrying to a lecture. Was there a music college nearby? Piano music leaked from many of the rooms. And there was singing, classical opera and musical theatre; not a cacophony, more a mingling of styles, and attractive in its way. I wondered what the soundproofing would be like once we were inside our practice room. What I did not expect, on entering room thirteen, were the reflections. Two sides of the space were mirrored, floor to ceiling. I immediately felt exposed. I've always hated looking at photographs of myself, and here I was, full length, front and side. Terrible. My tutor also found the room intimidating. I was quick to reassure her that she was far more photogenic than I. We laughed. But for me it was not only my appearance that worried me. The reflection exposed my apprehension about the creative process itself. To write a song! Was I about to make a fool of myself? What on earth was I doing here?

'How did you get on?' she asked.

Reaching for my briefcase, I extracted my homework.

My tutor had advised not to write a complete song lyric too early in the process. I should 'write freely' about something I cared about and which 'meant something' to me and which I wanted to 'share with others'. I was to 'trust the process', she said.

I had written a short piece entitled 'Trees'. It went like this:

There is a tree.

It stands in a forest. An out of the ordinary tree. Not like any other tree. Not all all. Not one bit. Quite unlike those others.

The tree stands alone.

Surrounded by many other trees, yet so unlike them. A gentle wind rustles their branches. The tree is unmoved by the chatter of others. Rooted, still as the night. In the forest.

A tree is a living thing.

It has form, shaped by the ground from whence it came. Geometry. The tree grew as itself alone, not as any other. For this is no bland or uniform medium in which, as if a crystal, it emerges identically to all others. The medium we call the earth is a riot of chaos. Soil, stones, rocks, worms, crevices and fissures.

Where the seed that began this tree fell, there its form was cast. Predetermined. Its roots found their way, as all roots must. Feeling their way, avoiding ... obstacles. Stones. Crevices. Seeking ... water. Little by little, the tree inched its way.

Above and beneath, the leaves littered around its base, the tree was shaped by the progress of its life. Unique. The tree must surely be treasured. It stands, in a forest, magnificent in its singular form, glowing with spirit. An individual.

There is a tree. An out of the ordinary tree. Not like any other. Not all all. Not one bit. Quite unlike those others.

She loved it. I must admit I thought it was somewhat effective, but precisely how it could or would turn into a song I had no idea.

'Did you find its centre?' she asked.

I admitted I had struggled. The best I had come up with were four rather uninspiring and repetitive ideas:

Tree

A tree

There is a tree

Not like any other (tree)

I asked whether she thought any of those would work as a song title.

'Hmm,' she said, looking doubtful, 'that's not what I meant by "song centre". Titles come later. First, we need to know what this song is about ... what it is *really* about.'

I nodded wisely.

And she began to ask questions:

'Is this a story about trees? Or about people?

'Is there a metaphor here? What can we learn from your story?

'Are *we* the trees?'

I began to see what she was driving at.

She suggested we 'spend five to ten minutes brainstorming alternative centres for the song'.

'Shall we?' she urged.

I said, yes.

Anticipating that something of this sort might be needed, and true to my consulting background, I had brought along several packs of Post-it notes. Dividing the pads between us, we each set to work. Every thought or idea was placed on the mirrored wall to our left. It provided an ideal adhesive surface for the yellow stickies. Minutes passed in silence as, note by note, the Post-its were consumed. And it quickly became apparent who had the most ideas. She was on a roll, I was struggling. By the time my tutor called a halt, her section of mirrored wall, about a metre square, was covered in yellow. She then suggested we discuss each other's ideas to see which could be discarded.

'Let's go through them one by one,' she suggested, 'You go first.'

And we did.

The majority of our scribblings were, we agreed, not song centres. One was rather amusing: 'geo-me-tree'. Yes, that was mine; sorry. However, there was one Post-it in particular which stood heads and shoulders above the rest. Far beyond. It was:

As Trees We Stand.

And of course, this Post-it was written in her hand. We immediately saw the strength of the idea, all others now seeming tired, naïve or weak, or all three. There was really no other option, we had our song centre. It told my story in four short words. As … Trees … We … Stand. It was about us, not about trees, which, on reflection, would have been a tricky subject for me to tackle with a view to my first 'hit single'. The four words sounded good to me, but my tutor was quick to stress that, 'At this stage, nothing should be set in stone. There are no rules in songwriting. Anything can change, at any time. Let's be prepared to adapt, extend and enrich the idea as the song develops. Our centre is not yet a song title, but may become one.'

I could only agree.

The next hour was intense. Our initial brainstorm had occupied the first forty-five minutes of the two-hour slot I had booked. The piano, which I longed to touch, had not been used and all we had was a single line! As ... Trees ... We ... Stand. The more I said it, however, the more I liked it. Hey, I was going to write a song. A good song!

'So, what happens next?' I asked, impatient to move ahead.

'More brainstorming,' came the reply. 'We have to develop the imagery, drawing on the ideas in your original creative writing.'

Another pack of Post-it notes was opened and shared between us.

She went on: 'Let's write freely again. What does our phrase suggest to you? What associations does it create? Does it invoke any specific or unusual emotions? Don't worry about the poetry to come, just write whatever comes to mind on a new Post-it. Strictly one thought per sticky. Think of these ideas as lines in the song, if you must.'

I was encouraged to look again at my original story and consider how I might summarise it? What I had was:

A seed falls in a random place on the ground

The place where it fell determines its future

Working alone for the next few minutes, the mirrored glass filled again. And once more we dissected each other's ideas, focusing attention on those ideas which might – if given an imaginative shove – form the basis for a line of a verse or the chorus of our song. We were reaching for short lines or couplets that could be repeated. Here are a few we found:

We walk among each other as if through a forest of trees.

There are, among us, trees so beautiful it can make us cry.

Listening to each other takes time, time for us to grow.

A forest of people. We count ourselves as trees.

As individuals we grow, reaching to the skies, our roots firm in the ground.

Together we make a forest so magical it takes our breath away.

Where the seed fell upon the softened ground

A sprout turns into a branch, turns into a leaf, turns into gold.

Well, it certainly wasn't a song, but there *were* ideas here.

Lesson time was fast running out and there was still so much to do.

'We can get started on the lyrics,' she said, 'but only in outline. I just want to give you a sense of the process. Normally, you would work at this over a day or two.'

It fell to me to collect all the Post-it notes, take them home and complete the lyrics, to my satisfaction at least, based on one of the song structures she had suggested during our earlier tutorial.

'As songwriters,' she urged, 'we need to pay attention to the lilt of the words if we are to find lines of poetry that can be sung.'

Her explanation recalled something I had once read in a theory book: the importance of the 'natural rise and fall of the voice and the rhythm of spoken utterances'. Yes, prosody.

We now abandoned the Post-its, speaking our ideas out loud as they occurred to us. My tutor would suggest a line, then I another. Back and forth, over and over; it almost felt like we were singing a duet. And while we did so, she urged me to listen for the reusable elements strong enough to form 'repeats' in the lyric: short phrases which could start or end a chorus, or break out a series of contrasting verses. Listening to the way she explained the process, I felt it must be like, yet unlike, the methods poets use; another field I must explore. And, like magic, verses emerged. Fearing we might lose them, we scribbled furiously in our journals:

> There is a tree,
> And the tree stands alone,
> There is a tree, there is a tree.
>
> A tree is a living thing,
> Not like any other,
> A tree is a living thing, a living thing.
>
> If I were a tree,
> There is a tree for you and a tree for me,
> If I were that tree, unlike any other.
>
> We walk among each other,
> We grow as if trees,
> The beauty of another,
> And how they came to be.

Wow, almost a lyric.

Then a pause, before she suggested: 'We should read it out loud.

(And we did.)

'Do you think the sentiment is strong enough?

(Yes.)

'What do you like or dislike?

'Think back to your original story.

(OK.)

'Is the lyric rooted in your writing?

'Could you see these words in a song?'

And I could, I really could. But then I witnessed the real songwriter in the room weave her magic. It happened in an instant, barely noticed. A chorus was needed, something to separate the verses. And my unexpected friend, the songwriter who would one day bring my snowman to life, spoke out loud:

And together we are,
Together we can,
Together we stand as trees, strong.
As trees we stand.

There it was. Our song! Two hours, end to end. And I had never touched the piano, and she had never opened her guitar case. I expect you can guess what my homework was?

We had no music.

33

EAR TRAINING

> 'Heard melodies are sweet, but those unheard are sweeter. Therefore, ye soft pipes, play on.' – John Keats, 'Ode on a Grecian Urn'

The next month flew by. Whether it was productive is quite a different matter. By the date of my next songwriting class, I needed to have finalised my lyrics and have concrete musical ideas on paper from which we could work. Yet four weeks seemed far too long to agonise over a few verses, a handful of chords and a sketch of a melody. Songwriting, while important, was only a part of the work I needed to get through each day. Theory, improvisation, technique, ear training; all had to progress if I were to advance as a musician. Ah, ear training, what to make of that?

Flashback. One year earlier.

I had been aware of the need to develop my ear for over a year. It was not coming easily. If I could not remedy this weakness, it would limit me on so many fronts. Without a serviceable ear you are not a musician, it's that simple. Whether just setting out or about to take up a place at college, I cannot emphasise it more: ear training will help, even if you never aspire to play a concerto or compose a song. It took me a long time to bottom out what ear training actually was. I had been listening to music all my life; but was I *hearing* it?

During the first few weeks with my adult piano teacher, he had tested my ear on several occasions. Could I recognise musical intervals with my back turned or eyes closed? Was I able to tell a major third from a minor?

What about the distinct sound of the 4th? Could I distinguish it from the 5th? They sounded remarkably similar to me. It did not help that inversion muddied the waters. C-G was a fifth, G-C was a fourth, same tones, different interval. And what about the reversal of the 3rd, the inverted 6th? After a few weeks of these and other tests, my ear had improved. But the small step up amounted to little more than a blip. A more thorough examination was needed. My ear was being probed.

Could I, my teacher wanted to know, distinguish the three inversions of the major and minor triads? What about 7th chords comprising four notes? Was I able to differentiate the major 7th and the minor 7th, in each of their four inversions? Could I hear the interval between the bass note and the tonic in each? No, I could not.

I tried. I did. Practising at home, in the semi-dark, I must have played a hundred variations of such intervals, listening meticulously, trying desperately to distinguish their quality and colour. What I found shocked me: I had a terrible ear. Anything more complicated than the intervals schoolchildren learn, I was flunking. As a result, when playing a melody by ear, I was mostly picking random notes until they 'sounded right'. The trial-by-error process was painful, frustrating and long-winded. Worse, when I improvised a melody of my own, I was hitting 'avoid notes' more often than a discerning listener would appreciate. Somehow or other I needed to 'hear in advance' and go straight to the correct place in the scale, or, if the mood took me, to the non-scale notes that nevertheless 'worked' over the chord I was voicing. But how?

Enough was enough: this ear training stuff needed to be taken seriously. I was only too well aware that a smattering of aural training was included in all practical examinations and that aural played a prominent role in grade seven theory and beyond. Without a trained ear, how could I ever complete or harmonize a melody in the examination hall, where not even humming was permitted? Which exposed another hornet's nest: sight-singing. Could I sing a notated tune from sight? I could pick it out on the keyboard and *then* sing it, but this would not be allowed during an exam. No, I had to be able to 'sing in my head' without actually singing. Try it. I found it more than hard, next to impossible. Without exercising my vocal cords it was tricky to pitch even a single note, let alone a tune.

What to do? As so often before, I set out to find a helpful book. A quick search revealed a pile of them, but one series stood out. It had many positive reviews, and I immediately ordered grades one to six, intending to work through each systematically. What I found was disappointing: I would fail a grade three ear training test.

I shared my dismay with my teacher. He suggested I go back to the drawing board, start over, and begin by distinguishing tones from semitones, at as many points on the keyboard as I could muster. At first, I simply alternated notes E and F and B and C, immediately switching to notes a tone apart. I performed this ritual daily for a couple of weeks and found the test straightforward. My teacher then suggested playing in different registers: one, two or even three octaves apart. That was tough. Try distinguishing a tone from a semitone when one note is two octaves below middle C and the other two octaves above! The remedy? Singing suddenly starts to make sense. I have the most dreadful voice, but this hardly mattered. I was now singing the melody line of almost everything I played (when people were out of the house). As a result, my ability to pick out the notes of a previously unheard song improved. For simple melodies, I was now note-perfect. The trick was to listen to the song through once or twice, hear its root, decide which scale it was written in by identifying a few notes, and then keying into that mode. If the piece was in E♭ minor, for example, I knew from my scale work which notes to use, barring any accidentals. Those proved challenging. I should have guessed; being able to recognise chromatic notes 'out of the prevailing key' is inherent to all music. Few tunes, if any, stick strictly to the diatonic; most steal tones from parallel and relative minors. Classical music modulates to related keys and back again. Jazz and other contemporary music continuously shifts to new – often surprising – keys. Even pop tunes modulate, if only by a tone. An ear able to move freely among keys is a mark of the advanced musician.

A smartphone app helped enormously. It offered an extensive (and I do mean extensive!) set of 'graded interactive exercises' that grew in complexity as I was learning. The clever software played individual notes, pairs of notes or chords, in varied sequences, and asked the listener to either 'check the box' corresponding to the intervals they think they heard or to 'pick out notes' using an on-screen piano keyboard. The software created variety by using inversions and randomly moving them around the keyboard, in the mid-range, in the high and low registers and by altering the number of octaves between note pairs. Obtaining 100 per cent success in the tests was next to impossible. But over time I improved again. Six months later, I was reaching 95 per cent in most exercises.

Listening to music 'ears open', my teacher assured me, would secure further benefits. Well, I had indeed heard a great deal and had done so since childhood. I loved music, but perhaps I had never 'heard' the music as he did and as every other competent musician has learnt to do.

'Howard, your ear has improved beyond recognition,' he reassured me. 'Now its time to focus on hearing the harmony,' he said.

Could I, he wondered, recognise when 'the changes' occurred? That's the term jazz musicians use to refer to a chord progression. In jazz, there is often a change of harmony once or twice in every bar; sometimes on every beat. He suggested I start with the 2-5-1, the ubiquitous progression he had taught me how to play during the first few months of our work together. And yes, over time, I did come to recognise the 2-5-1 whenever I heard it. In fact, I could hardly avoid it! It became a family joke. Whatever we were listening to – radio, TV, CD – my ear had become super-sensitive to its arrival, to the point where I could overdub the music in real time, at tempo, with the words TWO … FIVE … ONE. My wife, a good singer, was also becoming skilled at this parlour game; once she realised what I was doing. And I had started to 'hear' and recognise a few other progressions. The 6-2-5-1 and the 1-6-4-2-5-1 were the next to fall to my enhanced ear. Where I fell down, however, and fell down severely, was hearing the bass.

I could hear a bassline in the sense that anyone can, but unlike melody, which I could now hear clearly in my mind, basslines never came into mental focus. They 'sounded' fuzzy, as if the bass guitar or double bass were playing in another room – wrapped in cotton wool. The tones were blurred, indistinct; I could not distinguish where they sat in the scale. To put it simply, I could not sing along with the bass as I could with the melody. Unless rectified, this disability would limit further refinement of my ear because the bass note determines so much about the flow of the music. For a chord in root position, the bass note is the root. For a chord in first inversion, the bass is the 3rd of the scale. And so on. Not to hear the bass was, in a real sense, not to hear the music at all! Again, I discussed this with my teacher.

'I find that my pupils are either top-down or bottom-up listeners,' I remember him telling me. What he meant was that most people 'hear' best somewhere in the middle of the mix. As they reach for other notes and develop their sense of harmony, some tend to be influenced by higher tones (melody notes), and others by lower frequencies (basslines). I was a top-down listener, he was sure, so I had to 'reach down' a long way before I could accurately hear, play or transcribe (I wish) the bass. As the bass is, by definition, the foundation of all harmony, any top-down weakness would also limit my sense of where the music was heading, a vital skill in any form of improvisation. As my penfriend put it succinctly, 'So are you telling me that a good jazz musician senses and hears patterns of music without thinking about which note it is they are looking for? Have they therefore reached the point where they can hear the patterns faster than they can predict what notes they will need?'

'Yes,' I replied, 'it does feel like that. And also, I need to hear the prevailing mode of the piece. If the music is in Dorian, for example, I must hear that distinctive sound – the presence of the major 6th – in the otherwise "minor" scale. Same with the augmented 4th, the signature note of the otherwise "major sounding" Lydian scale.'

There seemed no end to the depth of aural training. Music was, after all, nothing but sound. What else would I expect?

A useful exercise was to sing the 'inner voices' of a chord progression. Hard. Let's suppose I was playing a 2-5-1 using 7th chords. I would pick out the 3rd, 5th or 7th of the first chord and, singing it, would follow the inner line as it wove its way through the harmony. This allowed me to more clearly hear 'the changes', not via the melody note at the top, nor via the bass note at the bottom, but via the innermost parts (the equivalent in choral music of the alto and tenor voices). Once I 'heard' these middling notes, I better appreciated what it meant to be a backing vocalist or supporting instrumentalist. I was singing what they could be playing during a performance. All this helped enormously, and I was now singing everything I played, top lines, middle and bass. As a result, I was hearing how each voice 'moved'. That's the voice-leading I have mentioned before and whose importance my teacher drummed into me at every juncture.

So where am I now, in terms of aural training? My ear has improved, not doubt about it, but I judge that it remains to this day the weakest link in an otherwise advancing musician. Unless I find a remedy, I have no hope of progressing to the highest grades of theory, nor to musical transcription. My ear training must continue, but I admit I find it challenging to keep up the momentum and build the required time into daily practice. Listen, Understand, Play, Transcribe. How else can a musician improve? Simple pop songs, yes – even I could now join a band, jump on stage and jam along with the best of them. It would be embarrassing initially, I would make (many) mistakes, but I reckon I could get there. As to more complex music, and especially jazz, forget improvisation with others: I can hardly keep up with myself!

My teacher, also a composer and arranger, had an almost super-human ear. No matter what combination of notes I pressed on the keyboard (or how many), he could call them out. And sing them. And do so even when buried deep in a mix, within a complex arrangement involving several instruments and timbres. He once floored me. I cannot remember what we were listening to, but there was a specific bar where I detected that an unexpected note had sounded, tucked away alongside the others, hidden. He picked it out immediately, named the tone and played it. And then spelt out the chord it formed with the rest of the notes in the bar. Amazing. How my teacher developed such an ear is a mystery to me. He once claimed it was the result of working as a semi-professional bass player for so many years. He called it 'the power of the bass', the root of all harmony. And perhaps he was right. Did I need to play bass in addition to piano, like my teacher? Maybe the idea of crafting my own fretless five-string should now get underway; in my other woodshed? Right now, however, I had a song to write.

Back to the present.

Songwriting. What on earth had I been doing all month? I had not finalised the lyrics as my songwriting tutor had asked, nor did I have a single musical idea of my own to bring to the party. Why? Elements of my journey, previously front and centre, were losing their significance. Songwriting was changing me, providing a purpose to what had been, to this point, a mostly theoretical exploration. Sterile theory, scale patterns, chord shapes ... these no longer held my attention, leaving me bare and exposed. This was alien territory for me, a murky pool obscuring a previously uninterrupted view of what lay ahead on the escalator. I was to write a song. A song! How? The creative act I imagined was the polar opposite of everything of my past life in the computer industry with its rigour, logic and rationality. The change I sought in retirement was working out. I was letting go. No longer afraid to fail, I was about to 'put myself out there'. The inexorable forward motion of the escalator had run its course.

In a moment of sheer panic, I found a new focus. And it was thrilling.

34

UNBOUND

In which I fail to write a first song, yet unexpectedly succeed with a second. We rehearse in private. Further mysteries of songwriting are revealed.

With only a few days left before my next tutorial, and desperate to finalise the lyrics to 'As Trees We Stand', I was struggling. How can I describe the pain? Hour by hour, day by day, I tried to find some semblance of a progression or snatch of a melody to which our words could be hitched. Each improvisation felt, and sounded, artificial. If the chords worked, the lyric did not fit. If I played against the lyric, the music felt dull, awkward or worse. Nothing seemed to be working. It was like shoehorning two entirely incompatible components together that had been independently manufactured, with no correspondence between their fit, angles and joints. The result was either naïve, inept or malformed; often at the same time. How could I possibly write a song this way? And if I did, could it ever be beautiful? The emotional love song I aspired to write for my wife was not just far away, it was off the map.

The tutorial proved equally frustrating. My tutor liked the final version of the poetry I had settled on but pointed out that my verses did not have a regular spoken rhythm. This, she said, would 'complicate the music', and went on to show how I could recast the lines to be closer to the cadences of natural speech, by simplifying the couplets, heightening their dramatic effect, yet retaining their meaning. I made a mental note to read more poetry. Taking the first of my verses and the chorus as an example, she picked up her guitar and, without thinking, began to sing.

The melody appeared to come from nowhere and the chords 'just fitted'. She was doing what a jazz musician would call improvisation ... except there was no lead sheet. She was composing in real time, out of thin air. Remarkable. I could just about see what she was doing, but how I would ever do the same I could not imagine. The words had predated the music, but now they emanated from her as one, unified. As she sang, often just the first word or two, her hands would move or twitch on the guitar's fret-board as if in a moment of creation; hesitant, questioning, before making her next move. A chess game. Her face told the story.

'Could this work? What about this? Shall I try something different?' she seemed to be asking, although without speaking a word. She was holding a musical conversation with herself. So familiar was she with her two instruments – voice and guitar – that my friend was able to doodle tens of musical ideas in a minute or two, experimenting with each until the melodic and harmonic ideas clicked into place. She would then use the riff or motif and try it out with words from my other verses.

Then, suddenly stopping, she looked directly at me and insisted, 'Now you try. Forget what I just did. I want you to create your own music.'

Goodness.

She expected me to solve the puzzle that is songwriting in the same spirit she had demonstrated, and if I could not sing, or did not wish to, I should hum while accompanying myself at the piano. So this was it, the moment had arrived. I was to create music in front of another human being. I cannot overstate how excruciating this could have been. Yet it was a measure of our friendship – her calm, quiet, reassuring manner – that I found the courage to try.

I should explain that we often recorded these sessions together. I owned a handheld digital recorder and, attached to a small camera tripod, we generally turned the device on at the start of every lesson. On this occasion, though, I had forgotten. My tutor reminded me to do so. Leaning over, I pressed RECORD – bad idea. As I began to improvise, the device loomed large, chuckling to itself behind my back as I struggled to find creative expression. Was it the presence of the recorder, or simply my ill-preparedness for such a step? In any case it was an ordeal, and I was much relieved when we both realised it was nearly time to vacate the practice room. Another two hours had passed. We quickly agreed on a few final tweaks to the lyrics and jotted down the names of the chords I had found at the keyboard. It was not much; a ragbag of ideas. A month had elapsed since the Post-it note brainstorms that had led to 'As Trees We Stand', and now there would be another four weeks before we could meet again. How could I write a song this way, stretched out over so many weeks? Hadn't my tutor told me that many of her best songs had been written in a day, or less? One story stuck in my mind. During a radio show on which she was a guest, she had been asked to write a song as a challenge, there and then, in twenty minutes! And she had. Clearly, the month-by-month, step-at-a-time approach I was subjecting myself to was nothing like that. I could not reconcile the two.

After our lesson, over our usual post-lesson coffee, she told me more about how, from the age of twelve, she had always written songs.

'I've played and written hundreds,' she revealed, 'but only a few find their way to the studio. I'm working on my second album now and have fifty ideas already.'

'Really?' I asked, surprised and impressed.

'Yes,' she replied, encouraging me to be just as prolific. 'In your case, Howard, it should not matter how good or bad your songs are, but you must try to complete each one. That's important.'

She encouraged me to write a song – lyrics or music, or preferably both – as often as I could and no matter how trivial the sentiment might be. The process, she explained, should consist of an endless loop: create, throw away, create, keep, create, throw away, keep. As always with the advice she gave, I promised to try. And we left for our respective homes.

During future lessons, I did eventually become used to the recorder and managed to ignore it, but to this day I have not gone back and listened to the recordings of our time together. One day, perhaps.

At home, left with the remnants of the last tutorial, I wondered how I would ever finish 'As Trees We Stand'. A flurry of excitement one afternoon, a cute musical idea in Dorian mode appeared to fit … until I sang each of the verses. No, that did not work. The words would have to change again, and nothing I wrote that afternoon made any sense. I had drifted too far from the song I had envisaged. 'As Trees We Stand' was no longer a love song, if it ever was. And it was only then that I realised what the problem was. My lyrics were a sham. They may have been creative at the time I wrote them – I'll leave others to judge – but they were not from the heart and had been conjured up merely as fodder for a tutorial. My lyrics were shot through with artifice; I felt embarrassed about ever having written them. And so 'As Trees We Stand' remains to this day an odd-sounding poem, hidden away in my notebook.

I told my tutor of the unfortunate decision in an email, and she replied simply, 'It happens. I still love your words, though, Howard.' And so do I, if only because of the memories they evoke. There must be a song in there somewhere, it's just that I have no idea how to tease it out. Yet something of those early lessons must have stuck, for, a few days after putting 'As Trees We Stand' in the 'one day maybe' pile, 'Unbound' was born. And it came fast and furious.

My wife was out for the day. I made a large pot of coffee, disappeared to the woodshed and sat down at the piano. Adagio had joined me, as he so often did. Placing my pencil, eraser and a pad of blank stave paper on the music stand, I took a deep breath and played a C∆7 chord.

Two words popped into my head:

See me

And I sang them starting on the 7th, B (See), to the root C (me), ascending. And two more words:

Know me

Follow the circle. Follow the circle. F∆7. Reverse the melody. I sang an A (Know) and then an F (me). And there it was. I knew right away I had a song. Repeating the lines, I also knew in an instant where the music had to move to next: around the diatonic circle. Keeping the form of the music clear in my mind, I stepped away from the piano to complete the lyrics while Adagio watched from his basket.

Thirty minutes later and with a dozen sheets of paper strewn on the floor around me – hastily scribbled lists of words, rhymes, synonyms and acronyms – I had two short verses:

See me, know me,
Hold me close tonight,
Feel me, show me,
Take me to our light.

Help me, mould me,
Tell me how to be,
Heal me, lift me,
Listen to my plea.

It felt religious in tone. Was it the circle? Had my jazz teacher's roots in gospel music influenced my choice of chords? But this song was not a plea to a higher power. It was an honest and direct statement of fact, a message to my soul mate, my wife, the person who knows me best, suffers all my eccentricities and flaws and who is the only person who can, in the end, help me overcome them.

There was a song here, but all I had were two short verses. I needed a middle section and a chorus. New music was required, and the only tool I had to hand was the theory I had spent so long studying. Quickly, I dropped out of the C diatonic circle and into B minor. It sounded … mystical. And again, in a rush, words came to me fully formed:

Here I am, find me,
Corner of our room.

Sing our starlight sound,
Time together now,
Dream this dream unbound.

And the melody flowed naturally from the B minor harmony. I could not hold back my excitement. No exaggeration: electricity coursed through my body. Writing out the notes of my melody on stave paper, I spelt the names of the chords I had used along the top and wrote the lyrics underneath. It was a rough and ready lead sheet, no clearly marked rhythm, merely a couple of slurs to indicate the lilt of the poetry.

Singing the song under my breath, I was convinced it worked, but there was only one person who could confirm this: my friend and tutor. If I could have conjured her up there and then to give feedback, I would have, but I had to wait three more agonising weeks for that joy.

Unable to stop myself, I wrote to my penfriend with the news. I had written a song. Could I explain the harmony to him? I simply had to.

'The song uses the whole of the circle I told you about all those months ago,' I wrote excitedly. 'It's in C, but I omit the vii(dim) chord and instead use the second inversion of V (G over B). After this, the song segues into B minor, an unusual modulation, just a semitone away.'

Whether he understood any of this, I had no idea.

'In the middle section,' I went on, 'this creates a suspended sound to mirror the lyric at that point, "starlight sound", a suspended IV chord (E minor sus 4). I then shift briefly back to C via F∆7 (which is a tritone away from B and thus continues the ethereal middle-of-the-night effect as the line "Dream our dream unbound" is sung. Then it's back to C and the same circle of fifths as before.' Proudly, I added:

'To create variety, I use chords from the parallel minor. In other words, A♭ major (the VI-chord in C minor), and then return via substitution of the typical end-of-song cadence: dominant V to tonic I. Instead of the V chord, I use the flat-2 (D♭ as V): the tritone substitution in jazz.'

'The flat-2 dominant chord,' I explained, 'shares two essential notes with the usual V dominant chord. More overtones you see. This creates a cute dissonance at the end, holding the G throughout. And to create even more dissonance, I use the D♭ major-7th form of the chord. Throughout the song, I am using 7th chords to give a semi-religious gospel feel, rather than simpler classical triads.'

I so hoped my penfriend had understood.

Reflecting on the achievement, my refusal to allow the music and words to drift away from each other was the hardest part of the exercise by far. Had they done so, I would have been faced with the complex task of shoehorning one into the other. Much better to do as my tutor had demonstrated: to allow the song to emerge as one, music and words in tandem. All that was now left to do was to play her the song and witness her honest reaction.

We were in London again. The same basement.

She listened attentively as I picked out the chords and melody on the piano, pointing to verses of the lyric as I played along. She looked confused; had she not got it? My heart sank. Had I been mistaken and the song was a dud? Or was it my clumsy performance? The harmonies were unlike the folk-pop-inspired sequences in her music … would my style work for her? I suggested she sing the song through to hear my music (and harmony) more clearly. And she did, and I melted. Then, just as abruptly as she had begun, she stopped, looked at the lyric sheet and pointed to the last verse.

'This is sung to your wife, right?'

'Yes,' I confirmed.

'So, surely … in the final verse … isn't it "*You* show me, *you* know me" and "*You* help me, *you* mould me"?'

Of course. Silly me. Storytelling. The first verse made a statement. The subsequent verses revealed the answer. And with that slight adjustment to my lyric, the song was finished. My tutor loved it, and for the next hour we played around with details, she practising the melody with its sweeps and turns, me the piano accompaniment with its voice-led circle of fifths and modulation to B minor. Despite my nascent accompaniment skills, it sounded … professional.

Facing me from the opposite side of the piano, we rehearsed the song one more time. Maintaining eye contact throughout, the emotion of the piece – a plea to my wife and a reflection of my insecurity – overcame us. As my tutor sang the final verse, she blushed, and I looked away embarrassed. It was the power of my music. We broke off and fell about laughing. How on earth was I going to perform 'Unbound' for my wife? It was not the lyrics, though I do struggle with speeches at family gatherings, despite having spent much of my working life presenting keynotes at industry events. No, my apprehension about performing the love song was more prosaic than simple butterflies or stage fright. I could not sing.

FINALE

'Music isn't just a pleasure, a transient satisfaction. It's a need, a deep hunger; and when the music is right, it's joy. Love. A foretaste of heaven. A comfort in grief. Is it too much to think that perhaps God speaks to us sometimes through music? How, then, could I be so ungrateful as to refuse the message?'

Orson Scott Card

35

DREAMS AND COINCIDENCES

In which I watch, spellbound, as a delightful poem written by my wife turns into a song for our friends. We experience our first house concert. I get another of my crazy ideas.

With my first song in the bag, but with no way of performing it for others, the weeks passed uneventfully. I felt … on hold. Often alone in the house, and having nothing better to do, I was drawn back to the music room, where I would sit for hours at the piano, repeating exercises I could already perform. Desperately hoping for a breakthrough, but unsure of what I was looking for, the time I was investing added nothing to my nascent ability. Curiously detached from the escalator, this period of my journey was unlike the blocks I had encountered before. Whatever this new block was, it would not be resolved by disappearing for a day or two to the woodshed to chip away at a technical problem preventing my hands from doing something they were resisting. No, this block was different. It felt like a malaise, a disconnection from my journey; and it frightened me. I think Adagio sensed my unease. I may have imagined this, but on the occasions when all I could do was to sit in silence, staring at my keyboard, our cat grew restless, furtive, and quietly left the room. *Nothing to see here …*

There were mornings when, after a fitful night, I woke with a start, as if from a nightmare, believing I had decided to drop the whole idea of becoming a musician. The horror of repeating my childhood mistake terrified me. Would I be able to surmount my regret a second time? These disturbing and destabilising feelings came and went: spectres that I felt were close but could never grasp. Perhaps my reticence to push on further was a by-product of exhaustion from the time and effort I had already invested? Or was it, as I feared, something darker? Had I been using the journey, and its unrealistic goals, strictures and repeated routines, to mask something else altogether? What was I hiding? There was nothing I could pin down. But yes ... how easy it would have been to give up, call it a day. A song written but not performed. To pat myself on the back for a job well done. I had to admit I could now play the piano, after a fashion. I could write simple songs. Surely I could now amuse myself for the rest of my life? Couldn't I? No. I could not. Deep down I knew I would never be content to camp out in a peaceful meadow, melding a soupçon of mediocre music-making into the gentle pace of a 'normal' life. If forced to accept such a reality, I might just as well never have started.

As you can tell, I was confused. My wife noticed a distinct change in my character. Perhaps it was the emotional music I was listening to? Or was it that, despite the songs I had written, my heart was telling me the journey from here on in would be harder than ever and I would eventually succumb to failure. The warnings I had received at the outset about 'unrealistic goals' haunted me more each day. Had my penfriend and his wife been right after all? Pushing the unpleasant thought from my mind, I had to believe I could go on. I saw no way off the escalator on which I had found myself and onto which I had stepped with such alacrity. I'd glimpsed an alternative world, a world I so desperately wanted to occupy but did not know how to obtain: to be a musician.

The interactions with my penfriend during this period did nothing to resolve the situation. Despite a flurry of notes in which I tried to characterise my malady, none of my friend's replies helped to pinpoint whatever was screwing with my mind. In fact our correspondence only made matters worse. I don't know what I was expecting from him. And then, one morning, an answer came, and in the most unexpected fashion.

My wife had just woken. I was downstairs making tea. Returning to our bedroom with the steaming brew, my wife, sitting up in bed, pencil and paper in hand, seemed eager to share something. Ignoring the tea I had brought her, and holding a scrap of paper aloft, she explained:

'Howard, the weirdest thing … some words came to me all of a sudden. I've written them down; I've not had to change a thing. They just fell into place. Listen,' she urged.

'Of course,' I said, surprised.

I put down the tray of morning tea to signal that I was listening, and my wife read me … what? A poem? A story?

Her words spoke of friends, of how friendships carry us through uncertain times as we look to the future, reflect on our childhood and ponder what might lie ahead. As she read aloud, perhaps nervous of my reaction, I was transfixed. I did not admit it at the time, but the nostalgia of my wife's verse perfectly captured my feelings about the hiatus in my musical journey. She, of course, had nothing of the sort in mind. Her inspiration had come from the precious occasions when our friends joined us for dinner, and, sitting out under the stars, we would light a fire, huddle together and just chat, trying to make sense of whatever worrisome development was happening in the world (no doubt exaggerated by the pervasive presence of twenty-four-hour news, social media and the curse of smartphone notifications).

What surprised me about my wife's waking dream, if indeed that was what this was, is that she is not known for writing. Maybe as a child, like most of us, she had scribbled a few lines of poetry or the outline of a story she hoped one day to bring to life. Beyond this, I knew of nothing. Yet this morning, these words were … lovely. Fully formed, gentle rhymes, neatly structured. Hey, it was a song, right there! My wife had dreamt, or been inspired to write, a beautiful lyric. Either way, it mattered not. There it was, on the page. Ten minutes' work, no more, the time I had taken to visit the bathroom, put the kettle on, make tea and return to our bedroom. Neither of us understood how such a creative act could have occurred.

Over the following few days, we read the friendship lyrics again and again and came to love them. And the inevitable occurred to us … perhaps I could write the music for my wife's words: a song she could then sing and I could play?

We tried. Really, we did. But we could not. Whatever I composed – too grandiose a word by far – was not working. The musical ideas were tolerable as far as they went, but my wife had imagined a distinct and specific style for her poetry, a genre I could not emulate: I was not a proficient enough tunesmith. And there we left it until, a week later, I had an idea that would jerk my imagined musical life forward another notch.

With my next songwriting lesson looming large and failing to make progress on a new song of my own, I made the following suggestion:

'Why don't you take my slot, darling? Do it. Take your lovely words and see what my tutor can do. I am sure she would enjoy the challenge.'

My wife felt apprehensive about the idea, perhaps fearing that the tutorial would be awkward, embarrassing, ineffective, or all three.

'No,' she said, 'much better *you* take my words and see what the two of you can cook up? You have the rapport with her. You admitted your latest song is not coming together. My words are ready.'

And they were.

I knocked out a quick email to my tutor, asking whether she liked the sentiment behind my wife's writing and would she consider setting the words to music? Back came her reply. She 'loved them' and thought the idea 'simply wonderful'. And so my wife's lyrics became the raw material of my next songwriting class.

Two hours. One lesson. Is it possible to write a song in two hours? I saw it with my own eyes. Magic! I played no part other than to observe. I remember explaining the style my wife had in mind, but this instruction turned out to be entirely unnecessary. To a real songwriter the lyrics said it all, and by the end of the session they had been transformed, miraculously, into the most beautiful music, the guitar accompaniment beguiling. We agreed to call it 'Friendship Song'.

Lesson over, and more than excited, I raced home so my wife could hear the rough-and-ready recording. She was more than pleased. Her lyric, not a single word changed, had been brought to life, and just as she had imagined. And right there, right then, everything clicked into place.

Flashback. One week.

I had attended a folk concert in London: an artist my wife and I adore. She was to have accompanied me but had been struck down by a nasty cold. The gig was adorable and I so wanted my wife to relive it with me. As the final song ended, I stepped up to the stage and politely asked the artist when she and her band were next performing live.

'Well, we have a house concert next week,' she replied, 'I am sure there are a few tickets left.'

I asked where the event was taking place, and she mentioned a village in Sussex, on the South Coast. Something about the name rang a bell. My goodness, it was the community where my wife had been brought up as a child. Not only that, and much to our surprise, the house hosting the gig was on the same road – on the edge of the South Downs – where her family home had been and which held so many fond memories. I kid you not. The coincidence was too spooky by far. We snapped up two tickets and decided to make a day of it.

On the day of the concert, we travelled to the area early. Revisiting her old stomping ground, my wife thoroughly enjoyed herself, and yes, we eventually did find the house where she had grown up. Little had changed. And there, just a few doors away, was the venue for the evening's entertainment.

Greeted by the host as though we were long-lost friends, the atmosphere was immediately welcoming. There followed an evening of intimate and exquisite folk music, more than we could have hoped. A dream. And, as a by-product, we experienced our first 'house concert', where – yes – we chanted 'oms' – which I earlier presented as evidence of my penfriend's suspicion of the mystical. He was wrong about that. Wasn't he? This meeting of two worlds, separated by over four decades, was surely more than serendipity; it was mystical; other-worldly. To me, our attendance at the house concert on the edge of the South Downs was meant to be; the connection to my wife's childhood too strong to be denied. Had I not been in London the week before and asked that simple question of the artist, we would never have known about the concert, the village, the house, the road it sat in and its strange intersection with my wife's family. Moreover, the next thought might never have occurred to us: could we host a house concert of our own? Why not! All our friends would come, we felt sure. And as soon as we said it, all the ingredients fell into place. My unexpected friend, whom I had met by chance at a concert in London, to whom I had given a snowman, and who had become my songwriting tutor, could perform a set for our friends. She would entertain us with her beautiful songs and tell stories of her journey to music. Our son, an excellent drummer, would add acoustic percussion. There would be much food and wine. And the evening would end with my wife's 'Friendship Song', an ode to our friends, for whom the concert we imagined was dedicated. Perfect.

And sitting right there, tucked away at the back of my mind, unbeknown to my wife, was my song, 'Unbound', the words and music I had written for her, and of which she knew absolutely nothing. Here then was my opportunity to perform. My songwriting tutor would, I was sure, agree to be my vocalist. It was to be a night filled with the sound of songs, beauty and joy.

I could hardly contain my excitement.

36

THE LIVING-ROOM CONCERT

In which we manage to keep the lid on the emotional roller coaster, exhaust our artist, and find solace in talking things through with friends.

In the weeks leading up to the living-room concert I became increasingly obsessed with overseeing every tiny detail. Nothing escaped my attention, no matter how inconsequential. My wife found this, and I think me, wearying. For her, the evening was nothing more than an abnormally large party. For me, it was everything I had worked towards, the culmination of my time on the escalator. Despite my interference, much of the organisation fell to my wife:

> You are invited to an evening of friendship and songs.
> Buffet meal and drinks beforehand.
> Entertainment to include 'Friendship Song'.

Finding a suitable day for the event, convenient for our friends and our artist, was far from straightforward. As I saw it, there was no point concluding a concert with a song about supportive friends if the people to whom it was dedicated were absent. The to and fro of emails, text messages and phone calls, as we homed in on a date everyone could commit to, was no easy task; especially as we hoped our children – whose diaries were always overflowing – would be able to join us.

In total, thirty people were invited. A few had heard of my wife's sudden inspiration but not the means by which her words had been transformed. Intrigue filled the air. Everyone eventually replied in the affirmative to the RVSP. Among them – how could it be otherwise – was my lifelong friend whose correspondence over the preceding three years had led inexorably to this day and to this book. He was joined by his wife, the person whose searching question had revealed so much about my determination to become a musician. And, joy, our son and daughter were able to join us. Quorum!

A living-room concert is not to be undertaken lightly. Fortunately, I already owned the majority of the necessary equipment. This included microphones and stands, a mixing desk, amplification and speakers. To heighten the atmosphere I obtained a set of gorgeous fairy lights, a scattering of soft candles and a few coloured lamps, all to be set out around the periphery of our living area. Our TV and other unnecessary furniture was moved upstairs, out of the way. Chairs were pushed back against the wall and the centre of the room filled with large comfy cushions. Given the numbers we expected, it would be cosy. Just right.

Our artist arrived in good time, for an early lunch. We gave her an upstairs guest room in which to relax; my wife had placed flowers in front of the bedroom mirror – a lovely touch. In the entrance hall below, I set aside a table so my friend could display her CDs and guest book. A spare laptop was co-opted for a running slide show of her promotional videos and delightful animations. Among these, of course, was the stick figure animation that had first caught my attention with his simple message of 'Hello!' Without this connection, I would never have sent her the email suggesting our snowman collaboration, and much of what had transpired over the proceeding months would never have occurred. It is no exaggeration to suggest that, without her trust of a stranger, I might have tripped and fallen from the escalator a long time ago. A circle was closing. It felt like the circle of fifths returning to the tonic.

We spent the majority of the afternoon testing the sound stage, tuning guitars and practising the songs. Our son's cajón and other acoustic percussion was placed to the left of the microphone, my keyboard to the right. With everything in place, it looked for all the world as if we were a band. He had never played with her before and found she was, quite rightly, particular about the more unusual rhythms in her music. Fortunately, our son is a fast learner; I had complete confidence in him. I only wish I could have said the same of myself. It was mid-afternoon, and I was already nervous. My song, 'Unbound', would be an emotional roller coaster for at least three people in the room.

I was to perform a love song for my wife in front of her closest friends. Scary stuff. Worse, this was not a tune others would know or immediately understand the sentiment therein; the words were my own; I was baring my soul. If I had misjudged how to communicate my message, there could be considerable embarrassment all round. There was one silver lining: it was not me who was going to sing; that would have been truly awful for all. I was to accompany my songwriting tutor on keyboards: an elegant Rhodes sample I had prepared for the occasion. She was to sing the words of my love song. To my wife! That in itself could lead to misunderstanding. As the afternoon wore on and the reality of what was to transpire sank in, I began to have concerns about whether we would be able to keep the lid on the heady brew. It did not help that, a couple of weeks earlier, I had inadvertently left the lyric sheet to 'Unbound' lying open on top of our piano. My wife had come across it and could not avoid scanning the first few lines. She knew I had been working on something for the concert but had no idea the song was dedicated to her. That fact was now glaringly obvious. Guessing that I wanted it kept secret, she quickly averted her eyes, but the lines she had seen left her with an uneasy feeling about the lyrics. What did they mean? Why was her husband saying this, and what would her friends think?

Later that evening, my wife spilt the beans and admitted she had come across the sheet by mistake. More than a little apprehensive about having the song performed at the party, I think she would have preferred me to drop the whole idea, fearing it would turn bad on the night. I tried to reassure her, asking her to trust me, and explaining that any distorted impression she had of the song's intent was most likely the result of having read only a part of the poetry. In the end, of course, she let me go ahead with the performance and 'Unbound' was included in the evening's set list. However, I suspect she remained apprehensive right up to the moment we started to perform, and this only exacerbated my anxiety. The evening was going to be an emotional powder keg, one way or another.

As people began to arrive, the bustle of their voices, the warm conversation, distracted me from any residual fears I harboured. Delicious and ample food (prepared by my wife, ably assisted by our daughter) was set out on a large table, and the garden doors were opened for those who wished to relax outside. I was pleased to see my unexpected friend, tutor and vocalist mingling among our oldest and dear friends. The professional among us, she appeared unfazed by the ordeal to come. As she chatted to our friends and met our children for the first time, her manner once again reminded me of the stick man in her video, just saying 'Hello'.

With the meal over, we invited everyone into the living room: our stage for the night. And, as if at a real gig, 'doors' were opened at eight o'clock sharp. The atmosphere created by the glittering instruments, the fairy lights and the gentle glow of candles set the scene. Perfect.

'Oh, my! So pretty,' said one of our friends. And it was. Our home, or at least one part of it, had been transformed. My sound recorder, so often a feature of my songwriting lessons, was hidden, unseen, at the back of the room. I planned to cut a CD of the evening's proceedings and give it as a gift to our friends at a later date.

It proved a fabulous concert, everything I had hoped for, an intimate evening of heartfelt songs beautifully sung and simply dressed: shimmering acoustic music. Much applause was forthcoming and the room was filled with joy and laughter. I shall never forget it. Nor shall I forget the work my tutor put in. Knowing how much the event meant to me, she had spent virtually the whole afternoon in rehearsal with our son. I had hoped she would have time to relax in our garden before the evening kicked off, but she was having none of it. By the end of the night she was utterly exhausted: I had asked her to play (and therefore rehearse) every one of the songs she had ever recorded! The set list was so long that we had had to split the evening in two (an opportunity for our guests to return to the dining room for pudding). My song, 'Unbound', would kick off the second half. In this way, if things fell apart, as I feared they might, we could quickly move on to our artist's own songs, and by the end of the night any embarrassment would be forgotten.

It was time.

Pudding over, I called everyone back to the living room.

Crouching behind my keyboard, I sounded a few chords in a high register as a bell, and as people were traipsing in and finding a place to sit I began to tell the story of 'Unbound'. A few of our friends were aware that I had been taking piano lessons. No one, however, other than my penfriend had any idea that I had also been learning to be a songwriter, let alone that I had written a love song and that it was going to be performed this night. All they had picked up was something about my wife and a song about friendship. What was this new information? Murmurs of surprise and expectation flew around the room.

'As some of you know,' I began, 'a couple of years ago I decided to pick up from where I left off as a child and renew my interest in music. I wanted to do more than play, to explore every aspect of music-making, practical and theory … and, via a chance meeting with our talented artist tonight –' glancing at my friend '– I decided to find out about the mystical process she calls songwriting and I call voodoo magic.'

Hoping to lighten the atmosphere, I added, 'So here is my first song. If you like it, I shall write another. If you don't, I won't.'

A few chuckles were heard around the room.

'My song is for anyone who has experienced a period of insecurity in their life. Especially if they looked for guidance from those closest to them.

'It's called "Unbound",' I announced.

And the room fell quiet, expecting the two of us to play. I had forgotten to mention the context they needed to hear: the dedication. Fortunately, though, my vocalist stepped in and covered for the unfortunate omission, explaining how, all those months ago, I had come to her with a singular request: 'to write a love song for my wife'. Hearing this, more sighs of appreciation fluttered around the room, and then, as often happens at concerts, everyone fell silent in anticipation.

I played Rhodes, my tutor sang – minus her guitar. The room was hushed, reverent. And for a moment my mind flew back to childhood, to the times when my mother and father would sit, silent, still, watching some great pianist perform, broadcast to our living room in grainy monochrome on our tiny television. Now it was me being scrutinised. Unable to maintain focus on the music, I could not help glancing across the room to see people's expressions. One face drew my attention. Our daughter, sitting cradled in my wife's arms in the middle of the floor, watched spellbound as our artist sang her father's words of love to her mother. Weeks later, she admitted that, until that moment, she had never thought of her parents in that light; as having a romantic relationship.

As the final chords of 'Unbound' rang out, I heard a '*Wow*' from someone in the room and, in the delightful atmosphere that followed, my wife stood up, walked over to where I was sitting – hiding behind my keyboard – and gave me a deliberate and loving kiss. Was it a signal to her friends that 'Howard had not embarrassed himself or me any more than was strictly necessary'? Our embrace suggested: 'Emotion over. Phew, now we can relax.' And the public display of affection kicked off another round of murmurs of appreciation from our audience. My love song had worked, but it had been a terrible performance. I had fluffed a few chords, and, not able to look directly at my vocalist for fear our friends might misinterpret my gaze, the two of us were out of sync much of the time. Despite this, 'Unbound' had woven its magic around the room, the flaws in my accompaniment masked by the story, as in all theatre. I was already looking forward to the next opportunity to perform my masterpiece!

As the applause died away, and with a wide grin on my face, I glanced across the room to my vocalist, the first time I had dared look at her since we had begun to perform. I hope she knew I was thanking her. And then, like a real pro, she snapped out of the reverie and, picking up her guitar, re-tuned for the second half of our evening. As she began the next song, I could now relax, and we were treated to another hour of heavenly music.

As the set drew to its inevitable conclusion, it was thank yous all round: to our artist for the night; to the audience for coming out; and for my son's percussion. And then, as we had planned, our artist once again picked up her guitar, announcing, 'Hey, we are not done yet!' Adjusting her tuning for the last time, she introduced our finale: the 'Friendship Song'. Tripping over each other, eager to tell the tale, we tried to explain to our audience how my wife's waking dream has led to her lyrics, and how I had been working on another song but making limited progress and so was able to offer my wife a chance to attend a songwriting class. How my wife had declined the opportunity but suggested I take her words – and so on and so forth. Our friends, however, were having none of this and insisted they wanted to hear the story first hand, from the lyricist herself: my wife. What had inspired her? Why those words?

And so, tentatively at first, and then with confidence, my wife began to explain the campfire analogy and our uncertainty about the future.

'I think we have all,' she began, 'at one time or another, found it necessary to talk something through with our closest friends. Isn't this why each of us is here?' No one could disagree.

A calm then descended on the room and, with my wife's thought echoing in our minds, our artist began, plaintively, to sing:

The night sky was lit,
By our laughter and our wit,
As we sailed through the night,
On a banter of delight.

It is friendships that carry us,
Friendships that carry us,
Friendships that carry us through.

Looking back on the past,
Rose-coloured spectacles cast,
A favourable view,
Of the childhood we knew.

But what of the new dawn?
And the shadow it casts upon
Our future uncertain,
The new day a burden.

But our friendships will carry us,
Friendships will carry us,
It is friendships that carry us through.

As the song entered its final chorus, everyone spontaneously began to hum, sing or sway to the music. So natural – it was my wife's lovely words and my tutor's beguiling guitar accompaniment. I was transfixed. Stepping out of myself, looking down from above, I could almost see the campfire that had inspired these lyrics. And in that transcendent moment it struck me that everyone with us that night was so happy, all of us together, playing and singing music in our first living-room concert. In the throes of nostalgia for the evening we had so carefully crafted, I was unable to imagine how such beauty could ever occur again.

As our friends were putting on coats, hugging, saying their farewells and stepping out into the night, a mix of emotions boiled up within me. Had our first living-room concert been a signpost to, and confirmation of, the future I imagined and longed for? I had written and performed my first song. Was I now a musician? One phrase from my wife's lyric hung in the air:

> *Our future uncertain …*

37

SHATTERED

'Without music, life would be a blank to me.' – Jane Austen, *Emma*

Three weeks later. July 3, 2017. A Monday morning like any other. I was to drive to our local garage to drop off the car for a minor but irritating repair. As usual, I slung my pedal bike in the back. We live just a mile and a half from the garage, the majority of which is main road. During rush hour the traffic crawls, but I can bypass bottled-up vehicles using the dedicated cycle lane. My penfriend and his wife had stayed over on the Sunday night after a lovely weekend. Keen to get home to cook breakfast for everyone, I was riding hard and fast. I have always been a confident cyclist, even amid the dense traffic of urban London.

Noticing a traffic cone in my path some thirty yards ahead, I decided to mount the pavement; the next turn I needed to make blocked by road-works. The driveways to the properties along the main road offered a convenient on-ramp. I had made the same manoeuvre many times before. This time, my front wheel caught on the rim edge of the stone curb – no more than an inch, but at the speed I was going it was enough to twist my bike into the path of the traffic. The cycle buckled beneath me and I was flung over the handlebars and went down hard.

For a few seconds everything moved into slow motion. I was lying awkwardly, face down, twisted to one side, but (thankfully) on the side-walk and out of the way of oncoming cars. Taking stock of the situation, I noted blood streaming from my knee: I was wearing shorts and a T-shirt. Assuming I had suffered no more than cuts and bruises, I felt sure I would be able to walk home, drop into a hot bath, cover any damage with sticking plaster and all would be well. Not so.

I moved, gently, onto my left side in an attempt to sit, look over my grazes and consider how long I should wait before standing. As I hitched myself up, I can only describe the pain as excruciating. My right arm went into spasm. Using my left, and now lying on my back, I reached round to the elbow and immediately knew something was seriously wrong. Difficult to explain, but it was as if the joint was hanging off, out of place. I shuddered and lay back down, unable to shift my weight, let alone stand. And the pain intensified. Waving my good arm, I tried to attract the attention of passing cars. Try this: lie on your back with your legs twisted to one side. Then wave. It must have looked comical, but the situation was far from that. I needed help.

The traffic on the highway was moving slowly, less than ten miles an hour at a guess. My bike was lying a few yards from where I had fallen, strewn across the kerb, partly in the path of oncoming vehicles. Any driver would have spotted it, or me, and immediately understood that something was wrong. Surely? Yet to my surprise and horror, and despite peering through the side window of their vehicles, every driver simply turned away and drove on. There was no question about it, our eyes had met, these drivers had seen me gesticulating, pleading for help, but I was nothing to them other than an irritation, a distraction from their morning commute. Months later, in recovery, I reflected on what these motorists' lack of interest signalled about how society had changed, but right here, right now, lying on the pavement, things were desperate. My broken arm was moving further into spasm, locked at forty-five degrees to my body. I lay back in frustration, unable to hail the selfish drivers.

And then an angel appeared.

Pedestrians being few and far between, I had been lucky. A young woman, a passer-by, had spotted me. Speaking in an Eastern European accent, she asked how she could help. I was becoming incoherent. Then I felt a blanket being laid over me, and I suggested she could take my mobile phone from my pocket and place it in my left hand. But try as I might, one finger could not dial home. My saviour therefore took over the task and, after hearing the dial tone, handed the phone back. No reply. We tried ringing again, this time waiting longer. My wife had no doubt left for work by now, and my friends were either still in bed, in the bathroom, or, most likely, did not consider it their place to answer. We tried calling again, this time letting the line ring and ring and ring, until, thank goodness, someone picked up. Seeing that it was my number, my penfriend cheerfully enquired, 'Hi, Howie, what's up?'

I cannot tell you how comforting it was to hear his voice. Explaining that I had fallen from my bike, could not move and needed help, I asked him to come out to fetch me and pick up the cycle. More frustration. 'Sorry, Howie. What did you say? I can't hear you.' He kept asking, over and over, to repeat what I had just said. I blurted it out again and again, repeating the name of the road where I lay. Nothing made any difference, he simply did not understand what I was telling him. And then I heard the words I needed to hear. He had no clear idea of what was wrong but would get in his car immediately and 'drive along the main road'.

A second angel had arrived on the scene, a man. Something about his demeanour was reassuring. Calmly, he asked what had happened and seemed especially interested in whether I had hit my head. I thought not, but could not be sure. The man had been travelling to the local fire station, where he worked. I knew the place well, only a couple of hundred yards from where I had fallen. Trained as a first responder, he carefully moved me onto my back and placed what felt like a cushion under my head. It was his coat. I remember his words … 'Stay with me now.'

Desperately tired by now, to close my eyes would have been the easiest thing to do, but he kept speaking to me, asking questions about my life and interests. 'I love music too,' he said, 'I play the guitar. You?' and suggested that 'When this is all over we should get together and jam.' Was he serious? Or simply helping me stay alert? And then my penfriend arrived. He could not have missed the scene, and I need not have worried about not being able to tell him where the accident had taken place. A calm, rational voice as ever, he tried to reassure me: 'Everything is going to be fine, Howie ... an ambulance has been called.'

By this time a policeman had also joined us. Barring the paramedics yet to arrive, it is fair to say that a capable support team was now in place. How I would love to have witnessed the incident from the viewpoint of a drone flying high overhead: my decision to mount the kerb; the fall; the behaviour of the timid or selfish drivers who chose to ignore me; the angels who cared for me; and of course the arrival of my penfriend.

The intense pain had eased, mainly because my broken arm was now locked, immovable, and in a very odd position. My friend was now calling my wife. Naturally, she was unaware of the incident, having left for work an hour or so before I had set off to the repair shop. Once again, however, the mobile network failed us. It took my friend several attempts to get a connection. As before, when he did manage to get through, my wife was unable to catch what he was telling her, while he could hear her clearly. I had fallen in a cellphone dead spot, not uncommon in London. My wife later explained that the twenty-minute drive from her place of work to the scene of the accident had been surreal. She knew something terrible had happened but had few details. For all she knew, I could have been lying dead at the side of the road. Nor did she have any firm idea where I had fallen. But sure enough, half an hour later, she too was hovering over me, cradling my head, her eyes welling up. And at that moment, seeing her close, emotion overcame me. All I could do was apologise, over and over again, as if this ritual would wipe away all traces of the ugly drama. And then, selfishly, I blurted out, 'My arm. Piano.'

And burst into tears.

For ninety minutes I lay on the pavement before the ambulance arrived. Exacerbated by heavy traffic, or perhaps with more severe incid-ents to attend, it had taken them an age to reach me. Taking charge, the paramedics politely asked everyone to move away, and once again inquired about my neck and my head. Foolishly, I had not been wearing a helmet. I had been lucky. The concrete, the kerb, the brick wall of the adjacent house, its unforgiving edge only two feet from the pavement where I had fallen ... The instinctive reaction to protect my head meant that my arms had taken the full force of the fall. How hard? A few weeks later, I looked on my cycle's trip computer to see how fast I had been peddling that fateful day. Twenty-eight miles per hour: I had been racing. And there, on my smartphone, was the text message I had sent as I left the garage having dropped off the car: 'Racing home. See you soon.' The accident was no one's fault but my own.

Having moved me onto a stretcher, held securely by straps attached to the inner sidewall of the ambulance, I was taken to hospital. Once again, owing to traffic conditions, the journey took far longer than usual. My wife followed in her car, and when I was at last admitted to A&E I spent the next six hours being triaged through several levels of assessment. The break was bad: to save the arm, I was to be operated on the next day.

I hope you are not squeamish. The back of my elbow had sheered off. It was as if a knife had sliced the inside crease of my arm, through my funny bone. Yanked by the contraction of the muscles in my upper arm, it had also moved out of position. The surgeon explained that with such an injury he could not employ the more common 'pins' or 'cage'. Instead, he must fit metalwork under the skin of my forearm, reaching round to the back of my elbow. Leaning over the hospital bed, he predicted that I would lose some movement; permanently. I told him that I trusted him 100 per cent and knew I was in safe hands. And then told him I was a pianist; amateur, not professional.

'Ah, yes,' he said, 'I saw that in your admission papers. We have to take great care with pianists. We will do our best. The bone and surrounding tissues can sometimes dissolve, leaving little for the implant to fix on.'

Oh, Lord. Far from reassuring me, the pit in my stomach swelled. Would I play again? The piano was my life. Had my journey on the escalator come to an abrupt and premature end?

Lying in my hospital bed that evening and throughout the long night, I was able to pick up snatches and snippets of the stories of other men on the ward, each coping with their own illness or injury. In the bed next to me was a priest. Not old, maybe thirty-five, forty. Apparently, he was afflicted by a dreadful neuropathological condition. I listened as he and a visitor, another priest, prayed together. Across the way a young man, no more than twenty-five, was strung up on a frame, plaster casts covering his left arm and right leg entirely. Whatever had happened to him? I never did find out. And, tragically, in the bed directly opposite, an elderly man was suffering from what I guessed was advanced dementia. Critical of the nurses, and shouting at anyone who tried to help, he was without doubt the most challenging patient on the ward. I later learnt from a nurse that as a young man in the 1950s he had worked as a carer and support worker in a mental institution. The things he must have witnessed … Clearly, he knew what care was and, judging by his ravings, had decided he was not getting it from this particular hospital. It was a difficult night for all of us. My accident now seemed so trivial, and I felt ashamed by the way I had reacted to the self-inflicted misfortune.

The next morning, after a fitful night, I was moved to the operating theatre, where I once again met my surgeon. The austere white disinfected cleanliness of the pre-op room brought home the reality of my injury. Presented with the usual forms that absolved the hospital and staff from legal responsibility for whatever happened next, I fell under the influence of the calming anaesthetic, filled with remorse for my wild and irresponsible ride home.

A moment later, I was wide awake. Glancing at a nearby clock, I judged I had been in theatre for no more than an hour, maybe less. The complex operation had been, I was told by a junior doctor, a success. The titanium support was secure. I would now be in plaster for several weeks and would then be offered a course of physiotherapy. The positivity of the post-op team was infectious. Was that it? Was this over?

At home, in the rough plaster cast, my upper and lower arm was locked into a mathematically precise ninety-degree angle. This was its position for the next eight weeks. Unpleasant, hot, and maddeningly itchy at times, it ached. The powerful painkiller I had been given drained me of all energy. But life had to go on. My son's graduation from his Master's degree was, unfortunately, the day after my discharge from the hospital. A trip to London, to the Royal Festival Hall: there was no way any parent could miss that. With my arm in a sling, the celebration of the young people's academic achievements was nonetheless a joy. But sitting in a narrow seat for several hours did my arm no good at all: I was hurting and fought hard not to make a fuss.

I needed rest. Over the following days, I did little but sit in an armchair, Adagio on my lap, and lament my sorry situation. I hate to admit it, but I became a couch potato, watching hours of daytime TV, mindless repeats of 70s crime series I had enjoyed as a teenager. My life felt on hold. It was not only piano practice that was no longer possible.

I could not wash or take a bath by myself. I could eat with only one arm. While such temporary disablement was minor compared to that of others, I began to realise what it meant to *be* disabled. I was humbled.

Decisions about the next few weeks had to be taken. A holiday to celebrate my sixtieth birthday – a trip around Norway from coast to coast, up through the mountains and fjords, organised in every detail by my penfriend's wife – was in doubt. Would my surgeon allow me to travel? If we did get away, would I be a drag on everyone? What if my arm worsened while we were abroad? A change of plaster at week four offered some respite: a new orthopaedic cast – fibreglass. This was lighter, more comfortable, but permitted no more movement. Two days before the insurance policy's cancellation clause expired, the four of us took the decision to travel. I promised to behave.

Oh, how glorious our holiday was. Oslo, Bergen, Flåm, travelling on boats and trains, in and out of hotels. I cannot claim it was easy for me, but the pleasure of being with friends, the clear air, the early morning light, the evening skies and beauty of the surroundings, meant that our joint decision had been the right one. The holiday gave me a lift, though I cannot recommend sleeping next to your wife with an arm in plaster, locked at a right angle, disturbing her with awkward movements to find a comfortable position. Nor can I claim that walking the hills with your arm in a sling and encased in glass is a joy. And all the while, at the forefront of my mind, was my piano and what the future held. I tried to hide it, though probably not very well. Deep down I was worried, more than my wife and friends could know.

As we arrived back in the UK, the useful distraction of our vacation was already fading and the reality of what lay ahead hit me hard. When would I be able to play again, and how many skills, so hard won, would I have to regain? A depressing thought. Two more weeks of moping about and I needed something to cheer me up. Songwriting! After all, one arm should suffice to play a few chords? I wrote to my tutor for her opinion.

'Shall we meet? Is there anything we could work on together?' I put in an email. And, hoping to amuse, I added a list of jokey titles for books that would appeal to a one-armed pianist:

- One-Armed Pianism: A Primer
- Scales for the Singular-Limbed Musician
- Basslines and Licks: The Ideal First Step Towards One-Hand Virtuoso Piano Technique
- Opportunities with Rootless Chords for All Left-Hand Pianists
- Plaster Casts: Their Use and Abuse in the Playing of Block Chords
- Move the Keyboard Not the Arm: A How-To Guide
- Write Half a Song, but Gain All the Effect
- The Use of Rigidity in Chopin's Piano Repertoire
- Avoiding Arm Movement: Pentatonic Melodies in One Octave:
- What To Do With Your Right Hand When Your Left-Hand Takes Over: Hints and Tips
- Forever Left In Politics and Pianism: Multi-Disciplinary Studies at the University of 'Something Is Not Quite Right'.

Well, it amused me. As I pressed SEND, however, I felt shame once more. My insensitivity to those facing permanent disability, and to the predicament of the men with whom I had spent a night on the hospital ward, shocked me. As my penfriend reminded me, I had 'escaped a bullet'. He was right: I needed to put my injury into perspective.

The new songwriting class helped. My tutor was all ears, eager to hear the gory details of the sorry story. Straightforward as ever, her view was simple: 'Everything in life has its good and its bad; focus on the positives.' She was also right that I was moping. She felt sure that in some surprising or mysterious way the unfortunate accident would reveal its silver lining. And she started to list possibilities. Perhaps it would help my lyric writing? Or free up time to study more theory? 'Watching the healing process will be a valuable learning experience,' she suggested, looking for confirmation that I had taken the positive messages on board.

Before we left the practice room, I asked her to promise me.

'Will you,' I asked, 'tell me honestly when you think I have written a good song and when I have not?'

'Yes, of course,' she said, suddenly serious.

I went on: 'I would like to write three songs … an EP, if you like. Whether or not it is ever released, I need to know what it is like to be a musician … to … sorry, this is crazy, but let me go on … to take the songs all the way to the studio … everything … recording, mixing, mastering, production. I need to feel as you felt when you recorded your first music, using nothing but your voice, a guitar, a microphone and a computer. And if I am to do this, I shall need someone to guide me. I need you.'

A moment's silence.

'And because you have a reputation and I have none, whatever I write must be good enough that you would want to sing my songs and be comfortable if other people were to hear them.'

Expecting a complicated reply, she did what she always does, make everything simple.

'I shall,' she said. 'It will be an absolute pleasure. And fun!'

'And … you'll be my vocalist?' I asked.

'Yes.'

And with that we left. I had been saved by a blue snowman.

But then a new X-ray confirmed my worst fear.

I was back at the clinic. The bone was healing, but the surrounding soft tissue – ligaments, tendons and muscle – had been severely damaged.

In a matter-of-fact voice, my surgeon informed me that my injury was 'on the edge of the worst he had seen' and that 'unfortunately the elbow is a terrible place to be insulted'. Legs, arms, hips – all such breaks were, he claimed, more amenable to healing when compared to the sheer break of the olecranon. In frustration at this news, I posted a copy of a new X-ray to my Instagram feed, adding the following caption:

'Recommendation. Never ever do this. Ever. I mean it! Avoid at all costs. You won't like it, and things will never be the same again. Hashtag #elbow.'

Within minutes, a colleague from my old work, from our Swedish office, saw my post and, struck by the stark image revealing the detail of the metalwork and six bolts, added his comment: 'How? What?!!'

I explained in a follow-up comment the next day:

'Cycling accident at speed. Awkward break. Operation. Metal. Endless physiotherapy to come. Year-long recovery process. Limit on future movement. Impact on music yet to be determined. I call it "THING". Will one day write a poem.'

But poems had to wait.

The elbow had healed sufficiently for my cast to be removed. Another X-ray only compounded my anxiety about the future. THING, as I now referred to my inept, disjointed elbow, would not move. It hit a stop at each end of a narrow range of movement. Bedtime was difficult. No matter how I lay or what position I adopted, THING sat awkwardly or became trapped under the weight of my body. The pain was such that I often needed a sleeping tablet. Worst of all, however, was the waking period. As if from a pleasant dream, I imagined the joint had mysteriously fixed itself during the night and could now move freely. Not so. The involuntary tendency to straighten one's arms after a good night's sleep became a stark reminder of the consequences of my accident. Each morning, the inevitable stretch – which I tried hard to suppress but could not – caused considerable pain deep in my elbow. The dull ache depressed my mood for the rest of the day. I was not dealing with the psychology of my injury well. Sensing I was down in the dumps, my penfriend diagnosed that my response to the accident was, 'probably because, Howie, you have never had anything wrong with you in the past'. It was true. I'd not seen a doctor since I was a young man.

My arm was well and truly stuck. The longer it remained in this position, the less chance I had of making a full recovery. The Internet was a boon, serving up useful datasheets about my specific condition, the nature of the sheer break, and the appropriate exercises that could help restore normal movement. I began to work the elbow daily. It helped my mood, if not the arm, providing more reassurance than infrequent hospital check-ups could provide.

Fortunately, my tendency to tackle goals head-on – an attitude that had served me so well in the woodshed – began to kick in. Having cracked complex scales and arpeggios, I was sure I could recover from this injury. I had to. One physiotherapist proved a godsend. She was able to give me detailed information on the appropriate exercise regime and the expected outcomes. My elbow, she feared, had 'internal fixture' and therefore the work to rebuild would need to come from me. She would do everything she could, but it was likely I would 'lose some flexion'.

The arm, I was told, should have one hundred and fifty degrees of movement. At this stage in my recovery, I had less than fifty! This made even simple daily tasks impossible, let alone any meaningful piano practice. I could not lift two hands to wash my face; I could not reach the top button of my shirt. Wet shaving was nigh on impossible. And, comically, no matter how I tried, I could not raise a finger of my bent arm to lick off the marmalade when I had been a messy boy eating breakfast. I felt like a child. And then, to add insult to injury, I received a letter from the hospital. Assigned to a support group at the local out-patients department, I had been booked onto a 'Coping with Disability' class. This was the last straw. More than anything else, the letter reinforced my determination to recover my arm. There was no way, ever, that I could accept not being able to wash my face, let alone be prevented from learning to play the piano to a reasonable standard, a standard I was convinced was possible, even for someone my age.

My physiotherapist explained that I needed to step things up a gear. She asked me to do eight different exercises a day, five times a day. Detailed instructions and video demonstrations were provided. Each activity involved ten repetitions, with 'holds' between each. They came with esoteric technical names such as *elbow flexion/extension*, *assisted ROM flexion*, *facilitated ROM extension*, *passive elbow weight*, *elbow weighted extension*, *active elbow supination*, *assisted shoulder flexion* and, my favourite, *prehension with ball.* Four hundred movements per day. 'Hey,' I thought, 'I remember this: a quadrillion scales, finger exercises and chord shapes; I know how to do this.' I was becoming a physiotherapy virtuoso.

Time, as with all challenging pursuits, was the limitation. To perform these medical exercises – thoroughly – took between two and a half to three and a half hours each day. Sounds doable if, like me, you are no longer working a day job, but it left me drained of energy for much of the day. The combination of physical exertion and the body's natural healing process prevented me from doing pretty much anything else. But I remained resolute in my desire to move on with the healing and achieve greater flexion. To the strict regime I added hot baths morning and evening, suffused with salts and emollients both to reduce the scarring and so ease the tension in my elbow and surrounding soft tissue. I also dedicated half an hour to massaging the wounded arm with my strong arm, digging my fingers into the crease of the ailing elbow. I honestly felt I was doing everything I could to regain movement. But no, during a routine 'How are you getting on?' visit to my consultant surgeon, he suggested I 'swing my arm about' during the day, to further flex the joint.

'How often?' I asked.

'Every ten to fifteen minutes or so,' he suggested.

These non-stop exercises and weekly physiotherapy sessions continued throughout the hot summer. The bent arm, unable to hang correctly, was now starting to affect my shoulder on that side, which had stiffened considerably. This was 'typical', according to the medics. The disablement was clear to see. I could neither reach up or round to the back of my head, neck or body. Therefore, to the roster of elbow exercises, my physiotherapist added a cast of new characters designed to help my shoulder joint. A further six exercises, five times a day, ten repetitions ... and more obscure medical terms, my favourite being *assisted ROM abduction*, whatever that was! Oh, and she also suggested I 'start swimming, maybe a few times a week?' Lord. Perhaps I was taking her advice too literally; I felt as if I were Iron Man being rebuilt after a fall from the sky.

Under the intense regime, my flexion did increase, albeit slowly. The physiotherapist took measurements at the beginning and end of each session. Sometimes a degree forward. Sometimes a step back. But the trend was clear: there was a steady improvement; my arm was beginning to bend. It is not uncommon, she explained, 'for the healing process to take a year; or more'. One patient she had treated reported increased mobility over three years from the date of their accident. My rehabilitation, however, was plateauing.

Six months on from the accident, and I had not been brave enough to touch my piano. THING, while now able to bend sufficiently to perform everyday tasks, still operated in an extremely odd fashion. It felt to me as if the metalwork itself appeared was preventing normal movement, but I was assured by the clinic that this was not the reason and that it was 'much more likely' that it was 'only the internal scarring'. ONLY! At times, a jolt of pain shot through the arm to my fingers. Fretting about what was happening to my body, fearful of how this would limit my progress as a pianist, I was not fun to be around.

Imagine two pieces of wood, held together by a rusty bolt, the screws loose, allowing movement in one direction but operating only crudely in another. That is how my arm felt, and I succumbed to a growing depression. My fingers, thank goodness, *were* able to move as they did before, but felt bruised, degraded; imprecise. To sit at the piano, to attempt to play, was something I avoided. I had no desire to know how much coordination had been lost; skills I had worked so hard to acquire over almost three years. Frankly, I was scared witless. During a further (and final) consultation with my surgeon, he told me I would 'most likely need to retrain as a pianist once the healing was complete'. No way. If I waited that long, I would never be able to fire up the motors and restart the escalator that had carried me this far. And so, while everyone was out, I summoned the courage to sit at the piano.

Picking up my notebook, in which I had recorded my progress up to the point of the accident – three weeks after our living-room concert – I selected four exercises. These four, I felt, would reveal the most about how severely the injury had affected my facility. It was a struggle. My hands and fingers moved over the keys but did so as if a child were learning from scratch. Accuracy and speed had been lost. My ability to play scales, hands together, was no more. As I pushed my fingers into the keyboard, my elbow ached. After just thirty minutes of this agony, I was dog-tired. I documented the painful reality using a fresh page of my journal, detailing what I could and could not do. It did not make for comforting reading.

I estimated I had lost as much as three grades.

That cruel summer, when THING happened, wrenched my life adrift. I was reduced. My yearning to play the piano, the hard work of recent years, meant little now. I was spent; spoiled. Loss of skills; lost time to practise; months in re-training – what did it add up to? Eighteen months, two years? Time lost from my 'window of opportunity'. Worse, the joy of playing was gone. Before THING, I had been honed to the task. My progress had been measured, slow but sure. Now I had gone ... backwards. I no longer knew who I was, and I feared there could be no further advancement. I hated THING. I hated its insensate cruelty. THING had taught me to hate. And I cursed myself for my own carelessness.

In these dark moments, I finally understood that it was not the theory of music I craved. No. I loved the piano itself with all my heart, the intimate physical act of working with a musical instrument. And I longed for a reset button, for everything to be as it had been in the past when I would take myself off to the woodshed for hours on end, late into the night, lost in reverie. I'm sorry to keep using clichés, but my being, my essence – the post-retirement identity I'd worked so hard to foster – had been injured. I had tripped off the escalator as I had tripped off my cycle, and through no fault other than my own. Now I would never know what I could have achieved as a musician in this, the final third of my life. As my despair deepened, I needed a cushion to break my fall.

And so it was that I walked upstairs to my old work-study, fired up a laptop, opened a blank template and began to write this book.

38
GIG

> 'If Music is a Place, then Jazz is the City, Folk is the Wilderness, Rock is the Road, Classical is a Temple.' – Vera Nazarian

Fast forward. New Year's Day, January 1, 2018. I woke early, to the sound of birds singing. Sunlight lit the room, glancing through slatted blinds. It was the day of our gig. We were to perform in a large church in central London, support act to a well-known jazz collective. Proud of our five tunes, we had released an EP. It was getting positive reviews online.

I remember the bustle and anticipation of the days leading to this, our debut. Practising together, marking up lead sheets, curating set lists, finalising lyrics … so this is what it is like to be a musician. Adjusting and locking down patches on our keyboards, choosing effects, organising cables, mics and stands, deciding who would bring what to the venue; endless tasks. The paraphernalia we had seen in the window or tucked away in the dusty corners of the music shops we had frequented on our journey now made sense. We were performing musicians.

Expecting a lively audience, and given the profile of the main act, the rumour was the event might attract a few high-profile music journalists and other bigwigs connected to the industry. Great for us. We needed to put our best foot forward, and spent the entire afternoon obsessing over anything and everything that might spoil our performance. Hours flew by, engrossed in last-minute rehearsal, perfecting our music, aligning mix levels and briefing the sound guy … so many details.

As the time of 'doors' drew near, there was palpable excitement and expectation. A large crowd had gathered. Standing space was already filling with the kind of folks who can only be in one place at a gig: up close and personal, just as I had been as a regular concert-goer.

At the allotted time, we trooped onto the platform, picked up or stood behind our instruments – keyboards, guitars and drums – and peered into the dark, blinded by the stark stage lighting. Then, a moment of awkward silence. The band had selected me to both introduce our set and thank the audience for coming out on what was a dull and very wet evening. I mumbled a few words of introduction. Would anyone ever remember our names? And then we were off, careering into our first number.

The applause was polite, but not overwhelming. Our second tune picked up the pace. By the end of our set, lasting just under thirty minutes, we were spent, dripping with sweat. Our relief was tangible. There was no call for an encore, but the whoops, whistles and cheers were more than we had expected or hoped. With our first public performance we had crossed a Rubicon. As creative musicians, everything that happened from now on was up to us and us alone. As we walked offstage we were already imagining our next event.

And with a start I woke from my dream.

THING was there, lying in wait.

Stretching from the night's uneasy slumber, muscles contracting, the elbow ached as it did every morning, reminding me of the permanence of my injury. Lying still, I carefully moved the arm back and forth, trying to get a measure of how it had fared in the night. A nodule under the skin at the back of the elbow clicked. Not a nice feeling. Despite this evidence of residual malfunction, I judged the joint to be a little better today. Teasing it back to life, I raised and lowered the appendage until it felt settled.

I got out of bed, put on a dressing gown and walked downstairs to make tea. Filling the kettle, I stood motionless, the only sound that of water coming to the boil. The ritual was soothing. As I swallowed the first mouthful, the warmth of the fragrant brew distracted me from my arm for a moment. I then disappeared to the bathroom.

Emerging refreshed, I felt that something about today was unfamiliar. I felt … in a rush. Breakfast, a bowl of cereal followed by strong black coffee, was taken standing up. As if in an altercation with an unseen presence, I prowled the kitchen, my mind distracted; but by what? Detached, unaware of what was going on, my wife and son readied themselves for work, ignoring me. Sleepwalking, I stepped back into the hall and entered the music room. The curtains were closed, but I did not open them.

My piano stood there, immobile. It had not been played for months, yet the lid was open. It had never been closed. Arms hanging limp on either side, I sat on the stool; and for a few peaceful minutes did nothing but listen to the rhythm of my waking body. Why was I short of breath? My heart was beating faster than usual. Why? Time passed. The front door clicked shut as my wife and son left for work. The house fell silent.

Focus. On this day, waking from my seductive dream – already fading, the details unable to be recalled – it was as if I were beginning my journey of three years anew. Everything I had learnt so far was, I judged, in the bag, done and dusted, no need to think about it. 'Put it all behind me,' I thought. 'Out of mind, out of sight. A new baseline.' Whatever had debilitated me since the accident could not be eradicated by putting up a sign and announcing that I was back in the woodshed. No practice regime could melt this block as it had so many others during my time on the escalator. Neither could my reticence to play be resolved by listening to the advice of others. No. A different strategy was needed.

I reached for an answer.

'Think, Howard …' Wasn't this as it had been when I first stepped into the music shop on the wrong side of town and asked for a lesson?

'One makes one's own luck in life,' I remembered. A blue snowman. What coincidences, dreams or teachers might lie ahead now?

Glancing up from the keyboard, hidden among the piles of music and theory books I kept on top of our piano, I found my old practice journal. Flicking through its pages, dense with three years of notes, I stopped at the page where I had recorded a final exercise, the day before my misjudged cycle ride. It hung there, waiting for resolution. Something about a suspended 4th? I had to know. And as if in slow motion, I turned to a fresh sheet. Picking up my pencil, I wrote in large letters:

TODAY, A NEW ESCALATOR.

ACKNOWLEDGEMENTS

Foremost, I must thank my teachers – offline and online – and especially a particular snowman. She, and they, know who they are. Not only did each of them inspire me as musicians, but they showed me an adult way to learn, distinct from the experience of children. I thank them for their patience. If my tutors had a plan for how to guide me, I apologise for self-inflicted changes of direction and persistent questioning.

How can I repay my penfriend's generosity of spirit? His patient replies to incessant communications over three years framed much of the inspiration for my book. He also knows who he is, and I owe him a considerable debt of gratitude; he wrote the book with me. Not only did our voluminous exchange of email sustain my journey, but it also acted as a memory jogger. Without that precious chronicle, I would not have been able to piece together the twists and turns of my time on the escalator.

My talented editor, Martin Ouvry, was a joy to work with. He took my brief and did neither more nor less than was required. It takes skill to avoid distortion of an author's voice. The result is my book, upgraded.

And surely I would be remiss if I did not acknowledge the angel at the roadside, fireman Jake Alexander, as well as my medical team: orthopaedic surgeon Mr Christian Kinmont and physiotherapist Penny Anderson. Each, in their own way, gave me back my arm.

Last, but by no means least, my wife and soul mate. Chrysogon is central to my tale. Not all partners have love songs written for them. Not all poetry exposes the writer's insecurity and is then performed in front of close friends. It must have been an emotional roller coaster for her. For keeping the lid on the frothy brew and enduring too many solitary weekends while I was ensconced in the metaphorical woodshed, I apologise. It inflicted a toll on our time together. Had I known of any other way to make progress, I would have jumped on it.

To everyone involved, through all my ups and downs, let it be known I am now a musician, of sorts, as I set out to be. I stepped onto an escalator and did that simplest of things, asked for a lesson. I urge anyone with a similar aspiration to do the same. It will be wonderful, I promise.

If you are curious about any aspect of my journey, do write. I would love to hear your stories and to learn from your experience; especially if, like me, you are bewitched by music and musicians, bothered by practice and bewildered by theory.

facebook.com/Note4NoteTheBook

NOTE FOR NOTE

POSTLUDE

HOWARD SMITH

Fairdene Press ♦ LONDON

'"Ah, music," he said, wiping his eyes. "A magic beyond all we do here!"'

J.K. Rowling, *Harry Potter and the Philosopher's Stone*

RIGHT TO BE WRONG?

I recognise that for some readers my book contains controversial views about teaching methods. Avoidance of premature rote, obsessive unblocking, imaginary pianos, mental performance, visualisation, out-of-body introspection … not everyone will agree. I hope, however, to have been respectful to all who bring the joy of music to their pupils. There are many ways to learn to play a musical instrument. This has been my story, nothing more, nothing less. It worked for me, as an adult … to a point.

Joss Stone, in her eponymous song, taught: 'We must sing our own songs. We may be singing out of key, but it sure feels good to me.' I felt her philosophy keenly during my time on the escalator. As the pianist Khatia Buniatishvili observed: 'Music is something very free, you have to have this capacity to think about things for yourself.'

Oh, and why the escalator as a metaphor? Have you ever tried to get off? It's virtually impossible. How could I have failed to turn up for lesson two? What would have happened had my first song been a one-trick pony? Could I have accepted failure, repeating childhood ill-discipline and regret? No. Embark on a journey like mine and you too will find yourself riding a bumpy, unpredictable, yet utterly unstoppable magic carpet. It's the music.

And so I shall now explain *what Katy did next*.

WHAT KATY DID NEXT

April 1, 2018. Three months after my return to the keyboard. Nine months since THING. Attempts to get back onto the escalator were not entirely successful, frightened as I was about what I would find there. I would step on and then immediately trip or fall back, unable to make a clean start. Other times the drive belt would fail to start or, if it did crank up, would come to an abrupt halt, causing me to fall. Over time, however, my balance returned and my footing became more assured. And one day it became self-evident, clear as day, that this time there would be no turning back. My injury had run its course. Despite six months of physiotherapy, I'd lost ten degrees of movement, permanently. The setback was real, there would be a significant period of re-training, but I could accept it. The physical and emotional jolt that was my accident, the writing of this book, and the loss of much time in the development of my nascent technique led me to realise what I already knew in my heart: I would now need a traditional piano teacher. No short-cuts. In effect, I must 'start over' to have any chance of mastering the instrument. I found a qualified teacher living locally, previously a concert pianist, and the owner of a gorgeous Steinway.

'Yes, you have some facility,' she confirmed. And by watching me play she determined which 'grade' I should shoot for.

It was this teacher who guided me through my first practical examinations and thus set the scene for further progress towards my 'unrealistic' goal. Our lessons together were the polar opposite of everything I have so far described: chalk and cheese. Theoretical meandering and freewheeling conversation about the physics of vibrating strings were not her thing. We agreed to focus on technique; studies and music that demanded attention to detail. And yes, J.S. Bach, the *Inventions and Sinfonias.*

'This is how I teach all my pupils,' she asserted, and nothing would shift her from that. It paid off. Bad habits, ingrained through unguided self-teaching, were slain. One example: a tendency to detach my hands from the keyboard between phrases was an unnecessary affectation which must have looked extremely odd to anyone watching me perform. Moreover, it complicated the work to align my hand for the next phrase. This and other deficiencies of technique faded as I learnt to 'stay close' to the keys. I was becoming a pianist, of sorts.

Despite the shift of focus to keyboard technique, the songs I had written before the unwelcome interruption of THING remained uppermost in my mind. Would I eventually be capable of writing and recording fitting accompaniments? I already had the vocal parts down pat, set against a metronomic chord-by-chord rendering of my music, intended more than anything else to give my adopted vocalist a solid foundation on which to sing. Based on a design I had found on YouTube, we had built a vocal booth at my home. The result was surprisingly effective, irrespective of the home-grown Blue Peter-style project. A more than semi-professional microphone had helped. But my metrical, over-simplistic accompaniment ... oh dear, it just had to go, to be replaced by something we could both be proud of. The beauty of my friend's voice demanded it. And so I tried. Two further weeks of experimentation, hoping to capture a 'take' that meshed with her subtle inflexion and singing voice, did not do it, my accompaniment skills falling short of the task. In frustration, I briefly flirted with the idea of outsourcing the job to a professional. I knew of a jazz singer and pianist, based in California and who taught on YouTube. She loved my songs, and hearing her perform them (via Zoom) was a joy. Encouraging me to take them into the studio and involve other musicians, the projected costs began to mount up. No, I must do this myself I told myself, the project was too simply personal. I was still far from the 'session musician' I had dreamed of all those years ago when I first met my jazz teacher and witnessed at first hand what it meant to improvise. And so my 'classical' training continued at full throttle. If I worked hard at grades, I convinced myself, the goal of recording the (planned) EP, without embarrassing my friend and songwriting tutor, would come to pass, just later than imagined. Notwithstanding this promising new phase of my journey, remnants of stilted childhood piano lessons – so limiting and uninspiring – never left me. And so, hoping for an elusive shortcut, I found myself scanning the web once again.

A piano circle, based in London. What was this? It sounded … intriguing. The group met monthly at a variety of venues, the only rule being that the room was equipped with a well-maintained grand piano. How does this work? Each 'member' pays a small fee to 'perform' and is allocated between six to ten minutes of performance time (depending on numbers and space). The group play purely for one another, and to practise in front of a friendly audience. No judgement. Introduce your piece, perform, the audience claps, the pianist smiles and bows with thanks. At the end of the evening it's off to the pub to ruminate on the mysteries of music. Later, a repertoire list magically appears on social media: a record of the group's work collated at the end of the year. What's not to like?

The venue turned out to be the expansive third floor of a converted light industry/retail premises in the heart of multicultural London. Now a stylish apartment, the proud owner's Steinway model D concert grand took centre stage. As it should. I expected to see the piano. What I did not expect, however, was an ex-work colleague, a technology manager, who, twenty-five years earlier, had rescued a complex pan-European research project I had won but had later screwed up: chasing the perfect as ever. Small world! We recognised each other immediately and exchanged the usual pleasantries. Our past was quickly set aside and any embarrassment quashed: witness the power of mutual interest in music. And of pianos.

One month later. A new meet-up, a new venue. And this time I had signed as 'performer'. An intermediate-level piece that I knew I could play perfectly well nevertheless fell apart. Decidedly so. My hands shook, the pedalling was dreadful. And what on earth was the juddering right foot? Mostly, however, it was the psychological trauma. Despite everything, the group clapped and, as they heard more of my 'performances' over the following months, assured me I was 'musical' and that it was 'only nerves' letting me down. There's an understatement. My performance anxiety became so intense that I found myself signing up for meet-ups only to bottle out at the last minute, feigning an excuse. How different from the living-room concert when I had accompanied my songwriting tutor in front of friends and family. There, I was not the centre of attention; she was. But here, at the piano circle, not only was Howard 'on show' but he was stretching himself (too far), performing music for which he was clearly ill-prepared. This debilitating anxiety impediment had to end.

The circle proved a valuable entrée to the wide-open space called 'returning adult'. Through this group, I found encouragement, mentoring, teachers, opportunities to perform and, most critical of all, the chance to observe others in their journey. Forever grateful, several became good friends: my newfound piano buddies. All had interesting stories to share.

In terms of ability (grades, diplomas, etc.), the members of this community were far ahead of me. Many had managed to combine the joy of piano with their working life. Those who had not had either achieved considerably more as a child than I or had not been foolish enough to leave a gap of forty years before returning to the keyboard. The most competent pianists had completed grades seven or eight as children and had returned to the piano in their thirties or forties; *not* in their fifties or sixties. And there it was, laid out before me, my regret in spades. What I learnt from these amateurs was that I was climbing a steep mountain: the proverbial 'late returner'. I'd always known this, of course. But as I watched a Diploma class, organised once a year by the group leader, the reality of my predicament intruded on the music, distracting me from the beauty of the participants' performances. What lay ahead looked more like the sheer face of the Dawn Wall than a day's hike to the peak of Snowdon. Sobering.

And there was more.

Sadly, among these pianists, the agony of my accident and its impact on my progress was not so uncommon. Several had their own THING, and not just physical injury but other medical conditions that would limit the ability of any pianist (young or old) to work hard and with sufficient discipline to make progress. Once again, the guilt I had felt so keenly during the night on the hospital ward awaiting my operation came back to haunt me. I had no right to complain. What I was now calling my 'adult amateur psychodrama' was null and void. Indefensible.

I had been with the piano circle for over a year. It had become my support network, mentor and agony aunt. As a result, I was seeing not one teacher but four! If this sounds extreme, you will be surprised to learn it is not so uncommon among more 'serious' amateurs. Most of us (I now counted myself as 'serious') see a regular teacher (once a week, every fortnight, monthly, whatever feels right) but also find it beneficial to 'dip into' complementary wisdom along the way. For example, I had met a talented young pianist and instrumental teacher who had progressed quickly to fellowship grade. The landscape fresh in her mind, she was able to describe what lay ahead, where another teacher might be unwilling to leapfrog the step-by-step 'grades' treadmill. We met up every few weeks. I shared my frustrations; she acted as psychotherapist and fixer. Readily identifying that my 'active listening' was weak, she insisted this was something I needed to work on. And she was never shy of introducing me to other teachers who could help.

'That is how I made progress,' she explained.

I went on to have occasional lessons with diverse tutors who specialised in practice methods, performance and theory. All had their own ideas on how to progress in the art of piano playing. Each, in their own way, helped me make the treacherous crossing that is the transition from intermediate to upper-intermediate and (hopefully) beyond.

Without doubt, a second escalator was in full flight, no more so than when I was persuaded to join my first Piano Summer School. The experience proved seminal: I was back at college, where I belonged. Playing in front of larger groups, helping others overcome their own anxiety, being exposed to professional recitals and top-flight teaching, all afforded me a clear picture of what lay ahead: Mount Everest.

So what is summer school? A holiday? A dream? Camaraderie? All this and more. Mental exhaustion? Yes. Tutorials throughout the day; recitals every evening. Practice rooms open early till late. End-to-end piano madness; be prepared to pace yourself. With so much talent on show, I felt ... inadequate, my journey just beginning. Watching the others – young prodigies, hard-working hopefuls and naturally talented adults – play the most exquisitely complex and intellectually demanding music, it was hard for me to come to terms with the truth. My contribution to the festival felt insignificant, despite years of obsessive practice.

My time at Summer School is best summed up by this exchange:

Pupil: 'I always get these bars wrong.'

Tutor: 'I see. Have you tried playing them right?'

And he goes on to explain how. And we laugh … but, I hope, also heed his advice. The efficacy of this medicine was borne out time and again as my experience grew. Whenever I lacked the self-control to play a pattern correctly, or failed to concentrate and went on to repeat a mistake more than once (hoping it would fix itself), I always regretted the ill-discipline. It would then take days or weeks to eradicate the routine from my muscle memory. My penfriend understood this from biology but had never experienced it himself. Had he done so, I believe even he, with his knowledge of physiology, would have been surprised by the agility of the brain to ingrain a pattern of behaviour, for good or ill.

So, what is a summer school? Essential. That is, if you also want to find out what lies ahead, just around the corner, waiting to pop up and poke fun at you. The experience taught me the joy of playing for others and to control, but not entirely eliminate, my performance anxiety.

Evening. The bar; chatting with friends. We had just been treated to not one but TWO concertos. Brahms No. 1 and No. 2, with full orchestra. A quiet lady joins us. I ask her what she had played to her study group. In an accent I don't recognise, she explains she had been too nervous. She has travelled to the summer school from Brazil. And not played! (other than to her assigned one-to-one tutor) Well, that anxiety had to end. Gathering up a colleague, and despite it being late (11 pm), I suggested that we grab a room and play to each other for an hour or so. And we do. And my plan works. She plays a complex piece by Villa Lobos. Slow and hesitant at first, but lovely. Half an hour later, she is demonstrating another work, rich in Brazillian rhythms. Mission accomplished.

At home, a few weeks later, these experiences at summer school gave me the confidence to try a performance experiment of my own. Could I, I wondered, give a mock recital, for our friends?

Our local church had been kind enough to let me use their piano, and at an attractive rate. The lovely building was a place of calm, and so long as I gave the bookings manager reasonable notice, she could usually allocate a few hours. The pastor was pleased with the arrangement. It provided a little extra income for the parish, and I got to play another grand. Unlike all other musicians (except organists), the pianist cannot carry their instrument with them and must develop the skill of quickly adapting to the unique (and surprisingly varied) feel and sound of the machine they are landed with. Imagine the impact on a recital or examination, if the pianist could not adjust. Coping with mechanical quirks is a necessity. Being able to play with feeling and emotion on an old or poorly maintained instrument is a skill in its own right. Indeed, there are exercises designed to help with this hurdle that every pianist will inevitably face. One involves sensing the action of an unfamiliar instrument by playing notes in high and low registers and at the extremes of dynamics: from ppp (pianississimo) to fff (fortissississimo) and everything in between.

I had been practising on the grand piano at the church for a few months. Our friends were due to visit in a couple of weeks and were able to stay over Saturday night. Could I book the church on a Sunday? It turned out I could, following morning prayers. Here was my opportunity. The audience, I admit, would be modest, a sum total of three: my penfriend, his wife and mine. I would subject them to a selection of my modest repertoire. Compiling the set list turned out to be harder than I imagined. My pieces covered everything from baroque, classical, romantic and twentieth century, including one jazz tune. Deciding the order of play was far from straightforward, given the diverse styles and key signatures. Should I start with old music and progress to new? Or vice versa? Could a piece in one key follow music in a harmonically distant tonality? One thing was clear, there needed to be both contrast and a sense of order to the proceedings.

In the month leading up to the mock recital, I practised incessantly and was surprised to find I had accumulated over an hour of music! Too much, yet I could not bring myself to drop a single piece from my programme. What would be, would be. As I handed our friends a professionally typewritten programme over breakfast on Sunday morning, I had the distinct impression they did not realise it was their host who was to perform. I love surprises.

We had the church to ourselves from one p.m. The four of us moved the heavy piano from a side chapel to the front of the main congregation. I sat down on the piano stool and my audience took their place in the pews. Oddly, they each decided to sit separately, my penfriend at the front, his wife halfway back and my wife to the side. As I had only printed one programme, two-thirds of my audience would have no idea what I was playing. Yet they went along with my game to a tee. As I moved through my pieces there was polite applause, and at the end of each section (by composer) I stood to take a bow. Twenty minutes in and I was exhausted. Push on. I only just made it through the first half. A short interval allowed me to recover my composure before heading into part two of the programme. Too much. A piece I knew perfectly well fell apart completely. I could hardly get through the opening few bars. Trying three times, I gave up. The next piece was a train wreck. Things picked up later in my programme, but overall I was not pleased with any of the music I had played in the second half. Returning home, I sank into a large armchair and my friends pampered me with kind words, tea and cake. I was emotionally and physically spent.

The following morning I received an email from my penfriend. 'Howard, it was not until we were driving home that we realised, for the first time, that we had witnessed a recital and not just your practice. Please believe us. You are now a pianist.'

Was I?

Fast forward. A new grade year.

Having selected my examination pieces, I opened the score in 'List A'. The Mozart did not look too hard, but after a few hours of work I was concerned. This did not feel right. The coordination issues I had experienced in the past were still hampering me. Surely by now I should be able to get a new piece 'under my fingers' more readily? Not so. Two weeks later and I was still struggling. Had I learnt nothing? Fearful, I opened a previous grade book and turned to the first piece I had worked on, recalling how difficult it had been to play the study well. Yet with my teacher's patient help I had finally mastered the music. 'Let me test myself,' I thought. Could I still play this a year later? Somewhat to my surprise, I found that I could. Sure, there were mistakes, but in terms of the flow of the thing, even the runs and jumps, I was doing OK. It felt nostalgic; comforting. I was enjoying this. And then it struck me: if I can play this study after such a gap, why are my new pieces proving so demanding? Had I come full circle? And those negative thoughts of rote learning came flooding back.

Had my success with the earlier study been nothing but the result of fanatical repetition and ingraining? Had I learnt nothing from its patterns that would enable me to tackle a new piece more efficiently? I could not bear the thought of having to work for months to bring one new piece to fruition in order to add it to my list of conquests. Days or weeks I could accept, but months? No. What was I doing wrong? Did I lack an innate ability that would forever limit access to the piano? In desperation I called my penfriend; this needed a voice conversation, not email.

'How, exactly, are my hands wired to my brain?' I began.

We'd chatted about biology, neurons and the learning process many times. On each occasion, however, we always ended up with the same conclusion: loss of brain plasticity as a result of the ageing process. This time, I decided to take a different tack. Explaining my struggle with the new music, yet the relative ease with which I could return to a familiar work, could he explain, in simple terms, what was happening? Stumbling and stuttering with no apparent 'facility' in my hands and fingers, the contrast with the music I had played so well in the past made no sense. The new music felt like treacle. The familiar – it just flowed.

'Why is that?' I asked.

'Well,' he began, 'first, there is no such thing as muscle memory, at least not in the sense most people use the term. Your ability to play the earlier piece comes from higher conceptual regions of the brain, not from your fingers. Without realising it, your hard work lodged the music's pattern and structure in your mind, permanently.'

That sounded comforting, but I was curious:

'What is it about the new music that I am finding so difficult? Is piano music ingrained to such an exact and fine level of detail that every new work is in effect an island, its own unique set of patterns? Does any past learning carry over to the new?

'That's an interesting question,' he replied. 'It must be the case. Otherwise, pianists would not be able to build an extensive repertoire?'

'Is this all relative?' I asked. 'The other day, a friend from the piano circle performed a rather complex work. I asked how long she had been learning the Ravel. She had first played it many years ago and had spent the last three months practising and refreshing her memory of the piece. Three months! And she is an advanced pianist.'

'Wow,' he exclaimed. 'That is a lot of work. Perhaps the piece is especially difficult? Maybe the coordination she needs is so complicated that even her years of experience are insufficient to reduce the required practice time substantially? Maybe music at that level is exponentially harder than the brain's ability to ingrain the movements?'

I felt he was pointing to something significant.

'You may be right. Certainly, every amateur pianist I have spoken to talks of the need for a high degree of repetition in their practice. But I think there is more. Reading between the lines, they emphasise slow and deliberate restatement, recapping and almost "playing" with the music. Not repetition for repetition's sake while daydreaming about something else entirely, but fully concentrating on the intricate movements and gestures. By doing so, are they pushing towards what you call "higher learning" to cut through the exponential complexity.'

'Yes, that would make sense,' he replied. 'Coordination comes from the mind, far less the physiology. Hand and fingers do change, as they are trained via practice, but to a far lesser extent compared to what is happening in the cortex.'

'I see. So the advice one teacher gave me, to spend time away from the keyboard – studying the score – would that help to embed the higher learning?' I suggested.

'Yes.' he replied, 'I think it would. You probably didn't do that additional work when you were rehearsing the early pieces. Nor would you, at the time, have understood how important such things could be. But the more conceptual, abstract learning must have occurred; otherwise, you would not be able to play the music a year later. If anything, it was the result of your excessive repetition, nothing more.'

'Guess so,' I replied, reluctantly accepting the truth of his statement. 'So, if I have this right, I need to bring higher-learning tools to my practice; if I am to get on top of new music with less effort?'

'Yes, I think that is correct,' my friend added.

The conversation brought to mind something I had once heard during a masterclass ... *'It's all in the mind.'*

Continuing, I explained:

'There are certain things I still find so difficult. For example, any music requiring large jumps of the position of my hands across the keyboard, especially if in both hands or employing chords of more than three or four notes. I'm not sure I'm any better today than when I first stepped onto this escalator.'

'I've never liked that particular metaphor, but I'm sure you have improved,' my friend replied, hoping to reassure me, adding, 'My immediate thought is this: our fingers and hands are designed for fine motor control. The elbow and shoulder are crude in comparison, but those joints are precisely what you'd be using for the larger jumps. Think about a bolt connecting two rods; a crude analogy but not far from the truth. Unless you are a trained athlete, any movement involving a large shift in position is likely to be harder for you than the tiny movements of individual fingers from one note to the next. Is this why concert pianists hardly look as though their hands are moving, even during a complex passage?'

'Ah, that's it, that's what I'm feeling', I explained. 'So let's get this right. Are we talking about a spectrum of capabilities? On the one hand, we have the pianist who takes as long to learn a new piece as the last: a flat-line graph. On the other hand, the more capable pianist who, with every new piece they tackle, learns faster and faster: a rising curve approaching the asymptote … and, take-off! I suppose every musician lies somewhere on the spectrum, even my teachers.'

'Yes. I think that is a good way to think about it,' he added.

'All else being equal: if a difficult piece like the Ravel is four times (howsoever one measures it) more difficult than one of your pieces, a pianist who is twice as good as you would still have to work twice as hard (and possibly twice as long) to master it. A pianist who has four times your facility would take as long to master the Ravel as you would take one of your grade pieces. Maybe there's a power function at play here? If so, as one moves up the repertoire to an András Schiff performance, for example, each level of complexity could be geometrically greater: four times as hard, or eight times more complex than the last, rather than linear arithmetic. And that ignores nuances of whatever it is that is challenging about the music and the extent to which different pianists may be variously gifted in each area of competence. Maybe this is why you tell me the more advanced pianists in your circle still report great difficulty in mastering new work?'

'Could be. Yes,' I replied. 'If the power curve is steep, could this explain why an experienced pianist can play pieces at my level almost at will?'

'Sure. Although it may also be they've played so many pieces during their career that the components of a simpler piece are so familiar that they come naturally,' my penfriend reminded me.

'In which case I need to find practice regimes that shift me from the slow-learner end of the scale to the fast-learner. You know, the more I think about this, I simply don't know whether it is physical coordination that limits me, or my mind ... or both! With your knowledge of the body's motor control, can you suggest anything? I asked.

'I suppose there might be something in the academic literature,' he suggested. 'My guess is that repetition of similar, short, simpler patterns will not be as effective, for you, as the repetition of more diverse, extended, complex patterns. In other words, tackling a complete piece of "unique" music won't necessarily build the mind's higher learning and pattern library. You do need variety, but not too much; a middle ground.'

'Ah, maybe this is why my teacher encourages me to play "studies"? Not that I like them. I find studies so unmusical.'

'Could be,' he replied. 'I bet you money that every time a composer in the past created a genuinely new or innovative musical form, someone else came along soon afterwards and published a series of "exercises" to help others learn how to play the novel style.'

Was my penfriend correct? I could not afford to waste time on mindless repetition at either end of the spectrum. The hunt was on for a middle ground that would cut to the chase. And yet … who said 'If you don't know it, how can you play it?'

Before I let the (more) positive tone of this endnote mislead you, let me be clear. While I did make progress, not all of the music I tackled succumbed so easily. Far from it! As I write, I am sinking under the weight of a stubborn block, a period in which nothing I try is making any difference. New music is not coming together. Old music is falling apart. Pieces once secure are no longer secure: no progress on any front. Just back from a short winter break, I had hoped a change of vista and fresh air would help. It did not. If I am to continue this treadmill of an escalator, something has to change, if only for my mental health. I have to know that the effort I put in – day in and day out – will, in the end, pay off. Time, as ever, rushes on, and my window of opportunity will inevitably close. Right now, it feels like 'Access Denied' lies in the road ahead, preventing further progress. And that was precisely the image I posted on social media, hoping my friends would notice and offer a diagnosis.

And of course they did, they always do.

'Please don't stop striving,' said one person. 'I've been through this more than a few times, and think I'm going through it again now. But I won't stop. Nor should you. The piano is too beautiful a thing to give up on. It will get better, I promise.' Others chimed in with 'likes' and emojis and agreement: 'Yes, me too! Keep the faith!' and 'We've all been there, Howard. It's part of the process. It will pass.'

One person suggested that 'a sudden increase in capability often follows a bad patch', pointing out that 'perhaps someone should do a scientific study of how long the brain takes to make new connections *after* a period of practice'. One for my penfriend.

The responses I received were encouraging. 'Pleasssse keep playing', they urged ... the tone of the comments suggesting a degree of frustration with my attitude. 'Stop worrying!' seemed to be the order of the day for this drama queen. But other than to 'push on', precisely what were these amateur pianists suggesting I do?

The general feeling was this: change something – habits, practice routines, choice of music or approach. Change. One colleague from the circle made this suggestion: 'Forget all the rules, Howard. Take a break from the formulaic didactic instructions of the score and the rigours of classical technique. Play in a disinhibited and reckless way for a while. Sing out loud as you play and enjoy the experience. It's your piano and it's your music. Order will be restored in a few days when you have recovered the joy and exhilaration that music can bring. Experiment a bit.' Her advice resonated with my mood.

At my next lesson, I explained these frustrations to my regular teacher. A stickler for technique, I'm not sure she was sympathetic. She had heard similar comments from me in the past. 'Have more faith in yourself!' was the extent of the solution she offered. 'You need to push yourself.'

My (other) occasional teacher offered a different remedy. She asked to watch as I mock-practised a short (and particularly tricky) phrase, elements I found particularly challenging. I fear I did not impress her.

'Have you forgotten how to practise, Howard? Do you understand the need to slow down? Read the score carefully. How many times did you repeat those bars? Do you break sections into management chunks? I get the feeling you are allowing yourself to rush, playing as if your practice were a performance.' She diagnosed that I was 'insufficiently disciplined'. To be honest, I did not feel this was the case but promised to renew my focus on the art of practice itself. To this she replied, 'You will know if you are concentrating with sufficient deliberation when, after only thirty minutes, you are utterly exhausted.' Wow. I had to admit, I was not achieving that degree of concentrated effort.

And so, as I write these words, I pledge a solemn oath: to slow down, be mindful, and to listen. Rest assured, Adagio will keep an eye on me. As my mentors keep reminding me, 'There is no goal, Howard, realistic or unrealistic; only the voyage.' The escalator. Or, as a friend from the piano circle once told me: 'It's our lot in life.'

So yes, I have booked into Summer School again. Wish me luck.

THE RETURNING ADULT

With time marching on, ambitious amateurs optimise their available practice time to attain the goals they set for themselves. Beyond a certain age, there is a finite window of opportunity to master any complex new skill, and piano is undoubtedly that. Eighty-eight keys. Two hands. Ten fingers. And pedals! More patterns than grains of sand on a beach. While age should be immaterial and attitude is all, our brains do lose plasticity over time. Having read my book, you know this reality played heavily on my mind; to the extent that was – let's face it – unhealthy. With that in mind, I posed a question to the piano community via social media. It asked:

'In addition to a regular regime of scales, arpeggios, studies and grade pieces, what else would you recommend for accelerated progress?'

The list below is a summary of the suggestions I received. Take from it whatever is practical for you. Personal context is everything: not everyone wants – or can allow – their piano to dominate their life. But for many amateurs it most certainly does. And we love it.

The 'advice to ourselves' forms a useful checklist:

1. Be clear about long-term goals; however, also define a few shorter term objectives. What do we want to achieve this month? Next?
2. The quality of our practice is more important than its quantity. Aim for what musicians call 'deliberate practice': mindful performance.
3. Maintain regular daily practice; at least five days out of seven. If possible, practise at the same time each day.
4. Hours-per-day is a debatable issue. Break up longer sessions (more than two hours) into chunks. Not everyone can work as if they are a concert pianist, though some amateurs do!

5. Combine different styles of practice each day: scales and arpeggios, specific exercises, studies, and of course the music we wish to perform.
6. Plan our practice time. Divide it between the many kinds of work and study required. Keep to the plan.
7. Create variety in practice: different keys, modes, contrary motion, legato and staccato, pulse (4, 3, 2), unison, in 3^{rds}, in 6^{ths}, chord inversion, and so on.
8. Practise slowly, building tempo gradually. Fingering should be 100 per cent correct from the get-go. Never ingrain a bad habit; not once.
9. Easy to forget: hands separately (HS) before hands together (HT).
10. Build sight-reading skills. Difficult for many adults, but essential.
11. Use any available time away from the keyboard for additional complementary study. Read and analyse scores.
12. Listen to as much good music as possible. Listen carefully. Listen intelligently. Watch professional pianists practise and perform.
13. Interweave a little ad hoc music-making into the everyday. No need to restrict ourselves to formal 'sit down' practice. Touch and stroke our keyboard whenever we can.
14. Learn to play in different styles and genres. If our preference is classical, try jazz, and vice versa. If we prefer modern music, try baroque. Mix it up!
15. Meet up with other musically inclined people. Join a piano circle. If possible, sign up for a masterclass or two. Consider enrolling at a summer school.
16. If possible, collaborate with other musicians: join a band, play duets, collaborate on songwriting, etc.
17. Record our practice and, if possible, our performances. Listen back. Compare ourselves to the recordings made by professional musicians.
18. Understand the score beyond the notes. Tease out the music's style,

patterns, contours, harmony, texture and structure. Theory is vital.

19. Look for supplementary advice to complement regular lessons, e.g. YouTube channels, blogs; other teachers.
20. Feel free to spend time in mindless wandering at the keyboard. Improvise. Have fun!
21. Always question our progress. Where are we weak or vulnerable? Ask our tutors to diagnose problem areas. Dedicate a lesson or two to this introspection.
22. Build a more robust technique. And strength in our hands. Yes, scales and arpeggios count. Articulate clearly. Legato and staccato.
23. Make sensible use of a metronome. Slow down for intense practice.
24. Short studies (or extracts of longer works) help build skills more quickly than extended pieces. There is value in practising tricky bars and phrases, even if not completed to 'performance' standard.
25. Observe other players; go to concerts, or watch online.
26. Choose repertoire we love and come back to these works time and again. Make a list of our conquests. They are our children.
27. Listen to what our teachers say, and do what they ask. Think like a child. Soak it up.
28. Play and improvise against recorded or computer-generated accompaniments – just for fun.
29. Try to hear the music in our head, feel its contours before we begin to play. Add landmarks on the score to help with memorisation.
30. Sing as we practice. Sing the melody line. Sing the inner parts. This will help to voice our chords correctly and bring out the melody.
31. 'Efficiency of practice' stated as a *goal* may not be a good metaphor. Enjoy the challenge of working on intricate 'impossible' pieces. Revel in the journey. Worry less about the future.
32. Being in a hurry can limit our development. Patience, yes, but keep an

eye on our progress. Is our practice approach working? If not, get advice, change the way we work.

33. Graded exams are useful milestones and evidence of our success, of which we should be rightly proud, although they are not for everyone. Time can be lost over-perfecting a handful of set pieces for a picky examiner.
34. Seek out high-quality challenging repertoire that gradually introduces new demands for the advancement of technique.
35. Always be on the lookout for new ways to practise. Be creative. Consider getting advice from teachers who specialise in pedagogy.
36. Never underestimate the benefit of correct finger, hand, arm and body movements. Healthy posture is vital. Eradicate all tension. Try Pilates.
37. Work with teachers who have ambition for us. Insist they push us forward. Look for what limits us, then hone our effort there.
38. Always have a sharp pencil and rubber to hand. Scribble all over our scores. Make notes on fingering, harmony, phrases and landmarks.
39. Invest in our memory. Practise memorisation techniques. Learn to perform without sheet music or lead sheets.
40. From time to time, return to and refresh and enrich our older repertoire; the works we cherish. How have we progressed? Give ourselves a pat on the back.
41. There are limits to learning the piano. It can rarely be rushed, and absorbing new patterns takes time. Try not to be too hard on ourselves.
42. Stay healthy. But don't forget to have a bar of chocolate or mug of coffee to hand; whatever your poison happens to be. But not too close to that precious piano!

CONQUERING ANXIETY

Like many adults, I found it surprising that I must suffer that most debilitating of all pianistic ailments: extreme performance anxiety. This came as something of a shock, having been a confident keynote speaker at many industry events during my long career. So what did I do? I posted a question to members of our piano circle and collated their collective wisdom into an advice note to myself. A picture emerged. Everyone had experienced anxiety at one time or another: it never goes away and has to be managed. Only repeated exposure to an audience can cure the afflicted.

ADVICE TO MYSELF

Confronting my fear and learning how to reduce and manage the nerves is empowering. I can become a more confident performer. There are two kinds of anxiety:

- Irrational anxiety: fear for no good reason. If I am well prepared, it should be possible to overcome natural concerns and butterflies.
- Rational anxiety: insufficient preparation. Maybe I was just lucky when playing at home in the practice room? Whereas, under the spotlight, things fell apart?

The combination of sufficient practice and resilience under emotional stress will help reduce performance wobbles.

Technical preparation is the bottom line. Stiffness, awkward movements and poor technique lead to complete dysfunction during a live performance; the mind and muscles (flooding with all kinds of harmful chemicals) will not be able to cope.

A series of flawed performances will result in a vicious cycle of doubt and negativity. I must build a record of success and avoid a narrative of failure. Consider techniques from neural linguistic programming or cognitive behaviour therapy. Turn negative messages and the 'toxic inner critic' into positive affirmation and confidence-boosting memes.

Strategies for coping with performance anxiety include:

1) ADOPTING THE RIGHT MINDSET

Accept myself for what I am. How well I perform is not a determiner of my self-worth.

A few mistakes are acceptable. Nobody is perfect. Most audiences won't notice, and the majority are non-judgemental.

Accept that a degree of nervousness – butterflies – is healthy. This is natural and affects almost everyone from time to time. If I am not nervous or am unduly overconfident, something is wrong. Adrenaline can be useful but needs a channel.

To build a narrative of success, seek out a graduated series of low-threat performance opportunities. Start with an audio recorder. Progress to video. Treat these sessions as if they were live performances. Stand and address the imaginary audience. Keep going, even if I make a mistake. Try to maintain tempo. Then move to the next level: a family member, a trusted friend or a musical associate. Then add more friends. And so on.

Each time I perform, think about what I found most challenging – not the music but the psychology (and physiology). Consider what new coping strategies may be required.

2) CHOICE OF MUSIC

The successful performance of any piece of music boosts my confidence and increases my emotional resilience in readiness for my next gig.

Choose music safely within (or ideally below) my grade: 'easy for me' pieces with which I am entirely comfortable.

Play at a tempo at which I can be confident I won't trip up.

Performing less well-known repertoire can help. Familiar music attracts a higher expectation from the audience, heightening the natural fear of being 'under the spotlight'.

3) Preparing for the Performance

Practise. Practise. Practise. Always be well-prepared. Eliminate anything and everything that can or could go wrong. Practise until I *cannot* go wrong.

Tip: A few days before the performance, identify the one bar (one) that I find the most challenging. Knock it on the head. Experience shows that this simple, practical solution seems to 'clinch' a sense of confidence after all else is said and done.

Perform whenever and wherever I can. Play on any 'found' piano, including those in public spaces. Play when my friends come round – whether they want to hear me or not. Join a piano circle. Tell my ad hoc audiences to accept my performance for what it is: the practise of practice! Doing so will help me to feel what it is like to be nervous. These 'safe' performances will reveal whether I am sufficiently prepared for whatever lies ahead: recital, examination, diploma or competition.

Practise in front of my teachers. Take their advice but ask them not to obsess about tiny details; it's too late for that. Ask them for their input on the entire sweep of my performance.

Work on my controlled breathing. Find the mind tools to redirect thoughts when they turn negative.

Be healthy. Exercise. Eat properly.

4) THE DAY BEFORE

Limit stimulants. Get adequate sleep.

Practise, yes, but avoid over-practise. Focus on the big picture.

Take a walk, jump up and down, shake out muscles, or do whatever feels right to ease any anxious feelings. Repeat nearer the time.

5) AT THE PERFORMANCE

If possible, warm up beforehand by playing a few scales. At the very least try to feel the action of the keyboard in advance. Play a few notes and chords, not forgetting the pedals. Adjust the stool; take my time.

Remind myself that I am well-prepared. Don't over-think what could go wrong. Foster a 'safe space' in which to perform. Get into 'the zone'. Centre myself.

Adopt an aura of confidence. Think of my audience as my friends. Connect with them – smile, make eye contact. Introduce my programme and do so professionally.

Shift the focus from my vulnerabilities towards the music itself. Close my eyes. Imagine my audience enjoying the music. Aim not only to perform correctly but also to communicate the emotion of the music: sadness, joy, profound feelings, and so on.

As I start to play: play with confidence. The success of the first few bars is essential to my surety throughout.

Play with passion! Play joyfully. Play as if I am giving a gift to my audience. Don't hold my breath. Breathe out; relaxing my facial muscles.

Perfection is not the same as beauty. Moreover, leave any ego at home.

As I play, listen but do not analyse. Focusing too closely on finger movements is not going to help at this stage. Communicate the 'story' of the music rather than its technical aspects. Allow the music to flow through me. Imagine I am a conduit rather than its deliverer or controller.

Play 'in the moment'. Don't anticipate the most challenging upcoming bars or tricky passage. Avoid thoughts such as 'I must avoid that risky chord or 'I must not trip up at bar 25'.

Tip: Imagine the score is a musical ticker-tape, inexorably moving forward. Let the music carry me along. Declutter my thoughts from the mechanical minutiae of performance. Bring my mind and hands together as one, not as separate machinery.

Concentrate as I play. Do not allow stray thoughts to enter my head. Chase them out. Focus.

If I make a mistake, which is certain as night follows day, I must pick up, recover and carry on – with the least amount of fuss. Never ever say 'sorry'. Keep going. Maintain tempo. Whatever happens, do not restart.

Have fun!

6) After the Performance

Don't dwell on what happened during the performance, other than to learn from my mistakes.

Plan for the next performance right away. No time to lose!

7) Additional

Minimise distractions. Find a fixed point in the distance. Focus on whatever makes me feel most comfortable. This might be a music stand, the keyboard, or an object beyond the piano itself (real or imaginary).

Be deliberate. When I step up to the piano, how exactly do I wish to sound? What, precisely, do I intend to communicate to my audience?

Visualise my success. Build the appropriate mental image: how I would ideally like to perform. Tell myself I am going to play brilliantly, with passion and clarity of dynamics. Think positive words such as *light fingers*, *smooth playing*, *even shifts*, *fluid movements*, *stable chords*, *quiet*, *calm*.

Performance anxiety creates muscle tension. Breathe from my diaphragm. Avoid shallow, rapid, chest breathing. As I breathe, focus on each group of muscles, releasing all tension as I exhale.

FURTHER READING

We live in an era of wonder, with so many precious resources from which musicians can learn to weave their magic: books, blogs, YouTube, etc. The titles listed below are those I own and have found particularly helpful. Omissions are my loss.

Harmony

Bach Riemenscheider: 371 Harmonized Chorales and 69 Chorale Melodies with Figured Bass, J. S. Bach, G, Schirmer, Inc.

Harmony in Practice, Anna Butterworth, ABRSM (Publishing) Ltd.

Music Theory Grade Six, Victoria Williams, My Music Theory (mymusictheory.com)

Revised Practice in Harmony, Grade Six, Josephine Koh, Wells Music Publishers

The AB Guide To Music Theory, Part I & II, Eric Taylor, ABRSM (Publishing) Ltd.

Jazz Theory and Practice

A Creative Approach To Jazz Piano Harmony, Bill Dobbins, Advance Music

Jazz Piano From Scratch: A How-To Guide for Students and Teachers, Charles Beale, ABRSM (Publishing) Ltd.

Jazzology: The Encyclopedia of Jazz Theory for all Musicians, Robert Rawlins and Nor Eddine Bahha, Hal Leonard

mDecks, Apps & Books for Musicians, mDecks Music (mdecks.com)

Solo Jazz Piano: The Linear Approach, Neil Olmstead, Berklee Press

The Diatonic Circle: Essential Exercises for All Jazz, Traditional, and Contemporary Musicians, Emile and Laura De Cosmo, Hal Leonard

The Jazz Language: A Theory Text for Jazz Composition and Improvisation, Dan Haerle

The Jazz Harmony Book, David Berkman, Sher Music Co.

The Jazz Theory Book, Mark Levine, Sher Music Co.

The Path To Jazz Improvisation: More than 30 lessons for all instrumentalists, Emile and Laura De Cosmo, Hal Leonard

ON MUSIC

A Musician's Alphabet, Susan Tomes, Faber and Faber (www.susantomes.com)

Comparing Notes: How We Make Sense of Music, Adam Ockelford, Profile Books

How Music Works: A Listener's Guide to the Science and Psychology of Beautiful Sounds, John Powell, Particular Books, Penguin

Play It Again: An Amateur Against The Impossible, Alan Rusbridger, Vintage Books

The Concise Oxford Dictionary of Music, Percy A. Scholes, Oxford University Press

The Cross-Eyed Pianist: Blog, Frances Wilson, Pianist & Writer on Music & Musicians (crosseyedpianist.com)

The Elements of Music: Melody, Rhythm & Harmony, Jason Martineau, Wooden Books

The Music Instinct: How Music Works & Why We Can't Do Without It, Philip Ball, Vintage Books

The Norton Scores: A Study Anthology, ed. Kristine Forney with textual notes by Roger Hickman, W. W. Norton & Co.

The Rest is Noise: Listening to the Twentieth Century, Alex Ross, Fourth Estate, Harper Collins

The Story of Music, Howard Goodall, Vintage Books

What To Listen For In Jazz, Berry Kernfeld, Yale University Press

SONGWRITING AND COMPOSITION

Chord Progressions for Songwriters, Richard J. Scott, Writers Club Press

Melody in Songwriting: Tools and Techniques for Writing Hit Songs, Jack Perricone, Berklee Press

Music Composition For Dummies, Scott Jarrett and Holly Day, Wiley

Tunesmith: Inside the Art of Songwriting, Jimmy Webb, Hachette Books

Writing Better Lyrics: The Essential Guide To Songwriting, Pat Pattinson, Writers Digest Books

TECHNIQUE & PRACTICE

By Heart: The Art of Memorizing Music, Paul Cienniwa, Self-published

Czerny: 101 Exercises: Op. 261, Augener Edition, Galliard Music Corp.

Czerny: Practical Method for Beginners on the Pianoforte, Op. 599, G. Schirmer Inc.

Foundations of Pianoforte Technique, Geoffrey Tankard, Novello Publishing

Fundamentals of Piano Practice (3rd Ed.), Chuan C. Chang, Self-published

Hanon Complete: The Virtuoso Pianist in 60 Exercises, ed. Allan Small, Alfred Publishing Co.

How to Memorize Music: A Practical Approach for Non-Geniuses, David Bolton, Self-published

How to Play the Piano, James Rhodes, Quercus Editions Ltd.

Piano Dao: The Way of Piano, Andrew Eales (pianodao.com)

Piano Technique, Walter Gieseking & Karl Leimer, Dover Publications Inc.

Piano Technique in Practice, Murray McLachlan, Faber Music

Practising the Piano, Parts 1, 2 & 3, Graham Fitch, Erudition (practisingthepiano.com)

Speaking the Piano: Reflections on Learning and Teaching, Susan Tomes, The Boydell Press (www.susantomes.com)

The Art of Piano Fingering: A New Approach to Scales and Arpeggios, Penelope Roskell, LCM Publications (peneloperoskell.co.uk)

The Complete Pianist: From healthy technique to natural artistry, Penelope Roskell, Edition Peters

The Foundations of Technique, Murray McLachlan, Faber Music

The Manual of Scales: Broken Chords and Arpeggios for Piano, Intro. Ruth Gerald, ABRMS (Publishing) Ltd.

The Mindful Pianist: Focus, practise, perform, engage, Mark Tanner, Faber Music

ABOUT THE TYPE

Fonts contribute hugely to the pleasure of a book. Mine is typeset in Adobe Caslon, a revival by the American designer Carol Twombly who studied specimen pages of the English typefounder William Caslon, printed between 1734 and 1770. Today, Carol is an independent artist, specialising in drawing and painting on textiles.

Titles are in Waverly CF. Designed by Connary Fagan, Waverly is a usefully constrained Art Deco font family with updated, clean letterforms.

Quotations, lyrics and poetry are Isabel. Designed by Eleonora Lana and Juan Pablo De Gregorio, Isabel glyphs weave their magic by combining the innocent elements of simple letters taught to children with the more conservative features of a readable book font. The effect is joyful, friendly and ingenious.

Printed in Great Britain
by Amazon

43468299R20209